The Contemporary Woman

First published in Great Britain in 2021 by Hodder & Stoughton
An Hachette UK company

This paperback edition first published in 2023

1

A CIP catalogue record for this title is available from the British Library

Paperback ISBN 978 1 529 35832 2
eBook ISBN 978 1 529 35833 9

Typeset in Bembo MT by Hewer Text UK Ltd, Edinburgh
Printed and bound in Great Britain by Clays Ltd, Elcograf S.p.A.

Hodder & Stoughton policy is to use papers that are natural, renewable
and recyclable products and made from wood grown in sustainable
forests. The logging and manufacturing processes are expected to
conform to the environmental regulations of the country of origin.

Hodder & Stoughton Ltd
Carmelite House
50 Victoria Embankment
London EC4Y 0DZ

www.hodderfaith.com

The Contemporary Woman

Can she really have it all?

MICHELE GUINNESS

HODDER

For Peter,
the man who shoved me through the open doors,
and for all men who do the same for women everywhere.

Contents

Preface from the First Editor

I've been raving about Michele Guinness' book, now named *The Contemporary Woman*, for many years. Being the editor for the first edition of this wonderful book was not only a delight but also important to me as a disciple of Christ and as a woman.

When I first came to the UK and spent some time at Ridley Hall, Cambridge, where my new husband was finishing off his training to be ordained in the Church of England, I chatted over lunch one day with the then principal, Graham Cray, about women and their contributions to the Church.

'So you believe women can preach and lead services?' I asked, not having seen this modelled in the church I came from Stateside.

'Oh yes!' he said, with a twinkle in his eye. As he shared what he'd found in Scripture to support his views, I felt a spark inside me alight. I wanted to know more.

A few years later, Michele gave me that 'more' that I was yearning for. For weeks I got to dig into her chapters on woman as God made her, delighting in Michele's Jewish way of opening up the Scriptures. Her chapters on Paul's view of women especially helped me, for I hadn't been sure about him or his message. What in his words was based in culture and what was him being God's messenger? Michele gave me the gift to embrace a worldview of freedom, grace and collaboration.

I didn't know when I was Michele's editor that her book would prepare me for life when I was no longer an editor. For not long after publication, the company that I was working for eliminated my job. I had thought I was at the pinnacle of my career as the UK commissioning editor for a global publisher, and then that position was gone. Yes, there were tears. Little did I know then that the grounding I received through Michele's book would set me up to pursue the work I'd longed to do. For I'd always wanted to be a writer. I started writing as a child but soon stopped, too self-conscious of my words and too fearful of not having anything to say. For me, becoming an editor was a way to bypass that fear (and in sharing this, I want to emphasise that many editors do *not* harbour these feelings). I could help gifted authors get their message out, and although it's more American than British for me to say this, I was good at my job and I loved it. But deep down, I wished I could be the one writing those books.

Losing my prized job started me on my journey of writing. It wasn't a fast process – it took ten years from my editorial job ending to my first book being published. I had to digest the wisdom that Michele advocates of women speaking forth life, each in their own way, before I could move forward in these scary but exhilarating new ventures.

I pray that *The Contemporary Woman* will continue to speak life and hope and truth into a new generation of women – and men. Michele's book can equip us, and those who love us, to live as life-giving, creative, affirming women. Read it, ponder it and share it with others!

Amy Boucher Pye, October 2020

Preamble: Sometimes it's
Hard to Be a Woman

'Blessed are you O God, King of the Universe, who has not made
me a Gentile, a slave, or a woman.'

Jewish Morning Prayer

I have witnessed in my short lifetime one of the greatest revolutions in
the history of the West: the immense change in the status of women.
Was it really more than forty years ago that I sat in a Manchester café,
and starry-eyed, told my newly acquired, long-adored man that I
could think of no more blissful future than staying at home to darn his
socks and iron his shirts? How old-fashioned and quaint it sounds now
– positively antique. To be honest, the self-sacrificial romantic idealism
didn't last long. For women of my generation the world was already
spinning on its axis. It was full of new opportunities we didn't want to
miss. And that caused some of us no end of heart-searching about
what it meant to become the woman we were meant to be.

I was a first baby and my father, like most Jewish men, had desperately wanted a boy. In fact he had a bet on it – £5 each way – with
his father-in-law. So when the formidable, starched-white Sister
crinkled her way into the hospital waiting room to tell the expectant
father he could stop pacing the floor because he had a lovely daughter, this skilled and competent physician asked her, 'Are you saying it
is a girl or you only think it's a girl?'

'Doctor,' she said disparagingly, for those were the days when a
senior nurse could reduce even a competent medical man into blanc-
mange with one twitch of her winged cap, 'we do have ways of
knowing these things.'

By the time I knew this story, my father not only had his son, but
had also discovered the joys of having an adoring daughter and,

though he dismissed women doctors as 'horses', had convinced himself that when I grew up I would break the mould, unlike my mother, whose choices were hidebound by the double whammy of being both British and Jewish, with aspiring middle-class expectations to fulfil. Ultimately, following in her footsteps and hooking a good catch were more important in that community than a career, though it no longer excluded acquiring the best education and a university degree.

So despite being Jewish, I was sent to a Church of England private school for girls where careers advice, dispensed by tweedy Miss Calderbank in bun and brogues, consisted of, 'You have three choices my dear: teaching, nursing or the army.' That was how it was in the not-so-olden days. The sighing Miss Calderbank suspected that few of the young women sent her way would need her advice anyway, since they would not be reduced as she had been, by a world war, to the necessity of spending an entire life working for a living. Even the teaching staff appeared to resign themselves to throwing their gems before unappreciative little wretches who at the first opportunity would exchange their brains for something in trousers, and flush away a shining future to become wives and mothers – as their mothers had no doubt done before them.

My mother, in blue nylon overalls, dusting and polishing, cooking and cleaning and straightening pictures, armchair castors and curtain folds, was hardly the stuff of my or any teenage fantasies. 'What's life all about?' I asked her one day, in desperation. She was in the process of moving the left-hand candle of a pair one centimetre towards its opposite number on the sideboard, and didn't even look up.

'You'll meet a nice Jewish boy, marry, have a nice home, children, a car . . .'

'And then what?'

'What more do you want?'

I didn't know then that an enforced lack of fulfilment would generate a quest for perfection that would, in its turn, lead her, and other Jewish women, into an Obsessive Compulsive Disorder that was as restricting as any prison sentence. Was this, then, my destiny, this drudgery that my mother evidently resented, this frustration with her lot in life? Every day, as she banged his lunch down on the table in front of him, she would say to my father, 'Next time I'm coming back as a man.' She didn't actually believe in reincarnation, but she did believe in making sure her man appreciated her long-suffering and self-sacrifice. I always wondered why she bothered making him lunch if she hated doing it so much. Couldn't he get his own? But had he or one of his male friends ever learned to cook it would have meant the overturning of civilisation as they knew it. My father took his role as breadwinner very seriously. He was convinced that he worked far harder than she ever did in the home, and let her know without overtly saying so that she was lucky to be 'a kept woman'. That she didn't need to go out to work was the sign of the status that he, the son of poor Jewish immigrants, had won for them both.

My mother wasn't alone. Surveys in the 1980s, as gender inequality began to be a real issue, showed that men hardly ever wished they had been born women, while about 25 per cent of women, given the chance, would rather have been a man. Today, that is a possibility – though the process and the consequences are neither painless nor straightforward. But it has generated a whole new discussion on what it actually means to be a woman.

A new world for women – or is it?

I was born several years after the end of the Second World War, a time when men were away at the front and women had been expected to take on their jobs. But then the men came home and there was barely enough work for them to do, so it became socially unacceptable for women to abandon hearth and home and the love of a good man. Those who did were usually single, and were treated with a mixture of fear and pity – stern, forbidding teachers who terrified pupils and parents alike; big-breasted matrons who ran their hospitals with military precision, tyrannising the poor patients; the dedicated personal assistant who organised her male boss, bought anniversary flowers for his wife, birthday cards for his mother and Christmas presents for his children, hiding behind that obsequious facade the certainty that he was lost without her and, given half a chance, she might even do a better job than he. These women whose rightful husbands were lying in the graves of an unknown soldier in France, Italy, North Africa and the Far East were often seen as formidable, unfeminine, unnatural – battle-axes. No woman could possibly combine a career with a fulfilling emotional and domestic life.

But as women were given greater access to education, social attitudes began to be shaken. In the 1960s the contraceptive pill was supposed to herald a new dawn for women. The term 'sexism' began to be used. My mother opened a pram shop in a mining town in County Durham and turned out to be a shrewd, successful businesswoman until the pits were closed and people could barely afford a nappy, let alone a pram. She couldn't do much about that but, after all, my father said sympathetically, as his lunch was once again bounced on the table in front of him, she had only been earning herself some pocket money.

The first equal pay act was passed in 1970. And though to this day the reality doesn't reflect what was a radical concession, change was accelerating at such a pace that writer Gloria Steinem could say with satisfaction, 'Some of us are becoming the men we wanted to marry.' For many women, no longer being forced to depend on a man for status or fulfilment has been a liberation. Once upon a time, a wife, denied any outlet for her education, gifts and skills, was forced to invest all her ambitions in her man and achieve them through him. And if he didn't have what it took to fulfil her dreams, she ended up nursing a lasting sense of disappointment, while he was left feeling a failure.

Today, women no longer have to become nurses to grow up and marry doctors. They can become doctors. They don't have to marry into the Army for the excitement of an army life. They can become colonels. They don't even have to go to theological college to snap up ministers. They can be ministers in all but the Roman Catholic, Orthodox and Conservative Evangelical churches, despite the fact that women often run them, even if they don't lead them.

But those who hoped that equality in the job market would make for a nicer society were doomed to be disappointed. Swiss psychologist of the fifties and sixties, Paul Tournier, one of the first spirituality writers to challenge the Church's attitude to gender, believed that for centuries Western civilisation had been dominated by the cold, objective male values of reason and rationalism, while the 'feminine' qualities of emotion, feelings and relationship were dismissed as inferior, and that led to anonymous multi-nationals and uncaring bureaucracy. If women were allowed to be leaders in the workplace, a right balance would be restored. What he didn't foresee was the sacrifice that getting to the top would require – friends, family life, and even femininity itself. 'When a woman behaves like a man, why doesn't she behave like a nice man?' asked celebrated actress, Dame Edith Evans, shortly before her death in 1976.

And if opportunity began to tempt some determined egalitarians, women from poorer socio-economic backgrounds were still kept in their place – well below reach of a skylight, let alone a glass ceiling. A recent BBC documentary on the Yorkshire Ripper[1] described how his victims were divided by police and media into prostitutes or 'innocent victims', as if the former asked for what they got. Even women who went out to the pub alone were described as having 'loose morals'. Sexism was endemic in the police force, as well as in many other national organisations.

In the 1980s, like many other women, I believed that if we got to the top, the world would be a gentler place – for men too. Then came Margaret Thatcher! Our first female prime minister, with her shoulder-padded, power-dressing, and cut-and-thrust image put paid to that illusion. But while our differences from men are one of our strengths, they can be seen as weakness and used to keep us in our place, so it isn't hard to understand why some women felt they had so much to prove that they had to be tougher than the boys to beat them at their own game. Perhaps that's why so many wished they had been men.

By the turn of the century the 'stay-at-home mother' began to look like a dinosaur – though many chose, or were forced, to jump off the career ladder because 'having it all' in a world of crazy demands wasn't as easy as it was made out to be, and those 'family-friendly policies' in the workplace didn't stretch to a week at home when each child in turn had the norovirus. Through the offices of an egalitarian husband, whose job allowed for flexibility, I had managed to juggle the demands of small children, a full-time job in the media and running a vicarage, eventually, once the nest was empty, becoming Head of Communications for the NHS in Cumbria and Lancashire. I had never planned to rise to the lofty heights of senior management, and would never have done so without a spouse who opened the doors, then shoved me through them. I think now how much I admire many single mothers for getting there without that kind of support.

But surely, in the twenty-first century, our struggles are now over? Or are they? At the dawn of the century, while men in the West were beginning to come to terms with the idea of women's equality, it was still almost unthinkable elsewhere in the world. In Africa, 80 per cent of the food was produced by women, yet they could not own land and had no rights. Extreme Islam still denies women the right to drive, ride a bicycle or venture out with their faces uncovered. And even in societies where women did manage to break out of the restraints that deny them their freedom, and earn a little money, male fear and resentment bubbled over into dire and desperate aggression – such as in the Mexican border town of Ciudad Juárez, where, between 1993 and 2005, some 370 young women, mainly workers in the American factories just south of the border, were raped and murdered for no other obvious crime than taking men's jobs. It became known as *feminicidio* ('feminicide'), and it continues, unchecked if not at such a rate, to this day.

When I was first encouraged to consider rewriting this book, I thought long and hard about whether it was necessary. We had even outgrown the post-feminist era. Surely the subject was passé? For many young women 'feminism' had almost become a dirty word. They didn't want to be associated with the embarrassing, bra-burning excesses of their mother's, or even grandmother's, generation. Men were now friends, not the enemy. As far as the Church was concerned, since women were bishops there was no further equality to fight for. In 2017 Professor Stephen Hawking suggested that since five of the most powerful people in the UK, including the Queen, were women, it represented a seismic shift in society.[2] Women had become the CEO of General Motors and YouTube, the managing director of the International Monetary Fund, head of MI5, and commissioner of the Metropolitan Police. But the fact that they were few enough in number to be named so easily seems to say it all. Not only that, but General Motors is an American company with an American CEO, Christine Lagarde, the then managing director of the International Monetary Fund was French, and the Queen really has very little power at all.

In the land of make-believe they were even Dr Who. Reflecting on the new tough media image for women, Daisy Goodwin, who wrote the TV serial, *Victoria*, claimed that a great deal of film and drama lulls us into a false sense of reality. 'Splendid as the notion is that women are now seamlessly integrated into every aspect of authority, it is at best wishful thinking – and at worst undermines the fight for equality.'[3] And she cites Carol Howard, who was the poster girl for armed policing, and then, in 2014, in an employment tribunal, won her case against the Met for sexual and racial harassment.

The BBC itself, that bastion of forward-thinking British life, and weaver of fantasies, was exposed for large pay differentials and ageism. So it seems there was more than just an element of truth in Goodwin's article. Men in fact still earn on average 18 per cent more than women. Women are three times more likely to be responsible for childcare. On average two women are killed every week by a current or former partner, and the number is rising. Women are scared to walk alone at night. In the churches where my husband ministered, where there were large numbers of students, it was not uncommon to see young women at the communion rail stretch out their hands to take the cup, and as they did so, baggy jumper sleeves would fall back to reveal an angry criss-cross of welts on their wrists. Self-harm is one of the most recognisable signs of previous abuse.

More than eighty women have made sexual harassment claims against film producer Harvey Weinstein – allegations he denies. It generated a tsunami of similar accusations. When actress Alyssa Milano invited anyone who had experienced unwanted sexual behaviour to reply to her tweet with '#MeToo', a phrase first used in 2006 by American social activist and community organiser Tarana Burke, half a million women responded in the first twenty-four hours. The hashtag has been used in more than eighty countries, initiating a movement that encourages women to speak out about sexual harassment and assault in the workplace, politics, finance, wherever it raises its ugly head. '#ChurchToo' began trending on Twitter in November 2017.

In 2017, the day after the inauguration of US President Donald Trump, millions around the world took to the streets for the 'Women's March' to support the women of the USA in highlighting women's rights, which they believed would be under serious threat in a Trump regime.

In August 2018 a member of the French parliament was arrested in Paris in connection with an apparently random attack on a woman in a café. Marie Laguerre said the man made a number of degrading comments and obscene noises as she walked past the café on her way home from work. She told the man to 'shut up', and he threw an ashtray at her head. They then traded insults which culminated in his slapping her across the face with his hand. Unfortunately for him, he was caught on CCTV, and Europe was outraged. But how was that kind of abuse imaginable in today's world? Presumably because the whole question of women's place in the universe is as valid as ever.

In many ways it seems today as if technological advances have contributed to the use and abuse of women more than ever before. Pornography cheapens and demeans us. We are exchangeable, dispensable and disposable. If a young man's main source of sexual information comes from his phone or computer, he may find a real relationship disappointing, and secretly wish for the kind of fake or pseudo variety he saw on screen.

No-commitment sex may not be all it is cracked up to be. In *How Was it For You? Women, Sex, Love and Power*,[4] historian and writer Virginia Nicholson questions whether the swinging sixties, rather than heralding female liberation, weren't actually responsible for some of the constraints women face today. She believes it encouraged a sense of male entitlement, leading them to believe they could have what they wanted when they wanted it.

Even so, a 2018 YouGov poll in the UK and USA found that only 34 per cent of women in the UK would actually call themselves a feminist.[5] It seems there is a problem with the terminology, rather than the concept of equality. We may not like the old stereotype of being a man-hating, hairy-legged harpie, but women are certainly not prepared to settle for the injustices of old-style, institutional misogynism. And it certainly hasn't evaporated into the ether.

Take, for example, the forty-year battle to make GPs and gynae-cologists face up to the damage done by the vaginal mesh. A review in July 2020 found that women whose bladder or uterine prolapse had been treated with this procedure had suffered years of such atro-cious pain that it had ruined their lives. Most doctors had dismissed their complaints as 'women's problems', and this 'arrogant attitude' had left women traumatised, intimidated and confused. Baroness Julia Cumberlege, who chaired the review, said their suffering had been caused by failures in the health system, and had been entirely avoidable. According to a BBC report, Kath Sansom, founder of the Sling the Mesh campaign, said: 'The report . . . makes it very clear that our medical establishment is deeply entrenched in institutional denial and misogyny.'[6]

According to the Royal College of Surgeons, in 2016, 58 per cent of students accepted to study medicine or dentistry were female, but only 11 per cent became consultants. That had risen to almost 13 per cent in 2019, which means that parts of medicine are still very much dominated by men. Not only that, but male patients are taken more seriously, possibly because being brave and macho means they are less likely to go to the doctors' in the first place. A study in 2018 on the differences in the way doctors treated pain in men and women concluded that although more women suffered with pain than men, 'women's pain reports are taken less seriously, their pain is discounted as being psychic or non-existent, and their medication is less adequate than treatment given to men'. In fact, women are often treated as hysterical, emotional, complaining, or simply as malingerers.[7]

'GPs and surgeons didn't believe me. They just looked at me like I was mad,' said June Wray in the BBC report on vaginal meshes. It seems we haven't come very far since the days when Freud attributed most of women's problems, psychological, physical and sexual, to hysteria. At least he attributed them to past trauma which could be treated! When it comes to women's issues, it seems there is yet much land to be possessed.

All about image?

For centuries Orthodox Jewish men have thanked God daily that they're not a woman. Today, under a barrage of criticism that the traditional morning prayer is misogynistic, rabbis claim that it is simply a chance for men to thank God for the many religious responsibilities they have been given. To me, that sounds too much like a cop-out. But having partnered periods, pregnancy and childbirth, my husband wryly thinks the prayer may be appropriate.

When the children were at school and I first re-entered the job market as what was known as a 'woman returner', being a woman seemed to have some advantages. As a researcher and presenter in the media I could be as feminine and flirty as I chose, and wear virtually what I fancied, while the male managers were condemned to a working life in almost identical dark suits and chafing, stiff collars. Simply excusing a cranky day with 'women's problems' would incur sympathetic nods from a fleeing man. If a spot broke out on her chin, a woman had ways of concealing it. A girlfriend would always tell you if a piece of broccoli was stuck between your front teeth. And a new lipstick could give you a whole new lease of life.

No access to instant brotherhood for the men, no sharing recipes and shopping tips, no whingeing about the way the wife's snoring kept him awake at night. No giggling in the Gents about the predictability of the opposite sex or sharing his anxieties about his prostate. Men certainly didn't have access to the kind of understanding among women that can unite virtually complete strangers. A compliment from another man would leave him back against the wall with a look of wild panic, a clearing of the throat and immediate recourse to the subject of football, decent beers or advances in technology.

I still thank God I'm not a man, but entering the higher echelons of management in the NHS made me see how often the advantages I enjoyed could be used against us. There was a dress code for women too. Short skirts were acceptable, along as you survived the day without a ladder in your tights. Small earrings, not the frivolous, dangly variety, were as much a symbol of professionalism as a tie. Discreet make-up was fine; anything more might be construed as tarty. And periods or the menopause could be used as reasons why women didn't make suitable managers.

It is important to celebrate our femininity and sexuality in a world where youth and body shape matter too much, and a woman riper than forty and bigger than thirty-six inches in the key places can feel she has been weighed and found wanting. We're robbed of our delight in being who and what we are. Few women are satisfied with their bodies. On a recent television programme about self-image one woman claimed she had believed life would begin when she got down to a size fourteen, but having achieved her goal, she was still waiting.

A text over a beauty salon in Uganda reads, 'With God all things are possible'. They are indeed, but God has made us – warts, skin tags, stretch marks, solar keratoses, scars and all. And I have plenty. I would have loved an English rose, rather than swarthy semite, complexion, a straighter nose, smaller ears and legs that don't end at my husband's knees.

Why are 'petites', as we're patronisingly called, condemned to neat, boring little separates in black, while flamboyant style and colour are reserved for larger ladies? As a local radio presenter, I had a regular guest with her own retail chain for the 'big girls'. She always arrived at the studio in bright red suits and clinking jewellery, turning every head as she marched past. 'I've never been short of a cuddle from the men,' she said on air, 'whereas if we were in Africa, the Oxfam lorry would be calling at your door.'

The cult of youth and beauty isn't new. A popular ditty of the 1940s urged women to 'Stay young and beautiful, it's your duty to be beautiful if you want to be loved'. We have been selling ourselves a lot of rubbish for a very long time. Perhaps it isn't surprising we have begun to believe it.

These days a facelift gets more tempting by the month – if I had the cash – though my beloved daughter and daughter-in-law insist that 'natural laughter lines' (read wrinkles) are much more attractive than a taut and permanent look of surprise. Even so, at certain stages of her life a woman seems to become invisible – when she pushes a screaming toddler in a buggy around the shops, when she's post-menopausal grey, when her figure sags and her varicose veins make the back of her legs look like Doncaster Station, or perhaps when she's too old and frail to stand up for herself. If women are 'past it' at forty, past what, I want to know? What can a teenager do that I can't, and a whole lot better because I have experience and wisdom and maturity on my side? In her sixties, Gypsy Rose Lee, the stripper, said, 'I still have everything I ever had twenty years ago. It just happens to be two inches lower.'[8]

Looking through the newspaper obituaries and noticing that three out of four of them were of men, the journalist Irma Kurtz came to the conclusion that only men die; women go through the change. Do we become worthless when we can no longer procreate? According to an article by Rosa Silverman in *The Telegraph* in 2018, following the launch of their Women Mean Business campaign that aimed at closing the funding gap among female entrepreneurs, one-sixth of new businesses in the UK were started by women, predominantly the over-sixties. 'Olderpreneurs' they are called and their businesses appeared to have a 70 per cent chance of survival, compared to 28 per cent started by their younger counterparts.[9]

So what is a woman?

Maya Angelou's wonderful poem 'Phenomenal Woman' is a celebration of womanhood, especially she who isn't pretty, slim or young, but whose sexuality expresses itself in the 'reach of her arms, the span of her hips, the stride of her step, and the curl of her lips'.[10] In other words, her power and presence emanate from her being comfortable in her female skin. Society's meagre stereotypes of the beautiful woman are pathetic compared to this embodiment of sexiness. 'The swing of my waist, the flash of my teeth and joy in my feet', are enough to drive any man to his knees.

Most dictionaries describe woman as 'an adult human being who is biologically female'. That definition is disputed today by those who feel gender is a matter of choice, rather than birth.

One day, one of our friends came to see my husband Peter and me, to tell us something she felt we should know. Lesley was attractive, vivacious and fun to be with. But on that particular day she appeared nervous and uncomfortable, fidgeting on her armchair and barely raising her eyes to look at us.

'There is no easy way to say this,' she said, 'but for the sake of honesty in our relationship, I feel there is something I need to tell you.'

We waited in silence for some time as she struggled to find the words.

'The truth is I was born a man.'

I wasn't shocked, but I was surprised because she was such a convincing woman that I had never once doubted her gender.

'I haven't had the final op,' she added quickly, 'and I don't intend to take such a drastic step, but that's hard because I know I can never let myself be loved. How could I do that to any man? Or even any woman? So mine will be a life of celibacy.'

'And of great loneliness,' I thought to myself. This was the first time Peter and I had been face to face with an issue that would a few years later become mainstream. But this wasn't 'an issue'. This was Lesley, and I felt a deep sadness at the cost to her of such a decision. But her parents had accepted it, and if Jesus treated each person as an individual, how could Peter and I do any other? She continued as an active church member, but when she moved away we lost touch, and I have always regretted it.

I learned from Lesley what heartache gender dysphoria is, how unforgiving society can be if we don't live up to the expected norms and don't quite fit the accepted appearance of womanhood, even if most women resent having the stereotypes of female behaviour and manner thrust upon them.

Very few men could ever be as convincing a woman as Lesley. Men and women were created different – bodily, biologically and physiologically. Lesley cannot have periods or ever give birth, and it's a tough and incomprehensible reality for someone who feels female inside. Lesley only responded to her gender dysphoria after years of heart-searching and counselling, when she knew she could live no other way. There was no question that Peter and I would reject her or not go on loving her. She wasn't in fact asking for our opinion, and so we didn't give it. But we do still wonder where she is and hope and pray that life, and the Church, has been kind to her.

Yet many young people seem to be making that life-changing choice at a very early age with minimal professional guidance. Peter and I have met several who have set off on the journey and have even had years of hormone treatment, but then turned back, because it didn't actually deal with the problem they were trying to solve. But those who critique that freedom to choose, as Germaine Greer and J. K. Rowling have both done,[11] worrying that women may lose their privacy and private spaces and run the risk of being abused by a man, become the butt of many a brickbat.

Meanwhile, I thank God that I'm comfortable with that je ne sais quoi that makes me a woman – 'the inner mystery', as Maya Angelou calls it, that men cannot fathom, that makes each of us uniquely feminine – that bodily feline quality that is not simply dependent on appearance, but seems more innate, more of a feeling than a fact.

So what of the Church?

A poster distributed by the Equal Opportunities Commission many years ago said, with failed irony, 'Prepare your daughter for working life. Give her less pocket money than your son.' If equality is still lacking in society, the Church, as ever, lags even further behind.

In the Church of England, when both husband and wife are ordained, the wife is often expected to work for no pay at all – as a voluntary, assistant curate. When I asked my daughter Abby why she never considered becoming a minister, she suggested the Church should have its own version of the equal opportunities poster: 'Prepare your daughter for Christian ministry. Don't give her any pocket money at all.'

Even when women had become head teachers, chief constables, CEOs and prime ministers, some churches and Christian organisations persisted in refusing them a chance to take any major leadership roles. It was a very strange sensation, at the consecration of a male bishop in Southwark Cathedral, to have to climb over two rather dour-looking clergymen in black suits who resolutely remained sitting in the pew during Communion. They couldn't take the bread and wine from the hands of the Archbishop of Canterbury as they were tainted when he ordained women to the priesthood. Surely their protest did not prevent them standing courteously to their feet to let me pass? The irony was that in the national Church diary it just happened to be a Feast Day dedicated to Saints Felicity and Perpetua, horribly and publicly tortured and killed in the third century, as Roman sport, for their Christian faith.

The Rev Joy Carroll, Richard Curtis' model for the Vicar of Dibley, told me that in the early days of her priesthood, some of her colleagues wouldn't as much as let her do a Bible reading at a deanery service, let alone preside. Before a cathedral service, our female curate was ordered out of the robing room by the male clergy, and told to go and put her gear on elsewhere. Exclusion could be total and was often irrational.

I heard recently that one of the newer, fairly large, non-denominational churches had refused an eager young woman any role other than helping in the Sunday School – on the grounds that she was single. And yet, some women, unqualified and unprepared, are given automatic access to key leadership positions in the Church through their husband's ministry. They may well be gifted enough, but it does make marriage the Church's new nepotism. This is just one story friends have told me about the battle their daughters still face in the Church simply to be treated as equals.

In France, where we live for several months of the year, I have waited thirteen years to be allowed to preach. I'm never officially invited, but 'steal' an occasional half of my husband's sermon time. And I still can't be an elder or lead services. What a stupendous battle it is to hold my tongue, but every now and then the frustration of being continually passed over makes me want to scream. Especially when I am forced to listen to a man who has no gift for it, but has been invited because 'we just don't have anyone else'.

Why is it that a Church called to follow its leader's radical example and stand at the cutting edge of society, demanding the equality of all human beings, regardless of colour, race or gender, is so often a reactionary, outdated voice, out of kilter with the contemporary world? For many years, while it has been led by men, it has been run by an army of dedicated women, happy to roll up their sleeves and do the menial tasks like dusting the pews and polishing the brasses, making the tea and attending to the flowers. Some of our best church cleaners have been men. They mend the vacuum cleaners, replace duff light bulbs and usually (pardon the stereotype!) are better than women at general maintenance.

Yet despite the breakdown of traditional roles in society, we often persist in the unspoken notion that women are more suited to certain roles – the caring pastor rather than the dynamic preacher or visionary leader. When we arrived at our last church but one it had never had a female churchwarden. 'Not a suitable job for a woman,' said the then churchwarden, 'she couldn't scramble up on the roof to check the gutters.' Within a year Peter and I visited Bath Abbey and in the bookshop met its feisty female churchwarden. 'The first thing I did on my appointment,' she confided, unprompted, 'was buy a boiler suit so that I could get up on the roof to check the gutters.' The very thought gave me vertigo.

Abby says she has met many young women who, though confident about their potential in the job market, struggle with their role in the Church. They suspect Paul was a misogynist. So either whole chunks of the Bible must be out of date and not worth reading, or they will have to limit their potential to meet with reduced expectations. Or, of course, abandon the institutional Church altogether.

If Western women are fed the myth that we're past our shelf-life at fifty, if the workplace hasn't always given us the opportunities we deserve, and the Church compounds the problem by giving us little encouragement to explore our gifting at any age, then why did God bother making woman at all? After all, he might have found other methods of procreation. Humans could have been androgynous, hatched from an egg.

But since woman was a vital part of creation, what might be his perspective on this particular half of the species? Apart from Emmeline Pankhurst and Elizabeth Cady Stanton, founders of the women's suffrage movement in the UK and USA respectively, and both mighty Christian preachers, the achievements of twentieth-century women of faith seem slim compared to so many of their fearless, outspoken, social-reforming, nineteenth-century sisters. So are the women of the twenty-first century still so busy recovering lost ground that we're not fit for God's purpose? These questions have pursued me. I have spent many years weighing up a mass of differing biblical interpretations, historical attitudes and cultural expectations in an effort to piece together a story of woman.

Time now to take a trip back to the original sources – the Hebrew Scriptures and the New Testament, the historic documents that explore her and not just his story. The Hebraic way of handling biblical material is to squeeze the text like a lemon until the juice flows, and when it stops, give it another squeeze just in case there is another nuance to be had. Sadly, the Church inherited a Hellenistic, or Greco-Roman, approach to all study, including theology. Learning is cerebral. The brain must be fed, reason satisfied. The Jewish tradition, in contrast, is to learn with practice in mind. Doing is more important than knowing. That's why story is the very fabric of the Hebrew Scriptures, and Jesus, immersed in that culture, continually resorted to parable. He knew that stories could be milked repeatedly and never run dry. Each time they are told they bring fresh revelation. 'With stories, you don't ask questions,' goes an old Jewish saying.

I apologise in advance if, as I share my own journey and write from my limited perspective, I may appear to overlook at times those with very different experiences from my own – the ever-increasing number of women who are single because of separation or divorce, or who have never married, or cannot marry because of their sexuality or gender, or perhaps because there is an imbalance in the number of men and women in the church; those who do not have children, either by choice, circumstance or in great sorrow; my black sisters, when my comprehension of their feelings and their battles comes only from a limited experience of anti-semitism. I hope nonetheless that much of what I say will be relevant to all my sisters under the skin – and to all the men who share our journey through the world.

My belief is that from the beginning of time, women have had an equal part to play in the story God was writing about his people – demonstrated by the extraordinary place they have carved out for themselves in history. I am constantly amazed by how timeless the Bible is, and how it is more, not less, relevant to our culture as we dig for the essence of what it really says. 'Women are there, defining history,' Rabbi Julia Neuberger once said to me, 'and finding them is like discovering precious nuggets of gold.'

By embarking on a romp through the biblical texts and history books, in search of the challenges, achievements, failures and joys of women as they have wrestled through the ages to take their place in the universe, this is above all a celebration of all that women have been, are and will be. The journey starts at creation, and continues on through the centuries to the place we have reached today. It's the story of tough Jewish matriarchs and risk-taking female leaders in the Old Testament, and determined, powerful women in the New. It encompasses a host of women down through the years who have inherited that same passionate determination to rise to the challenge of God's radical call, and discover what it means to be a woman in her right.

Today's woman of faith may not be able to have it all – at least, not all at once – but like her sisters past, present and future, she has the power to fulfil her God-given potential and change the world in ways he always knew she would.

Part 1

The Hebrew Woman –
A Matriarchal Heritage

Chapter 1

The Life-giving Woman

The book of Genesis ('The Beginning' in Hebrew) describes the start of history and her story. There is Adam all alone in a breathtaking, pristine, resplendent, new world. But there is no one to share his pleasure in the soft cotton wool balls that scud across the magnificent vault of a Wedgewood sky, or the diamond dew-drops that drip from the riot of multi coloured flowers nodding happily among endless acres of sweet-smelling grasses and stout, shady trees, or the foam-tipped aquamarine waters that lap gently around the borders of his garden. He tries to decide whether it's possible to have a meaningful relationship with any of the creatures that roam freely on his land, but, strangely enough, none meet his particular requirements.

The job spec is fairly straightforward at this stage – someone who will share his heart, body, soul and mind. Only later, after the loss of his golden paradise, does he add cook, dishwasher, cleaner, childminder and general drudge to the list, someone to run the home and kids to free him to be a successful leader, to iron his shirts so that he looks the part, to fill his belly so he doesn't suffer malnutrition on the way up, and to meet his bodily needs by metamorphosing into a sex strumpet when he returns from a difficult day at work.

For most of the twentieth century, particularly after two world wars when women showed how tough and competent they could be given the opportunity, a wife in the parlour contributed to a man's status in society. Marriage meant upward mobility. He, in turn, kept an insurance policy in the bottom drawer, providing for the little woman in the event of her being careless enough to lose him. I remember as a child that when my mother's friends did indeed face the trauma and ignominy of being without their breadwinner – for far less noble reasons than his unpredictable death – they often discovered that, despite their years of selfless service, when the bounder left them for a younger model they were in fact destitute and, since he hadn't done them the favour of dying, unable to claim the benefits of that insurance.

The last century could be cruel to women. Yet this rigid middle-class division of roles – the superior male doing the work, the inferior woman seeing to his domestic needs – was regarded as a Christian principle, supported by the Church and often based on an extremely convenient misinterpretation of the creation story itself.

Woman is the image of her father

In the image of God he created them; male and female he created them.

(Gen. 1:27)

The first account of creation in Genesis 1 reveals an extraordinary reality. Individually and corporately, men and women are reflections of their father-creator in heaven. We have his capacity to love, laugh and form intimate relationships. 'You want to know what I'm like?' God asks human beings. 'Then all you have to do is take a look in the mirror, or at the man or woman sitting next to you to see the pinnacle of my creative powers.' And that can come as something of a shock to the system.

God is neither male nor female, and is fully reflected only in both genders. Both are given dominion over the created order and told to reproduce. Both are made from the same design, and of the same stuff – two sides of the same coin.

So how was it possible for the great early church father, Augustine, to write in the fourth century AD, 'The woman herself alone is not the image of God, whereas the man alone is the image of God as fully and completely as when the woman is joined with him.?'[1] As early as the second century AD, the founder of systematic theology himself, Origen, said, 'What is seen with the eyes of the creator is masculine, and not feminine, for God does not stoop to look at what is feminine and of the flesh.'[2]

How could they possibly think that God was male, wilfully ignoring the wonderful first creation account? The key is in the writings of yet another second-century Christian sage. Clement of Alexandria said, 'Nothing for men is shameful, for man is endowed with reason; but for woman it brings shame even to reflect on what her nature is.'[3] The early church fathers, conditioned by their own classical Greek culture, admired reason above all other human qualities. Being made in the image of God meant that, unlike animals, man, but not woman, had been given an intellect. It was obvious: he was eminently reasonable, while she – it was abundantly clear to every man – was irrational and incomprehensible, given to sudden mood swings and strange intuitions. And so they made an extraordinary quantum leap – that she could not have been made in the image of God. Whatever the book of Genesis said, she was intellectually inferior and therefore a lesser being spiritually.

It never seems to have occurred to the early fathers that it takes a very practical, rational person to run a home, a husband, children, a dog, a rabbit and a budgie, let alone fulfil the other jobs most women do. It never seems to have crossed their minds that men simply don't understand woman's logic. Instead, her so-called moods, her contrariness, her sheer illogicality, they reasoned, must have something to do with that monthly mystery that they found so distasteful. Nowhere in the Bible is there any suggestion that female hormones, whether kind or contrary, have any major effect on our ability to make decisions. Yet until recently in the West, and still in many Muslim countries, the idea that women are unsuited to certain tasks – usually ones that involve thinking – persists.

The tragedy is that the clear creation message – the innate equality of men and women – should be obvious to those who love and grasp the Genesis story, to a people entrusted with eyes to see it, not blinkered by history and culture – in other words, the Church. Equality certainly has no place in contemporary Chasidic Judaism, Islam or Hinduism, which put a far greater value on boys than girls. For instance, from a Muslim point of view:

A successful wife is one that recognises the husband's nature. You should try and understand his temperament. If he is angry do not utter something that will increase his anger. Always watch his mood before speaking. If he responds to jokes by expressing happiness then continue doing so, otherwise not. If he is displeased with you, do not sit with a sullen face. Instead, plead with him for forgiveness and try to win him over whether it is your fault or not. This will result in his love increasing for you.[4]

Instead of proclaiming a radically different message, Christians, sadly, have tended to bang a very similar drum.

Even if our recent record is not quite so damning, we still do little to speak out for our sisters in a world where many women die in childbirth when the husband, who has first to give permission for a caesarian section, goes missing. After all, she's easy to replace. For Professor Anne Garden MBE, retired Dean of Medicine at Lancaster University, working in India in the early days of her career was a rude awakening. A reluctant feminist, it was seeing how disposable women could be that changed her mind. 'When men own women's bodies they abuse them,' she said to me.

In Afghanistan in the 1960s women had the vote. In the 1980s seven women were members of parliament. Before the mujahideen took power in 1992, 50 per cent of university students in Kabul were female. They were interested in fashion, wore make-up and mini-skirts and took education and a career for granted, much as women in the West. In 1996, when the Taliban filled the power vacuum created by the Russians, women were threatened with a lashing if they dared leave the home without being robed from head to toe in a heavy, scratchy burqa with its small, crocheted grille that barely allows the wearer to breathe or see. Professional women were denied any right to a career and ended up destitute, begging on the streets for food for their children. One in four women died giving birth in filthy, infested maternity hospitals. Education for girls was forbidden. Half the population became invisible. Farahnaz Nazir, founder of the Afghanistan Women's Association, said, 'Society is like a bird. It has two wings. And a bird cannot fly if one wing is broken.'

Today life is only slightly easier for women there and in many Muslim countries. Under Sharia law a man is entitled to have four wives, and a wife can do little without her husband's say-so. He is entirely responsible for the family's purse. A woman faces death by stoning for becoming pregnant after she has been raped. And men refuse to see that they are limited, earth-bound because of it.

But every now and then small signs of hope push their way through the unforgiving ground. In 2012, the Taliban shot fifteen-year-old Pakistani schoolgirl Malala Yousafzai in the head three times for demanding education for girls. After her recovery she became the world's most prominent campaigner for the right to education and was awarded Pakistan's first National Youth Peace Prize, as well as the Nobel Peace Prize.

In May 2017 Afghanistan launched its first all-women TV channel, in an attempt to highlight the rights of Afghan women. Presenters and producers regularly receive death threats, but won't let that stop them.

These are tiny jewels flickering in a dark world for many women, where there appears little political will or ability to act. Little girls endure enforced genital mutilation or have acid thrown in their faces as they walk to school, twelve and thirteen year olds are sold into marriage to much older men, their bodies unprepared physically to cope with rape and pregnancy. In her brilliant and carefully researched book *Scars Across Humanity*, which is a heart-breaking read, Elaine Storkey points out that in fact rape, domestic abuse, prostitution, honour killings and violence against women of every kind occur at all stages of life, and in all cultures and societies. And that the traditional patriarchy of the Church and the gender inequality it generated has in fact contributed to it.[5]

When the early church fathers countermanded the message of equality in Genesis they encouraged the reduction of women to a commodity, and the world was the darker and poorer. Throughout history, however, Christian women, largely acting alone, or in small, often despised groups, revived the radical flame and attacked basic injustices, achieved suffrage,[6] improved the lot of prostitutes, offered education to the poorest and proclaimed new freedoms wherever they went.

Largely, however, the Church dropped the ball. The late twentieth-century feminist movement caught it before it touched the ground and ran with it, rising to the challenge laid down by early Christian feminists. They changed basic attitudes to divorce, women's pay, child abuse and rape, and then went way beyond the God-given remit, claiming that women were morally superior and men dispensable.[7] In today's post-feminist era, men in the West are still struggling to redefine what it means to be a male, while the Church, always running to catch up, can, in many places, still be ambivalent about a woman's role, and blames feminists for creating the problem in the first place, rather than reclaiming the trophy that should have been ours.

Man's little helper?

It is not good for the man to be alone. I will make a helper suitable for him.

(Gen. 2:18)

It is the second account of creation in chapter 2 of Genesis that seems to have thrown the major spanner into the works. That little English word 'helper' became a justification for relegating woman to God's great postscript. Some might say that his first attempt at creating humankind was a trial run, that he took a look at Adam, stood back, scratched his head and said, 'I must be able to do better than that.'

The Hebrew word for 'helper' is *ezer*, used fifteen times in the Old Testament, fourteen of them referring to God himself, for example Psalm 30:10, where the writer cries out, 'O Lord, be my helper', and Psalm 54:4, where he calls God his helper. If God is our helper, is he then just a prop for the humans he created? Like any father, he sorts out our messes from time to time, but that doesn't make him subordinate to us, an assistant in all our little schemes, project, and ambitions – much as we would like him to be.

There is no hierarchical implication here in the word 'helper'. God doesn't establish a primary and secondary authority over creation, no chief executive and vice chief, no sheriff and deputy. Woman isn't created as backup any more than she is a helpless dependant. *Ezer* is a verb as well as a noun and means 'to protect, surround, defend, cherish'. These are powerful, active words for the way God

26

cares for us, and much more reflective of the text than 'backup' or 'support' – which Roget's Thesaurus also describes as 'crutch' and 'backbone'. Are men really spineless jellyfish who need a woman to lean on? If I help you cross the road, which of us is the stronger?

In 1971 at a Billy Graham event in the USA, President Richard Nixon said:

> We all think of Billy as a strong man. But as I look at the Graham family, if I am asked who are the stronger, Billy Graham or the women in his family, I'd say the women every time . . . God made man out of the soft earth, but he made woman out of a hard rib – the woman is the stronger of the two.[8]

Women often are resourceful and resilient, and when we really love, cherish and protect a man, it can transform him into the giant he was meant to be. That is a fearful responsibility, as we also have the means to reduce him to mincemeat. More on that later.

This 'helper' God creates is described as 'fit' or 'suitable' for Adam, both slightly inadequate translations of the propositional clause, *kenegdo*, not used anywhere else in the Bible. *Kenegdo* comes from the root word *neged* which means 'opposite'. A more accurate translation of *kenegdo* is 'opposite against', or 'standing boldly opposite'. In other words, Eve is right in Adam's face, nose to nose, eyeball to eyeball. They can gaze at each other with love and longing, but she can also confront where necessary.

Archbishop Desmond Tutu unwittingly described *kenegdo* when he spoke of his relationship with his wife, Leah:

> I have a very strong weakness for being liked. I want to be popular. I love to be loved. One has enjoyed the limelight. I am guilty of the sin of pride. Sometimes I find it very difficult to be humble – that is why it is so good to have Leah. She pulls me down a peg or two. To her I am not an archbishop with a Nobel Prize. I'm just a not-very-good husband who loves gardens but won't do any gardening. Your family is there to do what your guardian angel is supposed to do: keep your ego manageable and remind you that you are just a man.[9]

My friend Sharon, who had a number of partners before a God encounter turned her life upside down, waited a long time for a prince to arrive on his charger and sweep her off her feet. When he did, he was an available free-church minister in his forties who had ridden out the relentless advances of many a single woman in his congregations who fancied being the pastor's wife. But Sharon didn't simply swoon into his arms and let him carry her off. She had used the time of enforced celibacy to grow comfortable about who she was on her own. 'All these years,' he said to her, exasperated, 'I could have had any one of countless women who hung on my every word and agreed with everything I said – and God has to give me you.'

'Ah,' Sharon said to him, 'that's because he knew it was me you needed – for character-building.'

There's an unattributed quote that says, 'When women are bored we shop. When men are bored they start a war.' According to the biblical histories of the kings of Israel, it was a habit to go to war in the springtime. So sad to disrupt such a beautiful season with aggression and violence. But when King David decided to give the bloodshed a break, he ended up committing adultery and murder instead.

The ancient Greek playwright, Aristophanes, came up with the best way to put an end to this testosterone-fuelled madness. In his bawdy anti-war comedy, *Lysistrata*, he describes how one woman set out to end the Peloponnesian War by convincing the women of Greece to withhold conjugal privileges until their men were so desperate they negotiated peace. If the males can't be subject to reason, women simply find another way.

In his book, *Borderline*,[10] army veteran Stan Goff claims that war-loving and women-hating are two sides of the same coin, and stem from the same source – fear – a fear that rationalises conquest. Goff believes that confronting male contempt for women is also a way of challenging their senseless, wasteful justifications for war, so feminism is, inadvertently, a gift to men.

'No man is an island entire of himself,' wrote the roistering sixteenth-century Dean of St Paul's, poet John Donne, who seemed to spend a great deal of time in the bedroom trying to avoid that possibility. But away with the notion that God looks down on poor little man and says, 'Oh dear, you're all on your owny-oh. I'll make you a human teddy bear for company, to drive the nasty loneliness away.' God did not create woman because he knew Adam would be no good at keeping a social diary, or because he would never go out and buy himself a new fig leaf when the old one wore out. His intention was far more all-encompassing than simply satisfying the man's need for company.

In the garden were two trees with specific names: the Tree of the Knowledge of Good and Evil, and the Tree of Life. Before Eve's appearance Adam was told he could eat from the latter, but not the former. So why did he not help himself from the Tree of Life? Pastor Watchman Nee, who died in confinement in a Chinese prison in 1972, believed that Adam was only alive at this stage, but didn't have eternal life. 'From simply being created by God, to being born of him', Adam needed to eat from this particular tree, and Pastor Nee wondered whether it wasn't therefore a male tendency to be head-strong and independent from the very beginning. The Maker sees it and cleverly creates a being to meet his deepest need – someone who will look him in the eye and draw him gently out of his isolationism and self-sufficiency, so that they are more whole together than apart.

Here in Genesis is the answer to the question posed by *Bridget Jones' Diary*[11] as to whether men and women really need each other at all in this enlightened age of ours. Vexed female columnists denounced Bridget as a bad female role model for daring to suggest life might be better with a man. After all, countless women now choose to live and raise children without a man in their life. And others are happier and safer alone. But Bridget gets her man and life is richer because of it. Men and women were made for each other. But the full benefits of the relationship depend on our being lovingly face to face.

Kenegdo isn't simply about marriage. Although woman supple-ments and complements the male, Jesus never married and was certainly not incomplete. He had many significant, equal relation-ships with women that satisfied his practical, spiritual and emotional needs. Woman can be mother, sister, daughter, friend, colleague, confidante, ballroom dancing or squash partner – answering to the needs of the male in so many different ways.

So this is what I've been missing

So God says, 'Adam, I have the perfect answer. I will create someone who will fulfil all your deepest longings. She will be wife, friend, confidante, colleague and lover, but it will cost you an arm and a leg.'

'Tell you what,' Adam says to God, 'what will you give me for just a rib?'

Traditionally, woman was formed from an entirely dispensable part of the male anatomy, but forty-two other references in the Bible to the Hebrew word *sela,* used here for 'rib', are translated 'side'. More than 250 years ago, in his great commentary on the Bible, Matthew Henry wrote:

> The woman was made out of rib out of the side of Adam; not made out of his head to rule over him; nor out of his feet to be trampled upon by him; but out of his side to be equal with him, under his arm to be protected by him, and near to his heart to be beloved.[12]

When he sees the woman, Adam recognises that this is what he has been waiting for – 'bone of my bone and flesh of my flesh'. In other words, 'Nice as they are, God, the animals just didn't ring my bell, but this time you've excelled yourself. This one's just like me.' No mention here of physical, anatomical or biological differences, no pecking order or division of labour. Man and woman are psychologically, sociologically and spiritually the same, even if they are somewhat physically different. Human females are the only mammals to have breasts rather than teats, and evolutionists are not sure why. Nonetheless, it is the sameness Adam welcomes. The differences are only skin-deep.

Our Joel was three when his sister Abby was born. 'At first it was like having a human doll,' he said some years later. 'I loved it even more when she began to communicate in words I could recognise. She became a person just like me and it was so exciting.' All was well while she remained dependent, adoring and malleable. But imperceptibly the little girl with seraphic face and golden curls grew into an adolescent who rejected his protectiveness and pedantic ideas. She realised her big brother wasn't a giant after all, and developed a finely honed vocabulary that highlighted his foibles and failures and demolished him in front of his friends.

For two teenagers, loving was no longer automatic. It had to be learned. Once he was no longer threatened by her independent mind, and she by his need to dominate her, once they recognised their innate, God-given sameness and equality, a deeper relationship formed on the foundation of mutual respect. It amused me how fiercely they refused to enter into any inferred criticism of the other by a parent, and I loved that loyalty. He took a personal pride in her achievements, and she often turned to him for male support. Having discovered the benefits of having a strong and gifted sister for a friend, Joel couldn't bear to see restrictions on any woman simply on the basis of her gender.

Leaving, cleaving and coming unstuck

Adam calls his wife Eve, in Hebrew, *Chava*. Hebrew words are formed around a basic root and added to. Here the root word is *chai*, meaning 'life'. *Chai* is the root of the Hebrew word *Lechaim*, when you clink glasses of wine and say 'cheers'. It means 'to life'. The frequent biblical translation of *chava*, 'Mother of all Living', is insufficient. Eve is so much more than a walking reproductive system. In the Hebrew Scriptures the verb *chavah* is consistently translated as 'to declare'. In other words, the first woman's name has a verbal implication. It actually means 'spoken word of life'. Woman not only gives, she also speaks life to the man, and, subsequently, to all humanity. In the early days of development a foetus is neither male nor female. At sixteen weeks a sudden surge of androgens, the male hormone, precipitates the development of distinctive male characteristics in a boy, causing a slight thickening of the central column in the brain. It's possible the male's speech is more restricted to the left brain, while women find it easier to use both hemispheres at once, contributing to their communication and relational skills.

Many men do seem to find it harder than women to express their feelings. Domestic violence is often a result of an inability to express anger appropriately. On the other hand, some men, the Italians for example, appear to defy the 'Berlin Wall in the Brain' concept. Not that I've been close enough to an Italian to know whether they're as emotionally literate as they appear. On the other hand, I was a communications manager in the NHS for many years and know that boys generally develop motor skills much later than girls and that, from childhood, boys outnumber girls by as many as ten to one in needing the specialist attention of a speech and language therapist.

If woman is created to speak life, it can only benefit the whole of society, including men. Small wonder, therefore, that throughout history there appears to have been a vested interest in muzzling her. The Serpent, as he's portrayed in Genesis, set upon the downfall of humankind, seeks to sever it from all that is good, holy and wonderful.

At first all is well in the land of romance. Adam and Eve 'cleave' to one other. The Hebrew word is *dabaq*, meaning 'to cling, stick or adhere to'. Any parent knows that separating flesh joined by super glue can only be achieved with pain and trauma. The principle of leaving the parental home behind and cleaving to the new partner, reiterated by Jesus himself, is foundational. Adam and Eve had no parents to leave, but Adam seems to have been quite happy to exchange his nights out with the animals for evenings at home with the wife. In other words, Eve now has a prime call on his commitment, while he must be the priority in her life, even after the children arrive.

It is amazing how many relationships come unstuck on the leaving. My mother used to ring her mother every day for advice, support and commiseration, even though they lived a mere ten miles apart. My grandmother's word was law in our home. 'I've always been a better mother than a wife,' my grandmother used to say with some pride. 'A woman will always be better at one role than the other.' In her case it was a justification for ruling the roost in her home and ours, and not ideal for my father or grandfather.

So Adam and Eve are stuck to or with each other – naked and without shame. Some years ago I wrote an article for *Woman Alive* magazine about the extraordinary gift of the physical side of marriage. A woman wrote to me to say she could not accept that there could be any pleasure in sex. She and her husband had been so horrified at the sight of each other's naked bodies on their wedding night that they never managed to consummate the relationship. In our liberated society many have been robbed of the joyous freedom of being naked in the presence of the beloved by all kinds of abusive encounters.

The first couple's nakedness in the garden is mental, emotional, spiritual and physical. The man and woman have nothing to hide from each other. No past baggage, no rejection complex or horrible memory can rise up like bile to sour their spontaneous, joyous mutual discovery and companionship. Until one seismic moment of madness.

Where was Adam when Eve was deceived by the Serpent and took the fruit she knew wasn't hers to have? Was he at the bottom of the garden on a deckchair reading the newspaper or having a nap? Had he gone to the football match? The text says, 'She . . . gave some to her husband, who was with her' (Gen. 3:6). He was at her elbow. He doesn't seem to have tried very hard to fulfil his duty to protect this being who was his to cherish, or to exercise the authority he had been given over every living thing, including the Serpent. He is fully implicated in Eve's decision to ignore her Maker, and from that moment the relationship between men and women is doomed. One cock a snook at the Creator, and, 'It's all his fault', or 'She made me do it'. Farewell to trust, harmony and intimacy. Enter vulnerability, insecurity and isolation.

This description of a non-communicative husband by his frustrated wife, recounted by Paul Tournier, the Swiss psychologist and marriage guidance counsellor, says it all. When Tournier suggested she tell her husband how she felt, she blurted out, 'My husband is a mysterious island. I am forever circling round it but never finding a beach where I may land.'

'I understood her, for it is true,' Tournier said,

'There are men who are like mysterious islands. They protect themselves against any approach. They no longer express themselves, nor do they take a stand on anything. When their wife consults them on something important, they hide themselves behind their paper. They look deeply absorbed. They answer without even looking up, in a tone impersonal, anonymous and vague, which excludes all argument. Or else they make a joke of it.'[13]

'Yes, dear. No, dear. Three bags full, dear.' I can see my father now, sitting in his favourite green moquette armchair, his glasses on the end of his nose, vainly trying to hide behind the *Daily Express* from a verbal assault through the hatch that linked our kitchen to the sitting room, an expert at 'selective deafness'.

History goes pear-shaped

'I will make your pains in childbearing very severe;
with painful labour you will give birth to children.
Your desire will be for your husband,
and he will rule over you.'

(Gen. 3:16)

So much misunderstanding of male–female relationships by the Church is found in this one little verse. Commentators are divided about what it means, but it appears unlikely that the word 'desire' (Hebrew *teshuqah*) has a primarily sexual connotation. Experience should tell us which of the two genders tends to be the more predatory. The one with the testosterone, actually. Surely, God knew that would be the case, so had no reason to suggest the woman would be permanently on heat.

Yet throughout the tortuous history of the Church this verse has cast woman in the role of temptress, a misapprehension that began in the period between the end of the Old Testament and the beginning of the New, when some Jewish scholars were trying to square their Scriptures with tales of the pagan Greek and Roman gods and goddesses that were an inherent part of the culture. The biblical story of Eve was enmeshed with the mythical Pandora, a beautiful but deceitful woman sent to earth by the gods with a box of misery for the human race.

The Babylonian Talmud, a compilation of traditional Jewish sayings, passed down orally from one generation to the next, yet not

committed to writing until the seventh century, claimed that Eve –
or was it Pandora – brought ten curses on herself when she opened
the forbidden box. Number five is: 'Your desire shall be for your
husband', followed by a rather coarse and explicit description of
what that entails – enough to make a twenty-first century husband
reckon half a chance would be a fine thing.

The Apocryphal book Ecclesiasticus, written between 200 and
100 BC, first claims, 'From woman a beginning of sin; and because of
her all die,'[14] giving theological justification to an erroneous cultural
attitude prevalent at the time. Later, the Apostle Paul, in his letter to
the Romans, makes it clear that death and sin came through 'Adam',
as representative of humankind rather than the male.[15]

The King James and Revised Standard Versions of the Bible add
an English 'yet', before 'your desire will be for your husband', establishing a tenuous connection between childbirth and a woman's
supposed indefatigable sexual desire. A loose interpretation would
be, 'Sorry, girls, having babies is going to be horrible, but since
you'll go on having the hots for your man, you'll keep on putting
yourselves through that particular misery.' It's a link that isn't in the
original Hebrew. So what does the verse mean?

'I will greatly increase your pains (*itsavon*) in childbearing; with
painful labour (*etzev*) you will give birth to children'. *Itsavon* normally
means sorrow, and *etzev* toil. They are not the usual biblical words
used to describe the pain of childbirth. But they are poetic, a direct
parallel to Adam's 'sorrow' and 'toil' as he struggles to make the ground
productive.[16] No basic biological differences that predispose women to
running the home and men to running the world are enshrined here.
No emphasis on man's greater physical strength. 'Work' will involve
the same degree of sorrow and toil for both. In fact, of all mammals,
humans have the hardest time in childbirth, often needing help if they
or their baby's life is not to be put at risk. It probably takes more physical stamina and a higher pain threshold than most other human activity. I am rhesus negative, my husband rhesus positive. If I had tried to
have children a mere ten years earlier than I did, before the invention
of Rh immunoglobulin to kill my antibodies, I would have been
fortunate to have one live baby. Not to mention the placenta praevia
and prolapsed cord of my second pregnancy.

In the Genesis account the Serpent is cursed. The ground is cursed. But God will not and cannot curse the creatures he has created with such love and hope. Hard work and pain are the inevitable consequences of human determination to follow their own propensities. Eve is in fact blessed. Woman will give birth to the Messiah, the one who will ultimately grind the Serpent into oblivion and restore human beings to their original dignity and fellowship with God. With such a promise the process of having babies was never going to be easy. Since the Messiah will be born of a woman, 'the Serpent' will have a vested interest in making sure every birth is threatened.

I suspect this is the moment when the hitherto serene and seamless female reproductive system is completely scrambled. Periods never arrive at the right time; desire between spouses doesn't coincide; fertility is a hit-and-miss affair; pregnancy means nausea, stretch marks, high blood pressure, gastric reflux and the slow disintegration of the teeth; and the menopause brings on the dreaded hot flushes. When my husband says he sympathises with the prayer that thanks God he's not a woman, I'm tempted to think he grossly exaggerates the minor inconveniences. On the other hand, would men have coped with periods? The poet Carol Ann Duffy thinks not.[17]

> Then he started his period.
>
> One week in bed.
> Two doctors in.
> Three painkillers four times a day.
>
> And later
> a letter
> to the powers that be
> demanding full-paid menstrual leave twelve weeks per year.
> I see him still,
> his selfish pale face peering at the moon
> through the bathroom window.
> *The curse,* he said, *the curse.*

Some commentaries suggest the Genesis text means, 'I will greatly increase your sorrows and conceptions.' In other words, God never originally intended pregnancy would be the potential outcome of every experience of intercourse, ruining the enjoyment factor for millions of women down through the centuries, condemning them to serial childbearing and an early grave. Surely sex was given for mutual pleasure and intimacy, and not just to turn women into baby-making machines. Perhaps he was even rooting for us to invent contraception, creating hitherto unknown freedoms for twenty-first-century women.

Of course, it isn't only women who are blessed with problems in the reproductive department. When her patients complain about the lot of women, retired obstetrician Professor Anne Garden tells them to bide their time until that moment when they are tucked up comfortably in bed, and he is tyrannised by his prostate, trotting backwards and forwards to the loo.

So what is the woman's desire?

These days my desire for my husband flickers on in its post-meno-pausal, reduced state, but is probably not a reflection of this verse, since impregnation at our stage of life really would be a miracle. *Teshuqah* was translated 'lust' by Jerome in his Latin translation of the Bible known as the Vulgate, published in AD 382, as it was in the first English translation of the Bible in 1380 by Wycliffe. Gordon Wenham, in his 1987 commentary on Genesis, still seems to think that the word he translates as 'urge' has sexual overtones.[18] 'Women often allow themselves to be exploited ... because of their urge towards their husband: their sexual appetite may sometimes make them submit to quite unreasonable male demands.' Had it been thirty years later, I would have been convinced that he had been reading *Fifty Shades of Grey*. E. L. James's novel is deeply flawed. Women may fantasise about having a more aggressive sexual experience, but that's all it is – a fantasy. 'A psychologically healthy woman avoids pain. She wants to feel safe, respected and cared for by a man she can trust.'[19] In reality she will only submit to abusive male behaviour out of fear or poor self-esteem, for money, or in countries and situations where she has no alternative.

In the 1970s, responding to the growth of feminism, American biblical scholar Susan Foh agreed that *teshuqah* or 'desire' could not be sexual in this context, then argued that woman's real yearning is not for sex, but mastership.[20] Apart from the fact that it simply isn't in the text, there is no evidence for it. Until the 1980s there was no question of woman dominating her man, and there still isn't in much of the world. Imagine a young Indian woman, condemned to slavery in her in-laws' home for not having a big enough dowry, ever dreaming of being the boss.

The wonder of the Scriptures is their ability both in text and story to transcend cultural, international and historical boundaries. If it doesn't connect with my experience as a woman, wherever I live, whoever I am, it cannot truly be the inspired Word of God. But time and time again, as I dig deeper into the text, it challenges aspects, not just of my life but of every life, with a wisdom that belies its age.

When stuck with the interpretation of a text it helps to see what it means elsewhere. The word *Teshuqah* is used in two other places in the Hebrew Scriptures – in Genesis 4:7 where God warns Cain that 'sin is crouching at your door; it desires [it pulls] to have you, but you must rule over it', and in Song of Songs 7:10 where the writer says, 'I belong to my beloved, and his desire [longing or pull] is for me.'

In the amorous context of the Song of Songs the word 'longing' or 'yearning' may well have an erotic connotation – but it's healthy, happy and positive. In the bleak post-Fall context, it seems the opposite – negative and neurotic.

Missionary doctor Katharine Bushnell (1855–1946), who campaigned against the white slave trade and abuse of women throughout the world, shattered preconceived stereotypes of the role of women in 1910, in her book *God's Word to Women*. During her time in China she was horrified at the way culturally biased translations of the Bible brought women into greater, not lesser bondage. She was convinced that this was totally at odds with the liberating, healing power of the gospel, and spent forty years learning biblical languages and studying the original texts, so that women everywhere would have a solid, biblical foundation for their freedom. Dr Bushnell points out that most of the ancient translations of the texts, including the Septuagint of 285 BC, kept the literal translation of *teshuqah*, which is 'turning'. In other words, Eve is told that from now on her turning, or natural gravitation, will be towards man rather than towards God. She will, in fact, make an idol of him.

That translation makes a great deal of sense to me. As a single woman I relied on an hour of meditation and prayer each morning. Once married, especially when the babies arrived, there wasn't time. But in all honesty the erosion of that hour predated motherhood. In fact, it began on the first morning of our marriage. I simply didn't need that God-dependency in the same way – not when there was a flesh and blood source of wisdom, comfort and company sitting in the bed next to me. For some things a girl must be alone. But it was abundantly clear, as Peter picked up his Bible and tucked himself happily between the sheets, that he had no intention of vacating his warm little space to move elsewhere. That was the beginning of many years of negotiation for the quiet I needed to re-establish the primary relationship I had apparently mislaid.

It's all too easy to become a little dependent when you are married to a rock like my man. But it isn't only in marriage that women have a tendency to revolve around men like the moon around the sun. Not so long ago it was the accepted culture of the workplace. Nurses scurried around male doctors, air hostesses around the pilots, office clerks around male managers. Socio-economic independence for women in the West has modified that behaviour. But even so, there are still secretaries who would lie down in a puddle rather than let the boss dirty his shoes. In some churches, the minister still has a bevy of good ladies at his beck and call. A single girl is always being asked if there is a man in her life. It is too easy to invest our all – our attractiveness as women, our value as people, our justification for living – in male acceptance, pleasure and approval. And perhaps *teshuqah* does have a sexual component when a woman makes doe eyes at a married boss, colleague, doctor, vicar or any man she sees as potential for fulfilling her emotional needs.

Writing about the sexual revolution of the 1960s that followed the introduction of the pill, when so many women were deceived into believing they were now as free as they needed to be, historian

Virginia Nicholson said, 'As the prohibitive climate of the 1950s evaporated, women sleepwalked in sexual laxity. But their self-esteem was still predicated on pleasing a man.'[21] So no freedom from the tie that had women bound – *teshuqah*.

How well I remember the countless, boring 'snogging parties' back then – when couples spent an entire evening hunched up together, exchanging saliva because the alternative was to be the only woman in the room who had no knee to sit on, no armchair to share, no proprietary male to claim her. How I hated them, but how I feared being that lone woman even more.

So little has changed. Back from Soul Survivor, an under-canvas conference for thousands of young people, a friend described how the girls she took got up at 5.30 a.m. to get the hot showers, shampoo and blow-dry their hair and put on full make-up before the boys got up, while the boys didn't wash for a week and certainly didn't notice the efforts made for their benefit.

In its extreme form, the unspoken expectation that only a man can meet our deepest needs leads to an obsession with body image, the diet and fitness craze, and, ultimately, anorexia and bulimia. In developing countries, many of the inhumane practices imposed on women, such as circumcision, are condoned and even encouraged by women, terrified their daughters won't attract a man.

In a very popular TED talk on feminism of 2017, the hugely successful Nigerian writer, Chimamanda Ngozi Adichie, claimed that from their early years women are taught to compromise their potential. Instead of competing for career achievement, they compete for the attention of men.[22]

She followed that up in April 2018 in a book for a friend, who had asked her for advice on raising a baby girl to be an equal member of the human race. She called it *Dear Ijeawele: A Feminist Manifesto in Fifteen Suggestions*. One of her strongest directives is to encourage a daughter to reject likeability. 'Oh my God, all that time wasted,' says Adichie, 'that boys and men do not waste.'[23]

And what does the man do with the woman's desire?

'And so he will rule over you', says God, with a long sigh, I suspect. Her morbid craving for him makes her vulnerable to his instinctive domination and control of her. The secretary needs to be trodden on to feel a sense of worth, and the boss is happy to oblige, as it gives him a sense of power. The mistress stays with a man who has no intention of leaving his wife for her because any crumb of affection is better than none, and that enables him to keep her in a gilded cage. Women marry, not for love, but because they cannot face being alone. Co-dependency does not lead to healthy compatibility. It demeans rather than dignifies the other.

For God, this is a sad and sorry irony. Men were never made to be all-powerful. They were never intended to live a life imprisoned by the stereotypes of tough, unemotional, macho masculinity, nor the intolerable burden of having to fulfil a woman's every emotional need. They can be perfectly happy on their own little desert island, as Paul Tournier's client knew only too well – in front of a television or computer, absorbed by sport, lost in a piece of work brought home from the office, or pottering in the garden shed. Then he looks up and sees a boat coming for him. She's rowing for all she's worth, making dozens of different approaches in her determination to find a landing space. She finally gets there, and as she disembarks he throws up his hands in horror and heads for the trees. But the harder she tries to find him, the more determined he is to hide, for he knows that whatever he does, whatever he says, it will never be enough to fill what Jane Hanson calls 'the great canyon' in a woman.[24]

For the sake of self-preservation, he must find a way to keep her in her place, by becoming either the absent workaholic or the subjugating, desensitised male. How can the behaviour towards women of so many religious fundamentalists be understood, except by a deep-seated fear of the loss of power? They cannot live *kenegdo* with their women, for if she is allowed to express her views they may be forced to live with her confrontation, criticism and disapproval. And they may have to admit that they are not the perfect embodiment of divine authority and approval. Repressing her gives them the freedom to do exactly as they please, even if it means denying the tender, loving part of themselves.

Is it surprising that the leaders of the most repressive regimes in the world – China, North Korea, Russia, Syria, Sudan – determined to grasp complete domination of their people, are all men? It is disappointing that neither of the UK's two female prime ministers has been noticeably relational – but perhaps that's a reflection of a rather masculine concept of leadership in the party that gave them that power. On the other hand, the open communication skills of Angela Merkel, Chancellor of Germany for fifteen years and a respected, matriarchal figure, and Jacinda Ardern, the modern, dynamic Prime Minister of New Zealand, have assured their popularity and made them role models for intelligent, firm, but compassionate leadership. Nicola Sturgeon's handling of the COVID crisis in Scotland, with her clear, unthreatened and honest approach, inviting debate and welcoming feedback long before Boris Johnson got the message, earned her many more brownie points and the affection of the Scottish people.

At face value there seems little distinction between the man and the woman's sin and its consequences. Both make a bid for divinity, and both are condemned to hard work and grief. But in fact, as the story of woman unfolds, the initial failure and its implications are different. Woman is given dominion, authority, supremacy over the entire created order – with one restriction. She may not eat from one particular tree. She disobeys, takes what is not hers to have, and forfeits her authority, for man will now have a tendency to dominate and subjugate her. She who has the gift of speaking life, speaks death to Adam, and may now use her verbal skills to undermine, manipulate or domesticate men.

Adam, on the other hand, is given a relationship that is the very key to his wellbeing. He colludes with Eve when he should have protected her, and forfeits the benefits of that relationship. In dominating woman he loses an equal, a partner and a friend, unwittingly cutting himself off from the intimacy and closeness for which his entire being will always yearn.

The eternal tragedy of male and female relationships is encapsulated in this story for all time. Behind Adam and Eve the garden gate slams shut. No more frolics. Both are now condemned to the daily grind of creating a viable economy and raising a family. So why, when Genesis chapters 1 and 2 describe the intended created order, did the Church tend to base its concept of male–female relationships on chapter 3 which describes the Fall?

I was intrigued by a television series on Channel 4 called *Sex BC*. Professors of ancient history claimed that in the earliest recorded time, men and women were equal – hunting, gathering and cooking side by side. The women breastfed their babies to early childhood and it acted as a natural contraceptive. Then civilisation changed. Society became agricultural. A large workforce was needed to till the land. Babies were fed cows' milk. Women succumbed to one pregnancy after another, and their exhausted bodies often gave out in childbirth. Those that survived were domesticated, tied to the hearth. Woman's sexuality began to feel more like a curse than a blessing.

In the late 1980s, in the midst of the Church's debate on feminism, Professor of Psychology and Philosophy Mary Stewart van Leeuwen put it like this: 'The fall ripped apart the organic unity of homes and communities and turned us into a society of commuting wage earners (mostly men) and domestically isolated homemakers (mostly women).' In other words, man's dominion became domination and woman's sociability 'social enmeshment'.[25] We both became trapped in the cages that society, and often the Church, created for us. Men were locked into expectations of achievement, success and invulnerability, and women into nurturing, caring and self-sacrifice. And if we didn't fit the stereotypes, we felt more like Frankenstein's monster than God's created handiwork.

Adam and Eve before the Fall are male and female as God intended it, enjoying mutuality, compatibility and equality. We still catch a glimpse of what that can mean – in a marriage where we take the risk of exposing ourselves emotionally to our partner and it leads to a new and tender intimacy, or in a working relationship where, as colleagues, we use our gender differences dynamically to contribute to the success of a project and discover an almost heady satisfaction in complementary companionship.

Ultimately, it is the cross that grants a life-transforming redemption and restoration of the relationship lost through Adam and Eve's mutiny.

When a man hands over his autonomy to the man who wilfully surrendered his power and independence when he went to the cross, he no longer feels threatened when a gifted woman takes her place at his side, looking him straight in the eye. When God is the focus of a woman's life, the repository of her expectations, aspirations and desires, she no longer needs to drain a man with her dependency for her sense of self-worth. This is the key to a healthy relationship, for with dignity and independence re-established, women can turn the lock and release their husbands, colleagues, fathers, brothers, sons from any self-imposed isolation in the fortress of the mind, the cages built to protect themselves from hurt, pain and failure. We can take up the calling for which we were created and speak life into our homes, workplaces, communities and society.

A leading, liberating and life-giving woman

Every now and then, history seems to grant us an exceptional woman who, knowingly or not, lives out her theology in an extraordinary way.

Well before her time, one particular woman in the nineteenth century refused to let herself be defined by what was expected of her or to be subjugated by those who thought they owned her. Her faith inspired her to imagine a different world, a world where both men and women were entitled to an inconceivable freedom to become the people they were created to be. None of the huge risks involved could cow her spirit, as she spoke and gave life to hundreds of her fellow slaves, and earned the love and respect of the society in which she lived.

Born into slavery in the United States around 1822, life for Harriet Tubman was brutal and cruel. At the age of six she was rented out by her owner for sixty dollars a year to a plantation far away from her mother. The scars left behind from being lashed five times before breakfast never went away.

At the age of thirteen, sent to the dry goods store for supplies, she came across a runaway slave sheltering from his overseer. When she refused to help restrain the slave, the overseer picked up a 2lb lead weight and hit her across the head with it. From that day on she suffered from severe headaches, epilepsy and visions she attributed to God.

In 1849, hearing she was to be sold on again, she decided to take her chances and run. 'I had reasoned this out in my mind,' she said later. 'There was one of two things I had a right to, liberty or death; if I could not have one, I would have the other.'[26]

Her husband, whom she had married four years earlier, refused to go with her, but this was no helpless, dependent woman. She set off for Pennsylvania alone, following the northern star by night, and helped by the 'Underground Railroad' – a network of secret routes and safe houses, created by freed black people and white abolitionists dedicated to helping slaves to escape. After ninety miles on foot, she finally crossed the boundary from South to North, and could hardly believe she was free at last. 'When I found I had crossed that line, I looked at my hands to see if I was the same person. There was such a glory over everything; the sun came like gold through the trees, and over the fields, and I felt like I was in Heaven.'[27]

But instead of enjoying her safe, new life, she headed back to Maryland to rescue her family. Her husband, however, had married someone else in her absence. Refusing to be daunted by such a betrayal, she simply went on to save others instead. The passing of the Fugitive Slave Law in 1850, requiring escaped slaves sheltering in the North to be captured and returned to their former owners, robbed her of her new-found freedom, and made what had become regular trips to the South even more dangerous. But nothing would stop the mission that was her vision and calling. 'To this solemn resolution I came; I was free, and they should be free also; I would make a home for them in the North, and the Lord helping me, I would bring them all there. Oh, how I prayed then, lying all alone on de cold, damp ground; "Oh, dear Lord," I said, "I ain't got no friend but you. Come to my help, Lord, for I'm in trouble!"'[28]

So she rerouted the Underground Railroad to Canada, and over ten years saved so many that she became known as 'the Conductor', or often 'Moses', as she led her people to freedom. None of those she led out of captivity was ever recaptured, so in years to come she could honestly boast, 'I can say what most conductors can't say – I never ran my train off the track and I never lost a passenger.'

The Civil War of 1861–65 provided new opportunities to help liberate the South from the scourge of slavery. She volunteered for the Union Army as a cook and a nurse, but it was quickly recognised that she could be of more use in an entirely different capacity. Her knowledge of the plantations and her reputation made her the ideal spy. She became an armed scout and trainer of spies, travelling South by the Underground Railroad, then taking information from black slaves back to the confederate forces. She was the first woman in the war to lead an armed expedition. The Combahee River Raid saw the liberating of more than seven hundred slaves in South Carolina.

After the war her headaches became more intense and disruptive, and she 'retired' to the home she had bought on a small piece of land on the outskirts of Auburn, New York, from abolitionist Senator William H. Seward. It was unheard of for a black woman to own land, but this became a base for her family and friends, and for her fight for women's suffrage alongside the famous women's rights campaigner, Susan B. Anthony.

Despite financial difficulties, Harriet remained generous to a fault. In 1903 she donated a parcel of her land to the African Methodist Episcopal Zion Church in Auburn. It was on this site that she opened the Harriet Tubman Home for the Aged in 1908, and a free hospital for both black and white who couldn't afford health care.

She died in 1913 and was buried with full military honours at Fort Hill Cemetery in Auburn, becoming a legend and inspiration for generations of African-Americans struggling for equality and civil rights. But despite all the honours she received in her lifetime, the epitaph on her grave simply said, 'Servant of God, well done.'

Chapter 2

The Manipulative Woman

The women who followed Eve had no voice, no power and few rights. For many centuries they didn't appear to miss what they hadn't known, largely because they found subtle ways of exerting their influence. The tales of the four founding matriarchs of the Judeo-Christian culture suggest they resorted to the only means at their disposal – manipulation. Many of the matriarchs in my own family were masters of the art. Take, for example, my paternal Grandmother Rose.

Rose and her husband Michael were both asylum seekers from the aggressive anti-semitism of nineteenth-century Eastern Europe. Why Grandfather Michael chose to seek his fortune in the United Kingdom, rather than France, like most of his cousins, no one knew for certain, but he kept in close touch with them, and dog-eared sepia photographs testify that for many years they exchanged regular visits in the summer. He was an only child and they were the only relatives he had.

Rose, whom he met and married in Britain, was not an easy woman. Crippled by a badly treated hip injury after a childhood fall, she was aged before her time by arthritis and disappointment. I remember a small, bent old woman with a pudding basin cut of thinning white hair, whose eyes were like raisins in a sponge cake and whose tongue was as sharp as her nose.

My mother thought her the original mother-in-law from hell, forever critical and complaining. No one was good enough for my father, her only son, born unexpectedly eight years after his sister and the only glimmer of light in her world. When my mother told her she was expecting a third child, she snapped, 'How could you do that to my son?' My mother assured her that it took two to make a baby. But my father would make excuses for her. She had had such a hard and lonely life after Michael's premature death. But even he had no idea of the lengths to which her unforgiving nature had driven her.

Rose did not like most people, but especially her husband's family in France, so she began to intercept and destroy their letters. My grandfather was deeply saddened by their silence, and during the Second World War, when his letters were never acknowledged, resigned himself to the fact that they must have perished at the hands of the Nazis. After my grandfather's death, my father was deeply aggrieved that he had lost all his father's family in the Holocaust.

So when, some time after my father's death, my sister suddenly received a letter from cousins in France, we were all rather shocked. Peter and I went to visit them in Nancy. The tale they told was very different from the myth that had been handed down to us. They had indeed been in grave danger during the Nazi occupation, but had managed to flee to the Alps where they had been hidden for several years by a small community of Italians, unsympathetic – like so many Italians – to Mussolini. They had tried to reinstate the correspondence with their cousins once the war was over, and couldn't understand why their letters never received a reply.

I was horrified. What vindictiveness could have induced my grandmother to destroy those letters, year in, year out, when she could see the pain it caused?

I was nine when she died and all I remember of her are weekly visits to the bed sitting-room that was her self-inflicted prison in my aunt's house. She hated living with her daughter and son-in-law, and felt she should be living with her beloved son instead. He at least didn't cook bacon for breakfast and eat it after he had said his morning prayers and taken off his phylacteries. So she took her revenge, and on Christmas Day 1960 ended her own life.

For my father, no Christmas Day would ever again be without sorrow, regret and guilt. My grandmother was a master at family manipulation – and we all paid for it.

Four kinds of women

As a Jewish child at a private Church of England girls' school in Newcastle with predominantly non-Jewish friends, I was very conscious of how different the lives of our women were from the lives of the women in their families. Several of their mothers went out to work, mainly as teachers; one wrote children's stories;[1] others were stalwart fundraisers, local councillors, school governors or tireless volunteers for charitable organisations, making the most of the benefits a comfortable income bestowed on them. They attended coffee mornings, went into Newcastle to buy bits and bobs for the family cottage in Bamburgh, or a new evening dress for the Northumberland Hunt Ball. They took tea in town at Tilleys, eating little fancy cakes with a fork, to the accompaniment of a wizened, female string trio.

Not in my family. My mother socialised very little during the day. She was far too busy cleaning, tidying, organising and preparing for the next festival. In our home she reigned supreme. Her kingdom ran like clockwork. Well might my father be the omnipotent, omnicompetent local doctor. Once over the threshold of our home, he abdicated almost all responsibility.

The differences between our grandmothers were even more marked. My friends' grandmothers were sweet, self-effacing seventy-year-olds in black or grey, whose only mission in life was not to be a burden to the younger generations. Daughter of an immigrant clothes manufacturer and less genteel, my maternal grandmother was only in her fifties and a fashion guru. She smoked Woodbines, drank a great deal of whisky, expected a minimum weekly visit and ruled the roost in her home and ours.

The local women in the pit village where my father had his medical practice were more like her, tough and feisty. They controlled the purse strings. The men handed over their weekly pay packet and were given an allowance for drinking money. As the pits began to close there was less to give and life was hard. Those women shouted a lot, but unlike my father and grandfather, who wouldn't have dared answer back, their men told them to shut up and went out anyway.

Most women, it seemed to me, if they did have influence, exercised it from behind, rather than beside, the men in their lives. Most were too afraid of being found unattractive or unlovable to express their needs, wants or real feelings – unlike the women in my orbit. I couldn't help but feel the statutory bunch of flowers a man gave his wife every Sabbath was less a gift of love and affection and more a bribe to prevent several hours of haranguing or sulking.

I have a very vivid memory of a school friend's birthday party. She was the daughter of a consultant surgeon, revered by my father, as all consultants were in those days. I was about seven or eight years old, warned not to let my father down, and went feeling a little over-awed, but with high expectations. It was the most horrid party I ever attended. Mrs Consultant Surgeon, endowed, apparently, with every benefit of her husband's status, income and prestige, showed little evidence of enjoying it. Every time a record was played she had a fit of hysterics, whined about having a headache, swore she couldn't cope and demanded the music be turned off. Since virtually every game, from Musical Chairs to Pass the Parcel, required musical accompaniment, it left her plenty of opportunity to be the centre of attention in a room full of uncomfortable, unhappy little girls.

Later, when my father willed me to tell him what a wonderful time I had had, I simply nodded. It was my first conscious experience that all was not always well in the world of adults and I couldn't begin to put that into words – especially words he didn't want to hear. Yet in a strange way I was disturbed by the woman's obvious misery, and both embarrassed and sorry for my friend. What would induce a mother to spoil her daughter's birthday party?

As I reflect on it now, I can still feel the strange electricity that passed between the parents; he, impassive behind his half spectacles, she, demanding and difficult. What was she trying to tell him? Even then I knew the performance was for him. The relationship was the key to the woman's profound unhappiness.

Many years passed before the rude awakening that the strange behaviour of several of my school friends' mothers was a result of depression or alcohol. Now I understand that behind the facade of the perfect wife and mother, women of their generation had few means of keeping an all-pervading sense of boredom and worthlessness at bay, and were often deeply angry and frustrated. They had no choice but to resort to underhand ways of establishing their presence or achieving their own ends. It hardly led to open, honest, loving relationships. In fact, like my Grandmother Rose's extraordinary piece of deceit, it diminished all the people concerned in some way or another.

As society underwent a major upheaval in the 1970s and 1980s, women's expectations of both their personal and working lives soared. Legislation on equal rights and pay improved the latter, but change had to come from within as well as from without. To maximise the new opportunities, a new generation needed to gain a greater sense of self-worth, and acquire a more appropriate way of communicating. The apologetic stance, born of the need for approval, would have to go. Seminal books like *A Woman in Your Own Right – Assertiveness and You,*[2] by psychologist and counsellor Anne Dickson gave twentieth-century women a new confidence, and a new way of being.

I found the book empowering. When I ventured back into the workplace, it helped me regain the self-assurance that had drowned in the nappy bucket. But some in the Church, who were suspicious of any new-fangled, secular ideas, dismissed assertiveness training for women as a licence for domination and control. What a complete misunderstanding of the meaning of the word, defined in the dictionary as 'to state positively and confidently'. Anne Dickson's goal was to enable women to rediscover 'the art of clear, honest, direct communication'. To me, it sounded more like a call to re-appropriate God's gift to woman at creation, lost in the annals of male dominance and female co-dependency, or the old *teshuqah*. It was also consistent with the biblical injunction to be forthright and truthful in our relationships. If we are not graciously but firmly assertive, there remain only three unattractive alternatives: aggression, passive acquiescence or manipulation.

I've seen it so often, been there myself – Mum crawls in the back door after a manic day at work, laden with shopping, to find the sink stacked with dirty dishes, the ironing piled high on a food-bespattered counter, no sign of any preparation for the evening meal, and two senseless teenagers stretched out, glued to their mobiles or iPads.

Four reactions are possible. Three of them likely. An aggressive woman will have a rant, bang the doors, even threaten or kick the lifeless forms in front of her into action. The passive martyr will set to, tidy up, put the shopping away and the tea in the oven, sighing loudly throughout, then retire early to bed with a headache, feeling used. A manipulative woman will probably mutter, just loud enough for the children to hear, whine at them or nag, then look for some way of spoiling the meal for the whole family as a subtle form of punishment and revenge.

The problem is that none of these three reactions will bring any benefits for her or for her teenagers. She is left dissatisfied and they learn nothing about decent behaviour and meaningful relationships.

The assertive woman would say firmly, but pleasantly, 'Would you mind watching that programme later as I'm dog-tired and I'd so appreciate some help?' She might get a more reasonable response, not to mention a modicum of respect. On the other hand, she could of course make herself a cup of tea, switch on the TV, engage in whatever they're watching and wait until hunger forces them into the kitchen. But she might be waiting until bedtime.

To caricature an aggressive woman, she can appear competitive, domineering, sarcastic, cold or superior. She tends not to listen, states opinions as facts and is an expert at creating hurt and havoc. She may be the bullying boss who reduces her juniors to tears, the domineering wife and mother who always manages to get her own way, the committee chair who brooks no argument, and even the strident feminist for whom every innocent comment is a deliberate sleight. But that loud and forceful manner from boardroom to bedroom may well be a cover for a lack of self-esteem.

The passive woman feels permanently put upon, yet won't say so because she cannot cope with conflict. She sighs a lot – when people are there to hear it, and even if they aren't. She is the minister's wife who has allowed herself to become the parish doormat, wearer of cast-offs from the endless fetes and jumble sales she resents having to organise. She is the mother who always picks up the dirty clothes left in a trail up the stairs and across the landing, silently berating her selfish family. She is the office junior or PA who cannot get on with her work because the boss keeps sending her out for aspirin for his toothache or a birthday card for the wife. She is the teacher who always covers for sick leave because she cannot say no, but bitterly resents the way her good nature is exploited. At its worst, she is the subject of her husband or partner's violent attacks because she loves him. Ms Passive appears to be a pushover. She only wants to be nice, but she has 'victim' written all over her. Ironically, in the end, she loses the respect of those she sets out to please. She may well suffer from depression as a result of all that repressed anger, as passive behaviour often masks a great deal of repressed aggression.

Passive-aggressive behaviour is indirectly, covertly aggressive. That's because it may be the result of growing up in an environment where any display of emotion was discouraged. It was seen to be unhelpful, unladylike, unchristian in some cases, to lose one's temper – which is why passive-aggressive behaviour can often play havoc in a church, when being obstructive feels safer than confronting long-term frustration and anger.

The manipulative woman has different techniques for getting her own way. Like my Grandmother Rose, she uses cunning rather than resorting to open confrontation. Guilt is often her weapon of choice. A minister's wife couldn't admit she didn't want to teach in Sunday school any more; she thought up a dozen serious ailments and played on the sympathies of those she had in mind for the job, until one of them relieved her of her responsibilities. At her worst, like my school friend's mother, the manipulative woman may ruin her child's birthday party or even a child's life, for she simply cannot see how frighteningly destructive her behaviour can be.

I used to meet all three of those women every day, at work and at church. I see them in everyone except me. Yet most of us oscillate between those personality types all the time, and it's like trying to stand up in the middle of a seesaw. Frustrated with being passive, we swing in the other direction in an attempt to regain our power. But then we fear we're being domineering, so stagger back towards a more central position and try a more subtle approach to getting our own way. In the end, the seesaw swings to and fro at such a pace it leaves us feeling exhausted and giddy.

Assertiveness helps us keep our balance. Because the assertive woman accepts herself as she is, she finds it easier to accept other people as they are, with all their faults and foibles too. She doesn't need to put others down to increase her own sense of self-worth.

She doesn't think they're to blame for what happens to her. She doesn't make them feel guilty for not recognising her needs. She listens to what others have to say, and then expresses her own views openly and honestly, quite prepared to risk the rejection they may incur.

However, I don't think Anne Dickson has the whole truth. She claims that the assertive woman doesn't suffer from feelings of rejection because her self-esteem is anchored in herself. I know myself too well to have any confidence in that department. I will settle instead for the biblical definition of an assertive woman, preceding Anne Dickson's by several centuries. The assertive woman of faith is never completely crushed because her self-esteem is anchored in God. Her *teshuqah*, her cravings for love and fulfilment, are satisfied by him alone. She knows he loves and accepts her, and has only her good at heart. Therefore she can be as merciful to herself and to others as he is to her. No longer driven by her own insecurities, she is not afraid to speak out with dignity and clarity, or calmly stand her ground when necessary. If she is hurt, she works at forgiveness. And if she is wrong, she apologises with grace.

The Bible is full of assertive women of calibre – steady and wise, loving and good, open and honest, like Ruth, Esther and Hannah. These are women who know the will of God, adhere to it and speak up for it, whatever the risk, whatever the cost. That measure of godly assertiveness isn't achieved overnight. It requires patience and grace. Eve couldn't rise to the challenge, and, as far as woman's story goes, the plot was lost for a while.

Four great matriarchs

Jewish historians often ascribe the survival of the Jewish people, through thousands of years of persecution in the diaspora, to the Jewish Mama. I suspect this may be a rather romanticised notion. Personal experience tells me that if it's true, it owes more to a curious mixture of chicken soup and the art of emotional blackmail. Jackie Mason, a rabbi before he made a profession out of comedy, tells Jewish men to beware. Once they marry, their lives will be seriously proscribed. The Jewish woman is so house-proud he will only be able to sit in the one armchair she sets aside for him. The rest, kept in a pristine, plumped-up, grease-free condition, are strictly for guests. He recommends to Jewish men that they court a woman for as long as they like, but whatever they do, never marry her. 'That way you get to stay a guest and sit in whatever chair you like.'[3]

Eve's tragedy brought our family to this – to a grandfather who thought he had lost his only relatives in the Holocaust, and to my father restricted to one armchair in the multi-armchaired home of my childhood. The *ezer* or helper who has lost her equality is bent on regaining control. She makes her man think he is the centre of the universe, but it is the universe she has constructed and where she reigns supreme. The gentle art of *kenegdo,* of loving negotiation and healthy confrontation, has been lost. Be she mother, wife or colleague, when she manipulates he may wittingly or unwittingly submit, and the outcome, as in the case of my Grandmother Rose's meddling, leaves everyone the poorer.

According to tradition, Jewish Mamas have four role models – the four great, founding mothers of the faith – Sarah, Rebekah, Leah and Rachel. There is no doubt they were all exceptional, forces to be reckoned with. But women of faith? Their very problem was that they started well, with great faith, but then more immediate pressures crowded in and clouded their vision. In fact, like the many Mamas who followed them, they couldn't see beyond the end of their own noses. All that mattered was the success of their myopic, family-centred projects in the here and now, and that led them into a scant disregard for their part in God's far greater narrative. I often wonder whether that later, quintessentially British matriarchal figure, Prime Minister Margaret Thatcher, would have acted any differently had she been given a preview of how the history books and twenty-first-century TV documentaries would judge her. Perhaps we are all too blinkered, too tied to the mundane and immediate, to appreciate that whether we are a walk-in extra, have a tiny speaking part, or a main character role, our lives are essential to the bigger picture.

The Christian tradition has tended to pass over the four biblical matriarchs altogether. They simply don't fit our preferred conceptions of saintliness, our stereotypes of true spirituality – especially in a woman. They are tough, dynamic, fearless, outspoken, sensual, passionate, jealous, impatient, frustrated, rational, argumentative, entertaining – and highly manipulative. They are just too flesh and blood, too uncomfortably like us.

The level of equality and respect they enjoyed was remarkable for the time in which they lived, their husbands (apart from Jacob, and that was a costly, if unintentional, mistake) committed to a certain measure of monogamy. At the start of her married life each is definitely an *ezer* or helper, journeying side by side with her man, sharing in his pioneering adventures, enduring the dangers and discomfort without question or protest, protecting and confronting him when necessity demands it. And apart from Leah, though I suspect Jacob came to appreciate her gifts eventually, they were loved, valued and deeply mourned when they died.

But like a contagion, the consequences of humankind's fall from grace are already taking effect. Sarah, Rebekah and Rachel have problems with their reproductive systems and there are no fertility clinics to help – although surrogacy seems to have been in vogue, with consequences no less traumatic than they can be today. All four need to be the centre of their man's universe, and deeply resent any intrusion from an outside source – whether it be a slave girl and her offspring, a firstborn son or a sister. No matter how affectionate their husbands, their world is already proscribed by men – foreign kings and leaders, brothers and fathers. They have already become a tool, a bargaining point, property up for barter. Small wonder they become masters in the manipulative arts. Survival tactics are imperative.

The first great Jewish Mama

Sarah is my favourite – the quintessential Jewish Mama, rational and reasonable, wanting only the best for her man, going out to get it with the self-restraint of a steamroller running downhill without brakes – on the wrong hill. She must have been quite a woman. When Abraham sets out on his virtually incomprehensible mission from Ur to the land of promise, she accompanies him, despite the fact she hasn't yet managed to give him children. Why does Abraham keep a barren wife? What future is there in that? He must love her a great deal.

Sarah is such a stunning-looking woman that Abraham persuades her to tell the locals she is his sister. It is only a half-lie, after all, since she is his half-sister. That he exposes her to rape doesn't appear to bother him unduly. Twice foreign kings take a fancy to her and make off with her. On the second occasion she is well past middle age – an encouraging thought in our twenty-first, youth-worshipping century. It's a sad fact that where wolf whistles from workmen once made me bristle with self-righteous female indignation, they now make me purr with pride, for I know if the lads were closer to the wrinkles and droops, they would be horrified by their mistake. Oh the vanity of setting any store by fading female attractiveness. It is almost Sarah's undoing – especially as Abraham's duty to protect and cherish his mate is subsumed by his fear of confrontation. Fortunately, God defends his wife's honour, even if Abraham won't.

Sarah has discovered, probably with some disappointment and disillusionment, that her man is weak. He doesn't always make the best decisions. He opts for the peaceful life – compromise by any other name. And like so many women since, she believes that for his good, from now on she will have to take matters into her own hands.

Around twenty years ago an American writer, Laura Doyle, wrote a contentious book called *The Surrendered Wife* that attracted a great deal of publicity in the UK for its reactionary views, and spawned 'The Surrendered Wives' movement in the USA, still active today. For a new generation seeking equality with our men, some of her suggestions seemed like a rerun of old-fashioned Christian submission and are totally potty. For example, 'For greatest intimacy, agree with your husband's ideas even when it scares you.'[4] When did mindless acquiescence become an aphrodisiac? Manipulation is more likely to kill respect in a relationship than a little gentle confrontation. On the other hand, when, at the start of a televised group session, she told the participants that if they gave up their need to control their men, they might just forget they had ever thought them incompetent, I had to make a small concession. Sarah is concocting a recipe for disaster.

That same character flaw in Abraham makes its reappearance when he agrees, at Sarah's suggestion, to sleep with her Egyptian maid, Hagar, despite the fact that ten years earlier, he, not she, was told that Sarah's son would be his heir. Has he ever passed this piece of information on to her? I suspect not, for she is simply looking for a practical way to fulfil his hopes of becoming a father. It is a relatively unselfish gesture and he doesn't appear to have any objections – perhaps because ten years seems too long to wait for the fulfilment of a divine promise and he simply can't resist the attractions of a younger model.

When Hagar becomes pregnant and starts to laugh at Sarah behind her back, the scene is set for high drama and Abraham's peace is over. Living in close proximity with Hagar's humiliating behaviour must be almost unbearable for Sarah. After all, the girl was her protégé. She has been generous to her, opened the door of opportunity, and this is her thanks. I can't say I really blame Sarah for throwing Hagar out, though it isn't perhaps the best way to deal with the situation, and might not have been necessary if Abraham wasn't quite so passive, and sorted her out himself.

Hagar is allowed to return, and, for another fourteen years, remains part of the uneasy ménage à trois that Abe and Sarah's foolishness has created. But then, one day, listening behind the tent door – presumably the Old Testament equivalent of a keyhole – Sarah hears a strange visitor tell her husband that she's the one who will have the son of promise. She has to stuff her pinny in her mouth to stop herself laughing – and not just because even the menopause is a distant memory. Every preacher I have ever heard on this subject claims she says, 'But I am too old.' A delicate version of the truth, but too coy to be accurate. What she actually says is, 'At our age, are our clapped-out old bodies still capable of sexual pleasure?' (Gen. 18:12). The spiritual destiny of humankind is hanging in the balance and Sarah is wondering whether Abraham can rise to the occasion. Meanwhile, it is her faith that fails to rise to the challenge. But even her shallow cynicism gives way to wonder, when God reminds her that nothing – not even an anachronistic dose of spiritual Viagra – is too hard for him.

To her credit, Sarah's sense of humour never deserts her. She has the *chutzpah,* the barefaced cheek, to call her son Isaac, meaning 'laughter', for she knows that despite the hilarity her story will always induce, she has had the last laugh.

But there has been too much human meddling already for the fulfilment of the promise to bring this tense little family an unalloyed happy ending. With the arrival of a new baby the discord in the home spirals out of control. On the face of it, an apparently trivial incident lights the blue touchpaper that provokes the final explosion. In the Revised Standard Version of the Bible, Sarah sees and resents Hagar's child playing with Isaac (Gen. 21:9). The obvious implication is that Sarah is insanely jealous, a familiar typecasting of woman in the role of green-eyed monster. The New International Version, however, translates the Hebrew word *tsachaq* more accurately, not as 'playing with', but as 'mocking', or 'behaving with malice'. Ishmael is not a child. He is an adolescent, and that presents a serious risk to the baby. This is certainly how the Apostle Paul interprets events. In his letter to the Galatians, he writes, 'the son born in the ordinary way persecuted [or bullied] the son born by the power of the Spirit.' (Gal. 4:29). Ishmael's resentment of Isaac has probably been picked up from his mother. Children have a tendency to mimic their parents. But his aggressive behaviour is all his own.

Sarah's eyes are finally opened to the dangers that she and Abraham have unwittingly unleashed, and from which they will never now be free. The time for subtle manipulation has finally run out. Sarah knows there is no easy way to resolve the situation so, this time, to protect their baby, a reluctant Abraham has to act.

Hagar and Ishmael are banished once and for all. Abraham's reluctance is not because he cares for Hagar, but because he loves Ishmael, and would like to wriggle out of the consequences of his actions. 'Do what you usually do,' God tells him, with more than just a hint of irony, 'whatever Sarah tells you.' Within this apparently male-dominated story is a woman who repeatedly gets her own way. On this occasion her decision may not appear the most generous, but it is inspired. Speaking to the church in Galatia, Paul turns Sarah's relationship with Hagar into a picture of the ultimate triumph of true faith over oppressive, man-made religion. 'Get rid of the slave woman and her son, for the slave woman's son will never share in the inheritance with the free woman's son. Therefore, brothers and sisters, we are not children of the slave woman, but of the free woman' (Gal. 4:30–1).

However, Hagar and Ishmael are not left to die in the desert because they don't fit into the original plan. God is not taken in by Hagar's crocodile tears. After all these years in Abraham and Sarah's home, witnessing Sarah's extraordinary pregnancy, has she learned nothing of God's mercy? What does she take him for? God responds to Ishmael's prayers for help, not to Hagar's passive self-pity, and provides for both of them. But meanwhile, Sarah, for all her faults, her impetuosity, tetchiness, faithlessness, lack of vision and manipulative ways, becomes, with a wonderful touch of divine irony, a truly matriarchal figure – the mother of all who truly believe.

The second Mama's sedition

Rebekah is very different from the mother-in-law she never meets – self-assured and gracious. She doesn't stand on her dignity so that she cannot draw drinking water for a mere servant – and his camels (Gen. 24:46). She has learned that humility pays greater dividends than high-handedness. But she is no pushover. When she discovers the servant is looking for a wife for his master and that she fulfils the job spec, she pursues her destiny with single-minded determination. Why procrastinate?

Isaac recognises the outstanding inner qualities reflected in her external beauty and adores her from the moment he sets eyes upon her. It is a love that grows and deepens over the years. He still can't keep his hands off her well past their silver wedding anniversary, and is cavorting with her in a field when the king of the Philistines passes by and is appalled to see him in virtual flagrante delicto with the woman he has passed off as his sister. Evidently, Isaac has learned little from his father's mistakes. I imagine that when the king suddenly appears on the scene with a look of undisguised horror on his face, Rebekah rearranges her robe and stomps off with as much dignity as she can muster, leaving Isaac to wangle his way out of that one.

In fact, Rebekah eventually saves Isaac from far greater folly. Sadly, however, she doesn't do it *kenegdo*, or eyeball to eyeball. In most relationships there are times for straight talking, for gentle assertiveness in the name of common sense, but Rebekah opts for deception rather than reasoned confrontation. But then, she is a Jewish Mama, after all. Why change the habit of a lifetime? To be fair, like so many women after her, she probably finds confrontation difficult. Perhaps she tried it when Isaac suggested calling her his sister – and failed.

Men don't find confrontation easy either. We had a senior manager in my previous workplace who always resorted to manoeuvring behind his colleagues' back. He connived, wheeled and dealed, and usually got what he wanted, but in the end, turned us against one other, destroying trust and team spirit in the process. Not unlike Rebekah, who discovered that deceit and manipulation may seem the easier, even safer option, but that the long-term cost to relationships could be immense.

In her case, making a favourite of one of her two children was a fatal mistake. When it comes to children, women are at our most vulnerable. Mothering can turn an intelligent, rational human being into a fond and doting idiot. In my days as a youth worker it never ceased to amaze me that a mother would turn up for a court appearance with an absolute reprobate of a son, and still believe, just because he said so, that he had been wronged, yet again, by the criminal justice system. It was simply that her son had gotten into bad company. It never crossed her mind that he could be the bad company that everyone else's son was getting into. We may love our children, but we're not always good for them.

Isaac and Rebekah waited a long time for their twins, but the foetuses were fighting before they even left the uterus. The boxing match in the space between Rebekah's diaphragm and bladder is so intense she actually cries out in pain and is told there are two nations inside her – no wonder it hurts – and that the elder will serve the younger. They emerge with Jacob, the second-born, whose name means 'deceiver', hanging on to Esau's heel.

Was Isaac around at the time? Surely, he can have no doubt about the future of his two boys – yet he seems determined to thwart God's plans because of his own preference for Esau. Rebekah, because of her love for Jacob, cannot trust God to sort the situation out, so, repeating her late mother-in-law's mistakes, she decides to give him a hand. Although her intervention to secure the future of the dynasty is crucial in the light of history, neither she nor Jacob acts with love and generosity. Ironically, were she to challenge, rather than trick Isaac into giving Jacob the blessing of the first-born, such is his dependence on her wisdom and judgement that her husband may give her what she wants, and she would never lose her sons. But instead, she forges ahead and takes destiny into her own hands.

Every Jewish Mama knows the way to a man's heart – through his stomach. Esau is the Bible's answer to a celebrity chef and knows how to make his father's gastric juices flow. But *Masterchef* contestant Rebekah has no doubt that while her son is out hunting for game, she can reproduce the gastronomic masterpiece Isaac loves so much in a fraction of the time. Has Isaac's preference for Esau's gourmet cuisine stung her in the past? No Jewish woman can bear to hear an unfavourable comparison of her roast chicken or gefüllte fish. She'll show this foolish husband of hers how stupid he is to let his belly govern his heart and turn his appetite into an arbiter between nations! Was this the first man to be ruled and then defeated by his stomach? He probably wasn't the last.

Rebekah ensures that Jacob gets the coveted blessing, but he dare not stay to enjoy it. Esau is determined to kill him. Rebekah now sees that she is caught in a web of her own making. Her dysfunctional family is falling apart. She realises with the most dreadful, searing pain that through her own actions she must lose what she loves most in the world, and that her son's safety will depend not only on her manipulative skills, but also on every ounce of inner resourcefulness she can summon up. With a calm that belies her true feelings, she must untie her home-loving boy from her apron strings, and send him away as far as she can. But he must go to her family not as a fugitive, but with his father's backing, and Isaac, the old fool, must be made to believe it was his idea in the first place.

Using the excuse of Jacob's need for a kosher partner, unlike Esau's two common, local girls, she plays masterfully on the instrument of Isaac's self-interest. It is a stroke of genius. Isaac doesn't think much of his daughters-in-law either. The prospect of welcoming a third into the house, with more squabbling and rudeness, is altogether more than he can face, as Rebekah knows only too well. Her diplomatic triumph is complete. But the price is almost more than she can bear. She will never see Jacob again.

If Rebekah had not taken matters into her own hands, how different might history have been? Without doubt, God's intentions for the two boys, foretold at their birth, would come to pass. But Rebekah cannot rely on it, or resist the urge to be guided by her own cleverness. For her two sons, the result is a mess. She sows seeds of suspicion and hatred that will have repercussions for years to come. Throughout the centuries there have been many women, guided by the best and worst of motives, who have done exactly the same. Manipulation is a fearful and dangerous weapon in the hands of an unwitting expert.

My friend Janet, a minister's wife in the Midlands, claims it is an art passed through the generations from one woman to another. They learn it at their mother's knee. And she was no exception. By the time she grew up, the habit was so ingrained she couldn't admit its existence, let alone break its hold.

'Year upon year I watched my mother browbeat my father. Whatever she wanted, whether it was a new outfit, new curtains, her children's education or a holiday abroad, she would get. My father was a gentle, generous man, but if he expressed caution she would nag. If he endeavoured to open up a sensible discussion of the subject, she would throw a tantrum. Only once, after nearly forty years of marriage, did he ever admit the truth – that she simply wore him down.

'When I married Phil, that sort of behaviour was second nature to me. I knew no other way. As soon as he walked into the house from work I would hit him with my agenda. But I had a husband who recognised my behaviour for what it was and said, "I will not be manipulated." I was devastated. It left me completely powerless. I ground my teeth to such an extent that my dentist asked me what I was doing to them. Gradually I began to see that when I divested Phil of the right to any argument or debate I made him feel like a lion in a cage. Through counselling I learned the dangers of trying to use people to fulfil my own goals.

'But my need for control wasn't well and truly broken until a particular event in the church in which we ministered brought me to my senses. I'm still horrified when I think about what I did, even now.

'We needed a steering committee – I can't even remember what for – and a very shy, quiet woman in the congregation agreed to stand as secretary. She was a dear, faithful woman, but her shyness made her quite draining.

'There was another candidate, new to the church, vibrant, dynamic, impressive, and I thought, "This is the kind of person we need on the committee," so – and I can't believe I did this – I went around the congregation quietly canvassing on his behalf.

'He won the vote – with or without my help, I will never know – but he was a disaster. He left the church eventually, but not before he caused us the greatest heartache we had ever known in the whole of our ministry. Fortunately the woman was gracious enough to take his place on the committee, and was absolutely perfect for the job.

'I learned the hard way that we really don't need to do God's work for him. But we get it into our heads that we know what's needed, and I paid for my foolishness – but so did everyone else.'

A church with a manipulative minister's wife is in peril. I once attended a conference in York where a nun persisted in challenging me about my role. 'Yes, but what is your place in the church?' she demanded.

I blinked. It was obviously a leading question, and I was temporarily thrown by it. 'I suppose I'm a member of the congregation like any other,' I said.

'Right,' she agreed, triumphantly. It was evidently what she wanted to hear and I was relieved, but it left me feeling uneasy.

Only later did the truth dawn. It was naive of me to suggest I had no more power than anyone else in the congregation. It is not appropriate for me to sit on the church council or any other committee where I might be tempted to challenge my husband in public. I do not have access to the accepted channels for expressing a viewpoint. My democratic powers are severely curtailed. I am therefore not a member of the congregation like any other. But I also know from my experiences in the workplace that the person with the most power is she who shares the boss's bed. That gives me power in a league of its own. I can influence my husband's attitudes and sway his opinions simply by dropping in the odd word here and there over a meal or at bedtime. That kind of power, unrecognised, can easily be abused.

In the 1950s, lecturer in religious studies at Sussex University, Kathleen Bliss, claimed that because women had no real voice in the Church, they were all restricted to what she calls this kind of underhand, or 'irresponsible power'.

> It is nonsense to say that women have never had any power in the churches: they have had immense power, but power only in the form of influence, which is irresponsible power. Nobody can call to account the wife or mother who gets her way with husband or son and is known to be the real director of his opinion and vote. This is the form of power to which women, particularly very able women, have been confined by their exclusion from responsible power. Wherever democratic ideals prevail in society, influence of all kinds is discredited. Open attempts are made to prevent pressure on political leaders and on those who make appointments, issue honours and privileges and make executive decisions in every walk of life. That influence is influence with very great skill over the centuries and many still prefer it to any form of responsibility which brings them out into the open. But the choice between influence and responsibility is one that women have to make, and churches have to make in relation to women.[5]

For generations, from Sarah and Rebekah to Grandmother Rose, women resorted to using indirect, rather than open, methods of persuasion. Achievement and success could only be attained through a husband, brother or son. Necessity became a habit and, as Janet saw only too well, habits are hard to break.

Sleeping with the sister

Manipulation is self-perpetuating, even if it isn't genetic. It permeates and poisons whole families. Jacob, the master deceiver, son of an inspirational mother-teacher, is subjected to the ultimate deception by her brother. Welcomed into Laban's home, he falls hopelessly in love with Rachel, Uncle Laban's luscious younger daughter. For seven years, he subjects himself to abusive working practices to get the girl of his dreams, but they simply flash by in a haze of romantic passion. The wedding finally takes place and 'behold, in the morning, it was Leah' (Gen. 29:25). How on earth did he not know he had spent his wedding night with the elder sister? Whatever happened to sexual foreplay? I suspect Laban ensured that Jacob was very drunk after the wedding party. There was no electricity at the time and unless there is a moon, a tent in the desert can be very dark. But in the light of day Jacob's ignominy is complete. Our great romantic hero didn't even notice he had slept with the wrong girl. Since that day the bride's veil is always lifted during the Jewish wedding ceremony, for no Jewish man is fool enough to make the same mistake twice.

As for Leah – we can only guess at her feelings. Did she really have no choice? Or did Leah comply with her father's wishes because she had always found Jacob attractive and believed that she could make him love her in the end? Or, perhaps, knowing she wasn't as good-looking as her sister, she feared her chances were passing her by. Too many women find themselves in dismal, loveless relationships because they have married for similar reasons. Leah's hopes are doomed from the start. She is her father's pawn. Jacob finally acquires his true love too, and his penalty is life with two warring women. In fact, the consequences of the sibling rivalry are so catastrophic that marrying sisters in their lifetime is subsequently forbidden in the book of Leviticus.

I have often mused on what can be learned from Leah's plight and wonder whether her story, though desperately sad, isn't also tragically familiar. She is any woman locked in an unreciprocated, sterile relationship, denied the love and affection she needs. She is the woman whose partner walks out and abandons her for another. She is every woman who feels frustrated in love, rejected, let down and passed over. I had a favourite aunt, trapped by her lack of financial independence in a barren, desolate marriage to a rude, unloving man. He turned a vivacious, carefree young woman into a wistful, lonely hypochondriac. Nonetheless, she was a surrogate mother to me, and there were moments when her irrepressible generosity and sense of humour would break through – especially when we went on a shopping spree – and I loved her for it.

However it may seem, Leah is by no means divested of her worth. Status, dignity, acceptance and love are all hers, from a far more reliable source, if she isn't blinded to it by *teshuqah,* her need for affection from a man who cannot give her what she wants. God never deserts her. Seeing that she is passed over and unloved, he blesses her with children, while her sister, who has the looks and love Leah wants, remains temporarily infertile.

Nothing makes quite such a pathetic statement about her relationship with Jacob than the names Leah gives her first three sons. Reuben means 'to see', and is a prayer that Jacob will sit up and take notice of her. Simeon means 'heard', for now that she has given him another son, perhaps Jacob will not ignore her any longer. Levi, meaning 'joined' or 'attached', is a plea to Jacob to be part of her life, and to love, not use her.

With Judah, her fourth son, called 'praise', or 'worship', her focus seems to be shifting at last. Self-pity has given way to a glimmer of recognition that there are alternative blessings to be had that fill the void where Jacob's love should be, to replace the pain and humiliation of his neglect. She is given the significance her marriage has denied her. Even so, her obvious material success in biblical terms is not enough to stop her trying to manipulate Jacob back into her bed. She exchanges a night with him for mandrakes, thought to be a fertility drug, by an ever more desperate Rachel. Leah still needs human arms, human warmth, and God doesn't condemn her for that, for she has three more children, while, mandrakes or no, Rachel has none.

Eventually God remembers the oh-so-superior Rachel, and her two boys soon overtake Leah's children in their father's popularity stakes. Leah must seethes with self-righteous anger when she sees little Joseph being treated as the firstborn. Unfortunately, it's an emotion she communicates to her hapless boys, whose jealousy of their half-brother eventually fills them with murderous intentions.

But whether the actors see it or not, God's great historical drama is being played out and supersedes these minor domestic difficulties. Unlike Hannah in the Old Testament and Mary, mother of Jesus, Leah never grasps the great truth that it is the disparaged and overlooked who so often become the exalted in God's great scheme. And what sad irony, for it is she who becomes the mother of the priestly and kingly tribes. Jesus is descended from Leah, not Rachel.

On the official Guinness family tree and pedigree, a strange upside down triangle emanates from every married Guinness woman. They have progeny, but the tree doesn't say who and how many. Mothers and daughters are irrelevant. The woman's line of descent simply dies out, whether their descendants are more interesting than their male counterparts or not. Not so in Judaism, which is essentially matriarchal. Jewish identity is passed on through the mother's line. The four great matriarchs of Israel have a vital part to play in the history of the people of faith.

Whatever their failings and weaknesses, and however manipulative, they were formidable women, beloved and chosen by God, respected and valued by the generations to come. They could, however, have spared themselves and their offspring a great deal of *tsuris* (Hebrew for 'hassle'), had they chosen to be less manipulative and more assertive. Perhaps there is also a challenge here for men that living eyeball to eyeball with the women in their orbit and challenging manipulative behaviour can result in more positive outcomes.

It was the 1980s before Anne Dickson and many others took up Kathleen Bliss's call of the 1950s, urging women of my generation to abandon their mother's pattern, and reject 'influence' in exchange for responsible power and assertiveness. It may have come from secular, not spiritual, sources, yet it was a clear call for women to take up our God-given responsibility to speak love, life and truth. But it was already there for those with eyes to see it. Within a few years of the death of the matriarchs there arose a number of women, with equal courage and initiative, who provided a rather better role model of the best way to be a woman.

Chapter 3

The Assertive Woman

On a Friday evening in every Jewish home, when the family shares Kiddush, the traditional blessing of wine and bread, Jewish mothers pray for their daughters to grow up to be like Sarah, Rebekah, Leah and Rachel. Because the four women were so manipulative, former Rabbi Julia Neuberger prayed instead that the females in her family would grow up to be as assertive as the five daughters of Zelophehad.

I had to go and look them up. But there they are in Numbers chapter 27 – Mahlah, Noah, Hoglah, Milkah and Tirzah – who sound like an early biblical girl band. When their father dies, the five sisters are indignant that they cannot inherit his estate, as tradition insists it must pass to a male cousin. But these feisty women do not passively bewail their lot, or aggressively demand their rights, or wheedle some financial deal out of their cousin. They air their case before Moses and the entire wilderness congregation, holding out for their just and right inheritance.

It must have taken some courage to challenge the status quo. No doubt it later raised a laugh or two in the working men's club. Since when did a woman know anything about managing property? And just who did they think they were anyway? As the sisters came face to face with the rigid patriarchal system, they ran the risk of appearing difficult, demanding, grasping and unfeminine. That sort of behaviour could well have affected their chances in the marriage stakes. Yet Moses is forced to concede that they have a point. Tradition or justice? He must decide. Perplexed, he consults a higher authority.

And God says to him, 'Moses, do me a favour. Don't argue with assertive women like that!' or words to that effect. Not only is their case upheld, but it also sets a new precedent. Justice transcends tradition. From now on Jewish women have the right to inherit and own property, with all the status and freedom that implies. 'Zelophehad's daughters call us to take hold of life with our own hands,' says Rabbi Silvina Chemen.[1] If they hadn't risked asking, if they had simply accepted the conditions imposed upon them and submitted to a sense of helplessness, they would never have changed history.

By the time the book of Proverbs offers us 'the perfect wife' (Prov. 31:10–31), or *eshet chayil*, woman is actively involved in running the home, the family business and bartering for other people's land as well. The Hebrew word *chayil*, used to describe the wife as 'strong' or 'a woman of valour' in most translations, is often used to characterise male warriors. This is the original Superwoman. Every Sabbath Eve a Jewish man will tell his wife, in the words of Proverbs 31, that no other woman compares with his Superwoman, and will bring her a small gift, if he knows what's good for him.

Yet for another 4,000 years the non-Jewish nations in the West failed to recognise this essential, historical and biblical right. Everything a woman owned, earned or inherited belonged to her husband. In the event of a separation or divorce, mainly caused by his cruelty or unfaithfulness, she had no means of supporting herself, no right of access to her children, no say in their upbringing. It was nineteenth-century society beauty Caroline Norton, forced to flee an abusive marriage, who finally found the courage and voice of the daughters of Zelophehad. In a desperate bid to gain custody of her three children, she challenged and changed the British legal system forever. It was a hard fight, lasting many years. She became the constant butt of public and private ridicule. Her reputation lay in tatters. But in 1839 a new Act of Parliament gave a mother custody of a child under the age of seven. In 1873 the age was raised to sixteen.

Another nineteenth-century reformer well understood the limitations imposed by marriage, when a woman virtually became her husband's possession. The doughty, middle-class Florence Nightingale, who made nursing an acceptable profession for respectable women, was so afraid of losing her independence that she eschewed every attempt others made to marry her off, and encouraged her students to do the same. In 1867 she told the great reformer, John Stuart Mill, that she believed that owning property was more important for women than the right to vote. 'Till a married woman can be in possession of her own property there can be no love or justice.'[2] In 1882 married woman were at last granted that right.

It is their ineligibility to have any share in their own land or homes that keeps millions of women in developing countries subjugated and subservient, and it was never the intention of a God who gave Eve equal rights with Adam over the whole of creation. In 1993, a World Bank report concluded that promoting the rights and status of women would be a greater social investment in improving health in developing countries than pouring more money into health care.

In their continuation of the campaign initiated by Zelophehad's daughters, Caroline Norton and Florence Nightingale are reminders that the struggles of biblical women were not so remote from ours. Time and time again – as we shall see – the trailblazers in ancient society had their historical and contemporary counterparts – women who picked up where their forerunners had left off – even if it was centuries later.

My own first triumph in assertiveness didn't quite challenge the status quo as the daughters of Zelophehad did – but we all have to start somewhere. Some may find it hard to believe but I was a very passive young woman, a peace-loving pushover like my father who expected me to comply with my mother's wishes, as he had always done. I never stood up to anyone until I began to read about a different way of being.

It was soon after I started Anne Dickson's book that I bought a parka from a local boutique that cost far more than I would have usually paid. Fine if the family liked me in it, but they took one look and said, 'You look like mutton dressed as lamb – a middle-aged woman trying to be a trendy student.' With a sinking heart I trotted back to the shop to ask for my money back.

'We only give credit notes.'

I was about to concede and creep out when I heard Anne Dickson's words of wisdom resounding in my head – 'Repeat your wishes clearly and firmly,' and I heard myself whispering, 'I don't really want a credit note. I'd like my money back.'

The owner was summoned, and reiterated firmly, 'We don't give money back. We give credit notes.'

Everything inside me urged me to take the credit note and run. 'This is a local shop in a small town,' whispered an inner voice. 'You may want to shop here again. Don't make a fuss.' But I knew that would be a humiliating defeat. It would be the proof that all the lessons in assertiveness I was trying to learn didn't work. So, with my knees knocking below the counter, I took a deep breath and said more loudly, 'I don't want a credit note. I'd like my money back.'

'We don't give money back. We give credit notes.'

Jesus, I reminded myself, had commended a woman for her persistence with an unrighteous adversary. So I let the ridiculous verbal ping-pong continue, though ignominiously, as I couldn't think of anything more creative to say than, 'I want my money back.'

Eventually the owner turned away and ignored me, but I was not going to be browbeaten, and every time she turned back round I was still there, bleating politely, if feebly, 'I want my money back.'

'Oh, here it is,' she finally snapped, opening the till.

I was elated. Few transactions have ever given me such satisfaction, and as part of my new discipline, I made myself shop there ever after. After around ten years, I eventually got a grudging 'hello' from the owner when I walked through the door. This wasn't exactly a major victory as the world's great battles go, but I had taken my first faltering steps towards holding out for what mattered, and learned some tactics I have put to greater effect in the rather more important, life-changing confrontations that have come my way.

Deborah, the judge, and Mary Slessor, her successor

Israel's first great female leader refuses to be restricted by cultural expectations, societal limitations or her own insecurities. For the Egyptians the name Deborah denoted regal power. Its Hebrew root, *davar,* means 'to speak', but *devorah* can mean 'bee' or 'wasp'. This woman had the ability to sting her hearers into action. She was either married to or came from *Lappidoth,* or 'lightnings'. Was this a reference to her having divine enlightenment, or, as the rabbis believe, was she simply someone who had been given a rather menial 'honour' of attending to the lamps in the tabernacle?

Deborah manifestly led a very ordinary life before rising to be a judge. Her family was grown and departed, and her husband, if she still had one, didn't seem to be threatened by her new status. Would that workplaces and churches everywhere recognise the value of wisdom, age and experience! The basic organisational skills involved in running a home, a family or a voluntary group can be as good a preparation as any academic qualification for management responsibility.

Tracy Daszkiewicz, Deputy Director of Population Health and Wellbeing at Public Health England, refused to allow her status as a single mother to hold her back. She worked as a receptionist at a healthcare centre until her three daughters were grown up, taking a degree in Social Sciences at the Open University. In 2018, as the then Director of Public Health and Safety for Wiltshire, in post a mere three months, Tracy played a leading role in managing and orchestrating the response to the Novichok poisonings in Salisbury, and in keeping the city safe from the consequences of a chemical nerve attack. For Tracy, people came before the red tape, which she cut through when she had to. It was a remarkable achievement.[3]

I once heard a sermon to the effect that Deborah found herself a leader in Israel only because there were no suitable men available at the time, implying that poor old God, despairing of the weak, ineffectual male material at his disposal, was forced to scrape the barrel and appoint a woman. I defy anyone to justify that idea from the text in Judges 4. Deborah was leading Israel because she was the best man for the job. Her leadership qualities are plain to see. People mattered to her. She gave them time – one of the greatest gifts we have to give in this frenetic world of ours. Every day she sat beneath a palm tree, listened to their worries and problems and resolved their injustices. It may well have been unusual for a woman to have such power, but it only takes one to break the mould. From this moment on any biblical justification for banning women from access to leadership is rendered null and void by biblical history.

Deborah never apologises for her gender. With the man God sends as her sidekick she doesn't resort to passive tactics – 'Oh, Barak, I'm only a weak and frail little woman, so you'll just have to come and help me out.' She isn't aggressive – 'Barak, get your butt over here now, before I kick you into action.' Nor is she manipulative

– 'Barak, if you come and do this little job for me, I might be able to arrange that planning application for the new house you've been wanting.' Any of those approaches would have instantly destroyed the possibility of a positive, open, honest relationship. She simply tells him what she believes God wants him to do – to deliver the people from their Canaanite oppressors – and leaves the door open for him to say no. Unlike Sarah and Rebekah who dare not risk the potential failure of their plans, Deborah relies on the fact that God can bypass Barak, if he has to, and still achieve his goals. True visionaries know that no one is ever completely indispensable. There will always be an alternative way of achieving the necessary end. A prophet keeps their perspective. They always have the wider picture in mind.

Barak agrees to her commission – but with one extraordinary condition. She must go into battle at his side. Soldiers have always resisted the idea of taking women to war, lest they be distracted by the need to protect their weaker, feeble colleagues. But Barak is no macho man. He's frightened enough, and honest enough, to admit he cannot function without the authority, courage and confidence Deborah inspires in him.

This isn't exactly delegated leadership as Deborah intended it, and she warns Barak that it isn't the route to glory. In fact, and this is the irony, the final victory will go to another woman. Her name is Jael, and, according to Deborah, she is 'most blessed of tent-dwelling women' (Judg. 5:24). The English translation is inadequate. The Hebrew actually means 'most blessed of women in the tent', or, as an early Hebrew version puts it, 'blessed like a woman who attends the house of study'. There was a tent adjoining the Tabernacle known as the 'House of Study'. It was used as a place of quiet, much like a public library, so it seems quite possible that from very early in Israel's history, some women, like Jael, dedicated themselves to theological and religious study.

Yet despite Jael's brave and rather gruesome way of disposing of the enemy general as he sleeps, driving a tent peg through his head, and despite Deborah's leadership and initiative, it is Barak who ends up in the New Testament book of Hebrews as the hero of the day (Heb. 11:32), an example of faith in action. Once a task is handed over, when another takes up the responsibility for our ideas, we have to be prepared for the fact that they, not we, may get the kudos in posterity – however hard to swallow. And it does rather tend to be a man. 'Thank you for that excellent suggestion, Miss Briggs,' says the chair at a board meeting, in an old popular cartoon. 'Would one of the men here now care to make it?'

The Great White Ma of the Calabar

Deborah was referred to affectionately by the locals as a 'Mother in Israel'. In the nineteenth century the Okoyong people of the Calabar in West Africa called Mary Slessor their beloved 'Great White Ma'. In many ways, her life mirrored Deborah's.

Ma became the only woman judge in the British Empire. Her court was held in a thatched building in Ikot Obong. She sat at a small table surrounded by the local chiefs, who loved the sound of their own voices. If they didn't shut up when asked, Ma would get up and slap them, but they certainly learned the meaning of justice and mercy towards wrongdoers.

She sat through many long days trying cases, living on tea and biscuits and a tin of sweets. It took all her courage to cope with the stories of cruelty and shame that assaulted her ears and were especially terrible for a previously sheltered white woman to hear. In addition, she was not an expert in British domestic law, and there were no books to guide her in dealing with the cases, nothing but her knowledge of the laws and customs of the people she loved and her own good sense.[4] The other missionaries didn't know how she did it. Her only motive was to save her black sisters and child victims from the misery they suffered.

Born in Dundee in 1848, the daughter of a drunken Scottish shoemaker and a mother who supported the family as a weaver, Mary began work as a mill girl at the age of eleven. Even when she was very small she used to tell her older brother Robert that one day she would go to Africa to work with a wild tribe of people who killed their own twin babies because they thought they were cursed. He laughed at her and said, 'But you're only a girl, and girls can't be missionaries. *I'm* going to be one and you can come out with me, and if you're good I may let you up into my pulpit beside me.' But Mary had the last laugh, eventually becoming the first ever female Vice Consul of the Calabar.

At the age of 28, she had gone to West Africa with the Scottish Presbyterian Mission to work in an isolated missionary station with the Okoyong people. And from the start she openly challenged the prevailing cultural attitudes to human sacrifice, the killing of twin babies and the drunkenness that made life a misery.

At one time she even lived in a harem for a while, sharing her tiny quarters with the chief and his head wife, about twenty or so lesser wives, slaves, two cows, goats, fowls, cats, rats, cockroaches and centipedes. Her own room was divided by a makeshift partition of boxes and furniture, so that three boys could sleep on one side of the partition and she and two girls on the other. Every night her belongings had to be taken outside to make room for everyone. In the wet season they had to be dried out in the sun every morning before they could be taken back in. The idea of loneliness was unthinkable to the tribe, so good manners dictated the wives follow her everywhere she went. They were always bickering with each other, and the slaves were persistently being flogged. There was never any peace, privacy or sleep. Perhaps that's why the alternative became so attractive – to live alone like a native deep in the jungle.

In her adopted homeland a chief could do with his wife whatso-ever he pleased, including beat her to death if he chose. But if he died, one of his wives would be held responsible and would pay for it with her life. Mary Slessor's refusal to condone any behaviour that went against the basics of human decency and compassion, whether perpetrated by the tribal chiefs, the Mission or the ruling British government, ultimately earned her the undying love of the local people. It was the esteem in which she was so obviously held and her unique knowledge of local customs that encouraged the British Colonial Service to make her a government official in 1892. In the courts where she presided, women, and men too, were guaranteed a fair hearing.

By today's standards Mary's story may sound colonialist. But she integrated as totally as she knew how in the life of the local people, was never gagged by the confines of her situation, and in the world in which she lived was a radical force for that rare and precious commodity – justice.

Ruth, Gladys Aylward and adventures abroad

Several chapters after the story of Deborah, in Judges 19, there is a short account of an incident that is so unsavoury it seems strange that it's there – except that it demonstrates how the abuse of a woman can generate the first catastrophic breakdown in relations between the tribes of Israel.

A man and his concubine en route for home are given hospitality in Gibeah. Some of the local yokels, Benjaminites as it happens, take it as an opportunity to batter on the door and demand sex with the stranger. He, generously, hands over his concubine instead! When he finds her the following morning lying dead on the doorstep, a victim of the worst imaginable gang rape, he takes her body, divides it into twelve pieces and sends one to each of the tribes in a demand for vengeance. It is a sickening story, and it is there to shock. The message is clear – when people abandon a God-given moral code, women are treated as a commodity, and the ultimate consequence is a devastating civil war between brothers.

In the Old Testament accounts God may have had to shake a few of the male leaders like Barak, Gideon and even Moses into action, cajoling them out of their fears and inadequacies, dispensing with their unconvincing excuses, but he seems to have had a full quota of assertive, feisty women, ready to jump to his voice. They are risk-takers, ready to sacrifice their all if it is required of them – women like Ruth, the only non-Jewish heroine in the Old Testament, a favourite with Christian womanhood, I suspect, because of her sweet, humble, self-effacing, utterly feminine image. But it takes a great deal more than a passive, wishy-washy saccharine sweetness to do as she did. It takes courage, daring and an inner toughness belied by the stereotype.

Of course, the cynical view of the story is that Naomi and her daughter-in-law Ruth are simply two gold-diggers out to stitch up some unsuspecting rich bloke. But let's assume that what actually happen is that Ruth sees that her mother-in-law is devastated by the death of her two boys, in desperate financial straits and unable to cope. Ruth cannot let an embittered, unhappy Naomi go back to Bethlehem alone to fend for herself, so leaves her own family, friends, comfort and security, everything that is familiar to her, to accompany a lonely old woman.

'Where you go I will go, and where you stay I will stay. Your people will be my people and your God my God' (Ruth 1:16). The text is often used at weddings and it sounds so wonderfully romantic, but the reality for Ruth is very different. She has no idea what she is letting herself in for. 'Where you die I will die, and there I will be buried,' she adds, and for all she knows of their future, given their destitute state and the unlikelihood of meeting a male provider, starvation will make that a reality sooner rather than later.

Many of us have no idea what we're committing ourselves to, what the future holds, when we first say, 'Lord, I'll follow you anywhere, do anything you ask,' but unlike Ruth we tend to balk at the answer if it isn't as glamorous or as comfortable as we first expected. Ruth is prepared to do a dogsbody job. Gleaning, or picking up the leftover wheat after harvesting, is reserved for the beggar, the down-and-out, the rejects of society. Today's equivalent is probably cleaning the public toilets. In almost every church today it tends to be the Ruth-like people who set out the chairs, lever the chewing gum off the floor and take the tea towels home to be washed – the tasks no one else thinks about.

Not only that, but Ruth is the equivalent of an asylum seeker, foreign and vulnerable – subject to racist remarks, to accusations of 'taking our jobs', to acts of violence, even rape. Her courage and self-possession gain her the attention and protection of the landowner, Boaz, who turns out to be a relative. Now, as Naomi reflects on the possible ramifications of this extraordinary coincidence, it seems as if Ruth's past humility has merely been a test of her readiness for the real challenge. Perhaps, for us, there can be no real test of our faith and courage, no major commission, until we have proved our faithfulness in the humdrum, in getting on with the tasks we resent the most, which bring us the least kudos and satisfaction.

Naomi suggests to Ruth that on the night of the harvest party she puts on her glad rags, her make-up and perfume, and, when Boaz is asleep, climbs into bed with him. Even in our more liberal society this is not something a mother would usually ask of a daughter. If Boaz, finding a warm and willing woman at his feet, simply takes what's on offer – as many men would – without anticipating any further commitment in the cold light of day, she is destroyed. Her reputation would be in ruins, and she would lose everything, her means of earning a living, let alone her honour. It is an enormous, if calculated, risk.

Fortunately, Boaz's experience of Ruth's character alerts him to the cost and generosity of her gesture. He is touched that she has opted for an older man, not one of the handsome local lads. This is an offer he can't refuse, and as far as we know, the couple live happily ever after. The story with the happy ending is an object lesson in the benefits of rejecting personal gratification for what becomes a greater good.

Ruth becomes the mother of Obed, grandfather of King David, and in so doing earns herself a place in history as the only Gentile in the Messiah's family tree. Among Jesus' other improbable female ancestors are Rahab, a Canaanite prostitute who hides the Israeli spies who have come on a fact-finding expedition and converts to Judaism; Tamar, treated unjustly by a father-in-law she subsequently seduces; and Bathsheba, who commits adultery with King David, marries him, but to the very end of her life is always referred to as 'the wife of Uriah, the Hittite'. God, it seems, takes great pleasure in picking out the most unlikely candidates to fulfil his plans, particularly when it comes to women. These four women were all victims of their circumstances, but didn't allow it to cramp their style. They could have opted for a passive acceptance of their lot, but instead they rose up and grabbed their destiny by the throat.

There were a number of extraordinary women in the latter half of the nineteenth century and early part of the twentieth century who, like Ruth, left familiar surroundings and loved ones, sacrificed their creature comforts and even the possibility of marriage and children, risked ill health, loneliness, danger and death, to live among an unknown people. The most famous, portrayed by Ingrid Bergman in a hyped-up Hollywood version of her life, was possibly the most modest. When Alan Burgess wrote the biography of Gladys Aylward (1902–70), the Edmonton parlourmaid who became a missionary to China and helped bring an end to foot-binding, he could hardly believe how unassuming she was.

'But surely,' I said, 'in twenty years in China you must have had many strange experiences?'

'Oh yes,' said Gladys, 'but I'm sure people wouldn't be interested in them. Nothing very exciting happened.'

It was at least fifteen minutes before she confessed that she had once taken some children across the mountains. The rest of the conversation went in this manner, a verbatim memory which I have never forgotten.

'Across the mountains? Where was that?'

'In Shansi in north China; we travelled from Yangcheng across the mountains to Cian.'

'I see. How long did it take you?'

'Oh, about a month.'

'Did you have any money?'

'Oh no, we didn't have any money.'

'I see. What about food? How did you get that?'

'The Mandarin gave us two basketfuls of grain, but we soon ate that up.'

'I see. How many children did you say there were?'

'Nearly one hundred.'

I became conscious that I was saying, 'I see', rather often, and actually I was not 'seeing' anything at all, except that I was on the brink of a tremendous story.

It was not mock modesty on the part of Gladys Aylward; the stories she had been telling were, to her, the greatest in the world taken straight from the pages of the New Testament; that her own adventures might be worth setting down, she had simply not considered.[5]

Gladys Aylward's rescue in 1940 of a hundred children from the advancing Japanese was merely the culmination of her remarkable achievements. At fourteen, she had left school to work in the Penny Bazaar, the precursor to Marks and Spencer. Although she applied to the China Inland Mission she found studying difficult, failed her Chinese exams and was turned down. In the end she saved up her meagre parlourmaid's wages and went under her own steam.

The journey was horrific. She was imprisoned in Germany, almost raped in Russia and ended up in Japan, but finally made her way to China, where she quickly learned to speak the language like a native by living and working with the people. She even destroyed her British passport and became naturalised Chinese.

Foot-binding was imposed on women by their men to stop a wife running away, but it left even little girls crippled and in great pain. The government found a ban almost impossible to impose, and invited Gladys to be its spokesperson. That meant challenging rigid male authority in every traditional, rural community – an enormous risk for a woman. But, like Ruth, Gladys had a manner that was intriguing and an integrity and determination that was irresistible – winning over even the mighty, all-powerful rulers of the provinces where she lived and worked.

The friendship between the feudal Mandarin of Yancheng and the tiny ex-parlourmaid from Belgrave Square is probably one of the oddest stories in the history of Eastern and Western relationships. Although she spoke the language fluently it was years before she managed to grasp how his mind functioned. He was enigmatic, his thin face giving nothing away. A glossy pigtail hung down from his round silk cap; his gowns were embroidered in scarlet, blue, green and gold. To Gladys, he always looked as if he had just stepped out of an antique Chinese scroll. Little had changed in his style of ruler-ship since the time of Confucius.

There is little doubt that, to the Mandarin, Gladys Aylward was as alien as a Martian. She was female, which meant that she was socially and intellectually of less value than dust. Nevertheless, as news of her exploits reached him, and as, over the months, she continually bombarded him with applications, supplications, admonitions and near-threats, he simply couldn't ignore her. In fact, as their acquaintance increased, she became not only an adviser of sorts, but also a friend.[6]

Like Ruth, Gladys finally achieved her objectives, as in the end the Mandarin's profound admiration for this exceptional, assertive woman persuaded him to change the local laws, and foot-binding became a thing of the past.

Gladys was bemused and somewhat bewildered by the glamorised movie version of her life in *The Inn of the Sixth Happiness*. In today's world, so dominated by political correctness that women are inadvertently expected to live with so many abuses of their rights in the name of cultural tolerance, where celebrity status depends more on looks, riches and a good spin doctor rather than on character or self-sacrifice, Gladys Aylward's achievements might have passed unnoticed. She might even have been accused of being patronising or colonial. But it wouldn't have held her back. The lives of the little nobodies who risk their all to make their world a better place make a mockery of those who criticise from the safety of the sidelines.

Esther and Josephine Butler – where risk takes courage

The greatest of all the Jewish heroines is a little nobody plucked from nowhere. Esther's background was neither impressive nor devout. By the time of her birth most serious Jews had been only too glad to leave their place of exile behind and return from Persia to Jerusalem, where they rebuilt their precious Temple. A few, like Esther's relations, stayed behind, presumably because they were comfortable, happily assimilated into Babylonian society, much like the Jews of Austria and Germany in the 1930s, who dominated the professions and the arts, and thought they were safe. In other words, Esther isn't chosen to play a leading role in saving her people because of a pedigree in piety. Nor is she given a chance to suggest there must be a more suitable, holier person sitting in a synagogue pew nearby.

She even uses a Persian name – Esther, which means Venus – rather than her Hebrew name, Hadassah, or palm tree. Perhaps it's asking for trouble, but it's as a native-born Babylonian that she wins a beauty competition and finds herself with the booby prize – the king himself. King Xerxes' first wife, Vashti, has been too busy at her own banquet to turn up for his, so he decides to find a replacement in a cavalier yet fairly twenty-first-century manner.

This is no heart-warming, Cinderella, rag-to-riches story. Esther is a prisoner in a harem, with at least twenty other women all suffering at various times from boredom, competition and pre-menstrual tension. She probably cries at night with homesickness for her family, or for the local boy she loves and might have married. But there is no indication that she goes on lamenting the life she might have had, no evidence of self-pity or complaint. She makes the best of a difficult situation and earns the approval of Hegai, the eunuch in charge. She could have stayed on her dignity, and said, 'Actually I'm Jewish. We don't have anything to do with eunuchs.' But instead, she shows real humility in asking him to teach her about her new culture. It pays dividends in the long run.

She submits herself to the statutory aromatherapy – six months of massage with myrrh, and six with oil and spices. This lengthy procedure is repeated over and over again, until scent oozes from every pore of her body, and its fragrance trails after her wherever she goes. In biblical language, myrrh represents suffering and death, and oil is a symbol of the Holy Spirit. Esther is laying down her former life in preparation for something completely new – marriage to the king. It might be a parable of the spiritual life. There are no short cuts to being properly prepared and equipped.

After five years in the harem, apparently treading water, Esther's moment finally comes. One morning she finds her Uncle Mordecai sitting in sackcloth, weeping at the palace gate. Haman, the most senior politician in the land, doesn't like immigrants (what's new?), and has persuaded the King to issue an edict to destroy all the Jews. Esther, meanwhile, has lived quietly at the palace, submitting herself to the vagaries of her new life, manifestly keeping her Jewish identity a closely guarded secret.

Mordecai begs his niece to intervene and save her people. For Esther, it must be a shocking request. Any uninvited approach to the King risks the death penalty. She will have to expose her true identity. But so what? Mordecai tells her. 'Don't think you'll escape if your people are destroyed. But if you keep quiet help will come for us from elsewhere.' God, Mordecai explains to her, is not so dependent on one human being that he will allow their reluctance to thwart his plan.

She can, of course, still say, 'Not likely, Uncle. Why should I risk my neck when I've got this far? I think I'll sit it out and take my chances.' In one, almost mad, moment she makes the extraordinary decision to risk her all – position, status, reputation, and even her life, if that's what it comes to. And it's a decision that heralds a dramatic change in Esther. A fairly passive young woman at everyone else's beck and call begins to take control of the situation. She sends Mordecai to declare a fast, and to tell the people to pray for her. He does as he is told without question or argument, presumably responding with trembling excitement to that new authority in her voice. Traditionally, the Church equated passivity with femininity. Being 'nice' or compliant can seem one of the cardinal virtues of Christian womanhood. But to do what is necessary, what is required of us, may mean that, like Esther, we have to adopt a different, more assertive approach. The Holy Spirit is meant to strengthen, not stifle.

Esther takes a deep breath and faces the King and his possible wrath with her head held high. She doesn't flutter her eyelashes, flirt, flatter or apologise for disturbing him. She is no longer Venus, dazzling with youthful beauty; she is Hadassah, as stately and dignified as a palm tree. The King is impressed and listens to her plea. The Jewish people are saved from annihilation. Haman ends up on gallows he has built for Mordecai, and, with a nice twist at the end of the tale, Mordecai is made Prime Minister.

Like Esther, we all have to decide who has the ultimate control of our destiny and the destiny of the world in which we live. Mordecai reminds his niece, 'And who knows but that you have come to your royal position for such a time as this?' (Esther 4:14). In a world filled with suffering, alienation and injustice, even on our own doorstep, the challenge to give our all for such a time as this has never seemed more apposite. Yet we often hold back. There is too much to lose – our reputation, popularity, status, financial security, goals and ambitions. We fear making a fool of ourselves, making enemies, or not having the energy to see a project through. We tend to be more self-conscious than God-conscious, and it costs us an assertive stance, the determination to follow our calling, whatever the cost. 'Don't be afraid of those who kill the body, but can't kill the soul,' said Jesus. Instead, be afraid of the One who can kill the soul and the body in hell.'[7]

By the middle of the nineteenth century it was becoming acceptable, if not exactly desirable, for middle-class women to fight for higher education, better employment and more protection at law, but it was unthinkable to stand up for the rights of society's 'untouchables'. One woman dared to speak out against the wholesale abuse of the most dispossessed of her gender.

The Contagious Diseases Acts of the 1860s gave the police the power to drag any lone woman suspected of prostitution off the streets, so that they could subject her to the most brutal internal examination to check for signs of venereal disease. In reality, only a working woman would go out on her own, so only a woman of the lower classes, whether prostitute or an innocent abroad, could be subjected to this flagrant denial of her rights. She was held down on a surgical couch with her legs strapped apart, while instruments lifted out of boiling water were immediately inserted inside her. If she turned out to be a virgin and her hymen was ruptured, she would be told she was a good girl and given five shillings for a hot dinner. Some women miscarried. Others experienced permanent internal damage.

When respectable vicar's wife Josephine Butler (1828–1906) began her twenty-year fight to have the Acts repealed, she provoked a furore, which cost her her health, her reputation, her privacy and the quiet, precious life with the husband and children she adored.

When she realised how much her actions were costing her husband and children, Josephine questioned whether her campaign merited such a sacrifice. But they understood that she could not remain silent in the face of such an injustice and urged her to continue, even when they were the butt of verbal and physical brickbats. She saw only too well that the law was a thinly disguised form of persecution, enabling men to project their sense of self-loathing and disgust on to the victims of their lust. Josephine's crime was to say so in public. She dared to say that a woman could not pick up a sexual disease without the help of a man, and that he was guiltier than any prostitute he had used, for he had money, power and respectability on his side. Furthermore, she said it in sexually explicit language, exposing the hidden, shadow side of upright male society and the hypocrisy of much Victorian morality. Her honesty made Josephine Butler intolerable.

Raised in a loving, stimulating home in Northumberland where she wasn't penalised intellectually for being a girl, Josephine was encouraged by her father not only to think for herself but also to see her Christian duty as improving the lot of the people around her. She couldn't help but contrast the appalling poverty and deprivation in the north-east with her own protected, comfortable little existence. How could such inequalities exist? If God was a God of love, why would he tolerate such blatant injustice and abuses of power? Why was his Church so uncaring and ineffectual? She would shout out loud at God and beg him to come and show her what he wanted her to do. She felt at times she was going mad, but she couldn't contemplate a future that involved a life of meaningless domesticity simply because she was a woman.

It was her good fortune to marry a man way ahead of his time, both in his belief in the equality of women and in sharing her vision of a fairer society. George Butler was a gentle, likeable man, a clergyman and university tutor who was the perfect foil for his fiery wife. His fellow dons in Oxford were bemused that he encouraged his wife to take part in discussions on intellectual matters and to express her own opinions. For her part, she found them pompous and stuffy and was glad when George took up the post of Vice Principal of Cheltenham Boys' College.

It was in Cheltenham that the couple experienced the terrible tragedy that would change their lives forever. They had four children, three boys and then a much longed-for little girl. One evening, as they returned from a dinner party, their six-year-old daughter rushed out of bed onto the landing to greet them. But the bannisters gave way and she fell to her death onto the tiled floor at their feet.

At first Josephine couldn't believe a man could suffer the loss of a child as intensely as a mother. Then one day, in her husband's study, she found a scrap of paper in which he described his pain at the loss of his beloved little girl. He had kept all the little presents, drawings, pressed flowers and bookmarks little Eva had made for him. Sharing their sorrow drew them together into the deep and lasting bond that would keep their relationship strong and steady in the challenges ahead.

George was appointed Principal of Liverpool College and threw himself into his new job, but it compounded Josephine's sense of emptiness. Seeing that she needed some outlet for her pain, a wise old Quaker woman encouraged Josephine to go with her to the local workhouse where 4,000 destitute girls were housed in the most abysmal conditions.

For a well-meaning woman of Josephine's class to make benevolent visits to the workhouse, read the Bible and pray with the inmates, wasn't exactly unique. But whereas few survived the ridicule, and coarse language, it would take more than spittle running down the front of her dress to see Josephine Butler off. She not only weathered their initial rejection, but she also reached out her arms and held them as they poured out their problems. That a beautifully groomed and immaculately dressed woman would touch their filthy tatters said more to them about the love of God than anything her words could convey. And their acceptance began to fill the aching void in her heart. Their stories convinced her that prostitutes were not wicked, licentious women, but the victims of circumstances and preying men.

When a government committee, set up to look into disease levels in the Army and Navy, led to the first Contagious Diseases Act in 1864, she was horrified beyond belief. Her crusading reputation was beginning to be well known, and with a sickening sense of inevitability she guessed it would only be a matter of time before she was approached and asked to lead a campaign. She was right. A small, predominantly male, protest group had been formed, but no man could fight for the rights of prostitutes. That was a job for a woman, and Josephine was the perfect, possibly only, candidate.

She never doubted the cost would be immense, and she wasn't the only one who would have to pay the price. George had been tipped for a shining career in the Church. There were hints about him becoming a bishop, but not with a wife who publicly challenged the sexual status quo. Her three boys were now seventeen, fifteen and twelve and very vulnerable to abuse from schoolmates. And then there were her family and friends. Anyone who had any connection with her would become a pariah. She agonised over the suffering she might cause, but in the end it was George who encouraged her to walk, in her words, 'straight into the jaws of hell'.[8]

The cost turned out to be even greater than either had anticipated. In the first year alone she travelled 3,700 miles, largely in rickety carriages, and spoke at ninety-nine meetings. For the next few years she was constantly on the road. George ran the home and took care of the boys, an extraordinary commitment for a man of his time.

Josephine found public speaking an enormous strain, yet had the ability to keep a large audience enthralled. Had she been a portly dowager she might have been left to have her say, but her striking appearance and understated sexuality seemed to incense her enemies as much as her message. She was constantly harangued and heckled, interrupted by rude innuendo, raucous laughter and vulgar abuse. Mobs were hired to pelt her with dirt and stones.

At home, George received obscene drawings of her through the post. Rumours suggested their marriage was in difficulty – a cruel experience for such a devoted couple. Both found the extended separations unbearable.

But one foggy night in April 1883, after years of persistent battling, Josephine, now a middle-aged woman, made her way to the Ladies' Gallery of the House of Commons to hear the reading of a Bill to repeal the pernicious Acts. Down the road, in the Westminster Palace Hotel, George and a motley band of every class and status, male and female, had gathered to pray. She joined them for a while, and it was a sight she would never forget.

There were the poorest, most ragged and miserable women from the slums of Westminster on their knees before the God of Hosts with tears and groans, pouring out the burden of their sad hearts. He alone knew what their burden was. There were women who had lost daughters; there were sad-hearted women; and side by side with these poor souls, dear to God as we are, there were ladies of high rank, in their splendid dresses – Christian women of the upper classes kneeling and also weeping. I thank God for this wonderful solidarity of the women of the world before God.

Women are called to be a great power in the future, and by this terrible blow which fell upon us forcing us to leave our privacy and bind ourselves together with our less fortunate sisters, we have passed through an education – a noble education. God has prepared in us, in the women of the world, a force for all future causes which are great and just.[9]

At midnight she went back to the Commons, and was in the gallery at 1.30 a.m. when a majority of seventy-two gave her the answer to those prayers. Too overwhelmed to go back to the hotel immediately, she went out onto the terrace overlooking the Thames. 'The fog had cleared away and it was very calm under the starlit sky. All the bustle of the city was stilled and the only sound was that of the dark water lapping against the buttresses of the broad stone terrace . . . it almost seemed like a dream.'[10] They had done it. With God's help, and with a band of doughty supporters, she and George had made the world a kinder place for young women.

But that was just a beginning. 'The campaigns she spearheaded – against sex trafficking, child prostitution and state-endorsed brothels – continue today, and if she remains one of feminism's unsung heroes, it is probably because she was so eclipsed by both the drama and the relatively uncontroversial achievements of the suffragettes.[11]

Like Esther, Josephine Butler risked her all to save the young women she saw as her own people, her sisters. There are other assertive women hidden like golden nuggets in the text of the Hebrew Scriptures: one is Hannah, who has fertility problems, but doesn't slink away in shame when she is accused of drunkenness as she weeps in despair in the Temple, but ultimately gets the desire of her heart – a son, Samuel. Another is Abigail, the wise, who stands up to her fool of a husband who is too mean to provide food for David and his men, and then becomes David's wife when he is king. Still another is the unnamed woman in the book of Judges who drops a millstone from a high wall onto the leader of the army besieging her city. This really is strategic thinking. Since women don't have the brawn, they find brain works better.

Some women, whether key players or walk-on extras, make their mark on history when they give up the need to discover God's will for their individual lives, and ask instead, 'What is your will for this beautiful world which you have made? And what is my part in it?' They have a vision of the wider canvas, of the broader brush strokes used by the artist, and the importance of contributing carefully and accurately to the detail. They do what they know to be right and just, not what's expected of them, and that takes courage, self-sacrifice and a gentle but tenacious assertiveness. 'Unless a grain of wheat falls to the ground and dies, it remains only a single seed. But if it dies, it produces many seeds' (John 12:24).

Part 2

The Christ-following Woman – A Liberating Inheritance?

Chapter 4

A Woman of Little Status?

Jesus did not alter or override Old Testament theology. He taught it, interpreted it, enhanced it, divested it of the cultural flotsam and jetsam attached to it by the tide of time and human hypocrisy, and tempered it with mercy. This liberating, life-changing approach is particularly evident when he doesn't condemn the adulterous woman, but challenges her male accusers (indifferent to the fact her partner in crime has done a vanishing act) to cast the first stone if they dare. Given that the practice of stoning women has returned in some countries – even for the 'crime' of being raped – this story has a fresh poignancy today.

Nonetheless, I couldn't believe my eyes when I read an article on the web that said, 'Jesus related to women as he did to any other outcasts.' Which Old Testament woman would answer to the name of outcast? Ruth the asylum seeker perhaps, but she finds love, acceptance and respect. So how, suddenly, do Hebrew women become outcasts in the New?

To be fair, a great deal has been said and written down through the centuries about how Jesus is supposed to have raised the status of poor, excluded females who happened to fall across his path. Samaritan women perhaps, but knowing Jewish women as I do, I'm not convinced. Mary and Martha do not strike me as oppressed little creatures to whom Jesus gallantly and condescendingly offered his friendship, publicly lifting them out of a life of seclusion and servitude. He simply enjoyed their company. He probably enjoyed the food Martha kept putting in front of him too. I can almost hear her cutting into the flow of his stories with, 'So, eat; a boy needs his food,' just as my Jewish great-grandmother used to do. And I expect he obeyed with a chuckle and tucked in with relish.

In fact, Jesus never seems to stop eating. In the Gospels, more of his sayings take place around the meal table than in the synagogue or Temple. No wonder he made regular visits to that little house in Bethany. He wasn't trying to make a point. This was simply a chance to relax and unwind with special friends.

A number of misunderstandings about the place of Jewish women at the time of Jesus seem to have filtered through the decades into Christian consciousness from the writings of a Dr Leonard Swidler, scholar of ancient Jewish texts.[1] Based on misogynist sayings in the oral Jewish law, Swidler claimed that Jewish women were uneducated, downtrodden, segregated, banished to their homes and generally abused. The evidence shows this wasn't the case. Contemporary Jewish scholar Hyam Maccoby points out that a Jewish woman did not forfeit her property rights when she married.[2] She could also initiate divorce – for ill-treatment, incompatibility, an unsatisfactory sex life and her husband's body odour, if it wasn't to her liking. Although her world revolved primarily around the home, she came and went as she pleased. Furthermore, like the Superwoman in the book of Proverbs, she was honoured, respected and even revered by her man.

The hotchpotch of oral rabbinic instructions with their negative view of women were not formally transcribed into what became the Talmud for several centuries, and at the time of Jesus were only given credence by the most Pharisaic wing of Judaism. The Sadducees, who collaborated with the Romans and were part of the ruling classes, certainly didn't condemn women to a life in the shadows. In the Jewish quarter of Jerusalem, where a Sadducee house has been excavated and used as a museum, the personal belongings of the wife of the High Priest are displayed in a glass cabinet – her jewellery, elaborate combs, lipstick and kohl pencil. In fact, her make-up collection looked very much like mine, and I certainly don't put on full warpaint to sit at home and spin.

So, what was life really like for women at the time of Jesus and in the early days of his Church? And what impact did an encounter with this extraordinary man have, not only on their lives, but also on the lives of those who would come after them?

Banished to the gallery?

It now seems that women were much more active in the religious life of the Jewish community than they are today.[3] In Orthodox Judaism a minimum of ten men must be present before corporate prayers can be said. That was a real trial when my father died and tradition required prayers in our family home morning and night for 'shiva', the seven official days of mourning. We could guarantee a quorum every evening, but the early morning stint was another matter. My brother had to ring round all his friends to beg and bully enough men into stopping off on their way to work, otherwise we would have to do without a very meaningful ritual. But the idea that only ten males constitute a viable congregation isn't found in ancient sources until AD 500. Even as late as the twelfth century, rabbis agreed that a woman could count as one of the ten.

Participating in prayer was not the only privilege women shared with the men at the time of Jesus. During my first visit to Israel, we visited the ruins of an ancient synagogue, and the guide asked the party where the women sat.

'In the gallery,' we all said immediately, in unison.

'Which gallery?' he persevered.

We looked up, and the penny dropped. There was no gallery. No sitting up in the gods for the female members of this synagogue, ogling the talent below, as I did in my misspent youth. Galleries were not in fact added until around the seventh century, probably owing to the influence of Islam. One of the best preserved ancient synagogues uncovered by archaeologists, at Dura-Europos in the Syrian desert, dates from the third century. The congregation sat on two rows of plastered, tiered benches on all four sides of a rectangular assembly hall. There was no partition, no evidence of any segregation, either there or at the excavated first-century synagogue at Masada. Not only did men and women sit together during synagogue worship, but excavations in Israel have unearthed large stones bearing inscriptions such as *archisynagogissa* – a female 'Head of Synagogue', and *presbytera* – a female elder, or council member.[4] No one is sure what these positions were. Inevitably, some scholars have tried to suggest they were merely honorary. That seems unlikely.

There has always been more than an 'honorary' hint of matriarchal power within the ranks of the Jewish people.

Banished to the Women's Court?

It appears there was no segregation of male and female in the Temple either. Most public assemblies were held in an outer court where men and women mingled together. It became known as the Women's Court because the women tended to commandeer it, preferring to enjoy the familiar chatter of a female sisterhood than venture into the two more interior courts. It also made it easier to nip out to breastfeed or drag out a screaming child. In the same way, the Israelites' or Men's Court was given the name because the men from non-priestly families tended to congregate there, rather than in the Priests' Court. However, there was nothing to stop women walking through the Men's Court into the Priests' Court to offer sacrifices at the altar.

The only enforced separation in the Temple was for the seven nights of Tabernacles. The priest would return from the Pool of Siloam carrying a golden pitcher full of water, ready to pour on the altar the following day, and as he arrived the men began to dance, and danced all night. A gallery was temporarily erected in the Women's Court to allow the women to watch their men dancing in the great space below. Men and women could worship together, but dancing together was a step too far.[5]

The seventh day, referred to in John's Gospel as the 'greatest day of the festival', is the climax of the festival. As the people cried out for the coming of the Messiah, and the water was poured over the altar and flowed through the elaborate Temple drainage system down into the Kidron Valley and on towards the Dead Sea, it was in the crowded Women's Court that Jesus stood up and declared, 'Let anyone who is thirsty come to me and drink. Whoever believes in me . . . rivers of living water will flow from within them' (John 7: 37–8).

When it came to public worship, the only contribution allowed from a non-priest was to read the Scriptures. Although it wasn't expressly forbidden, women were not encouraged to put their name down for this particular privilege. As late as the eleventh century a famous rabbinic scholar was asked whether a woman might be called up to read from the scrolls. Rabbi Solomon came to the convenient conclusion that according to the law she could, but, out of respect for the congregation, she should not. It seems this was a polite way of saying, 'Sorry, girls, the men would find that just too threatening.'

No wonder the extraordinary events of Pentecost caused such a furore in the city. It seems quite possible that on that momentous Feast of Shavuot the disciples, many of them women, had gathered in a room at the 'House of the Lord' – the Temple.[6] Where else would good Jews have been on such an important festival?

There in the crowded Temple, as the traditional Scriptures rang out through the courts – the story of the giving of Torah on Sinai, when God appears in wind, thunder, noise and flames of fire – there is a simultaneous, audio-visual demonstration in an upper room. Both men and women are filled with the Holy Spirit and begin to worship God in unlearned foreign languages, and in public.

The RSV version of the Bible appears to dispute the idea that women were involved at all. Explaining the disciples' strange behaviour, the Apostle Peter is supposed to have said, '*These men* are not drunk, as you suppose . . .' But the Authorised Version's 'these', and the NIV's 'these people', translate the Greek accurately, because a masculine plural pronoun is used for a group of men and women. The same principle applies in French grammar where four women in a car are referred to as 'elles', but if one mere man were to join them, 'they' would become 'ils'.

It is because the Holy Spirit is poured out on women that the Apostle Peter makes the connection with the prophetic words of Joel. 'Your sons and daughters will prophesy' (Joel 2:28). This then was one of the basic differences between the synagogue or Temple and the brand-new church. Women were given, by divine appointment, an active role in public worship.

Denied an education?

Though Jewish women didn't have the same religious obligations as men, they knew their Scriptures. Mary, the mother of Jesus, may have been a mere peasant girl, but her Magnificat (Luke 1:46–55) is evidence enough that she had learned to read and had studied Torah. Mary not only knows Hannah's song of thanksgiving at the birth of Samuel, but also has the insight to apply it prophetically to her own situation during her pregnancy. So, even if Jewish women were denied the right to read the Scriptures aloud in public, they certainly read them in private.

If you wanted a woman to be a better mother and to raise children in the faith, educate them, said the Jews. Malala Yousafzai would have approved. 'One child, one teacher, one pen and one book can change the world,' she said to the United Nations on her sixteenth birthday more than twenty centuries later.[7]

Some of Jesus' innate respect for womanhood must have come from his mother. Did Mary sing the Scriptures to her boy at bedtime, helping him to learn them off by heart? He certainly expected women to know their Scriptures as well as any man, as his relationship with Martha clearly shows.

Martha and Mary revisited

Martha's education and intelligence is obvious when Jesus arrives at her home after her brother Lazarus has died (John 11). I love their relationship. It is wonderfully real and robust. While Mary sits quietly at home grieving, Martha marches out to confront him about his failure to turn up in time. She's the assertive, combative type, and I reckon when Jesus sees her coming, he knows he's in for a hard time.

'If you'd come when we first sent for you,' she snaps, 'my brother wouldn't have died.'

'Don't worry, Martha, Lazarus will rise,' Jesus reassures her.

Martha doesn't appear to have heard. She stands her ground.

'On the last day,' she retorts, referring to a verse in the book of Daniel,[8] with the unspoken but obvious implication, 'That's a fat lot of good to me, because meanwhile, Lazarus is dead and this isn't the last day.'

There is no sense here that Jesus treats Martha any differently from the way he would treat a man. She is no fading violet in his presence. She's a strong and sensible woman who isn't afraid to give him a piece of her mind, and he loves her for it. For now he tells her what he hasn't yet revealed to another living soul – that he is the Resurrection and the Life. And she responds exactly as he knew she would, in her usual forthright manner, becoming the first person to declare, 'Yes, Lord . . . I believe that you are the Messiah, the Son of God' (John 11:27).

In another encounter with Martha, she is so at ease with Jesus that she thinks nothing of drawing him into a family tiff (Luke 10:38–42). She genuinely expects him to tell her sister off for sitting around while she does all the work. And he knows Martha well enough to know she can take his criticism on the chest like a man when instead, he affirms Mary for giving him the gift of her attention. Martha probably goes on muttering to herself in the kitchen. She has given him the gift of her cordon bleu cuisine, for goodness sake, but then he is a man, after all; what does he know about the grind of the kitchen sink? And he would shake his head and laugh. It would take more than his gentle word of rebuke to flatten Martha.

Dorothy Sayers (1893–1957), bestselling detective story writer and creator of Lord Peter Wimsey, the new, caring, gentle, upper crust hero, could be as tart as Martha. The only child of a clergyman and former student of mediaeval French at Somerville College, Oxford, at a time when a woman wasn't entitled to a degree, Sayers continually prodded polite society, including the Church, over the subordination of women, begging for their gifts to be recognised. She lampooned the bishops and other male authority figures in her orbit who referred to 'the women, God help us!' or 'the ladies, God bless them!' In her most outspoken essay on the subject, 'Are Women Human?' first published in a volume knowingly called *Unpopular Opinions*, she said Jesus never mocked or patronised women because he had 'no axe to grind, no uneasy male dignity to defend'. He was completely relaxed, completely unselfconscious with them. No wonder they were 'first at the cradle, last at the cross'. (She seems to have overlooked the fact that they were the first at the resurrection as well.)

Dorothy Sayers herself was a thorn in the side of the Church of England. 'It is necessary,' she wrote, 'from time to time, to speak plainly, perhaps even brutally, to the Church.'[9]

> I think I have never heard a sermon preached on the story of Martha and Mary which did not attempt, somehow, somewhere, to explain away its text. Mary's, of course, was the better part – the Lord said so, and we must not precisely contradict him. But we will be careful not to despise Martha. No doubt, he approved of her too. We could not get on without her, and indeed (having paid lip service to God's opinion) we must really admit that we greatly prefer her. For Martha was doing a really feminine job, whereas Mary was just behaving like any other disciple, male or female; and that is a hard pill to swallow.[10]

Unfortunately for the Church, her popularity made her hard to ignore. I love Sayers' description of the discomfort of preachers trying to handle the Mary and Martha story, forced against their better judgement to disagree with God because they cannot break out of the confines of their own cultural prejudices. In her time, the late 1940s and 1950s, a 'kept' wife was a badge of status and success for a professional class or businessman, aping his aristocratic superiors. Meanwhile, poor women did the domestic donkey work. No preacher balked at their peeling potatoes, blacking grates, polishing the brasses or scrubbing floors. I still remember the large, rough, calloused hands of our 'daily woman', as my mother called her, when I was a child. In the eighties, when we arrived for Peter's curacy in a mining town in West Yorkshire, I was told you could tell I was middle class by the length of my nails.

For most of the century the Church was dominated by the middle classes and their cultural attitudes. On the positive side there was an army of women who had the freedom to work on a voluntary basis for the Church. Their loss, as younger women eventually took their place in the job market, has been incalculable. On the negative side, for centuries, women who went out to work, or who operated in any other than a domestic setting, were treated with suspicion, if not downright hostility. And the Church not only concurred, it also spiritualised the concept.

For years I got speaking invitations that read, 'Dear Mrs Guinness, Could you possibly come to speak at our women's group one afternoon? We realise you may be too busy what with running a busy home and parish.' The home was the least of my worries. And the parish was my husband's. But my job presented a bit of a problem. Employers were hardly happy to let me gad about all over the country speaking at Christian meetings.

In Jesus' day, although Jewish women knew their Scriptures, it was their duty to run the home. Theological study, to sit at the rabbi's feet and analyse their teaching, was a male prerogative. In his affirmation of Mary's unconventional behaviour, particularly in a middle-eastern setting where hospitality and good manners were intertwined, Jesus is making an important point – women don't have to be condemned any longer to a life of domesticity or social entrapment. The prime role of any disciple, male or female, is to spend time with the Master. For Jesus, the kingdom supersedes the kitchen. Fifty years ago, Dorothy Sayers wrote (but is it fully a reality yet?):

> It is strange, but it is true, that John Stuart Mill could not have written in Queen Victoria's day of the emancipation of women had it not been for this carpenter of thirty who told Martha, and no doubt certain listening disciples, that Mary had many gifts which must be given freedom to develop. The intellectual woman of every sort today, university graduate, writer, artist, musician, social worker, world traveller, may feel she goes forward in her work with the approval of Jesus Christ; that he looks for her part as a thoughtful citizen of his kingdom, and would miss it, were she not to use her talents. He sat down gratefully to Martha's good meal; he also took joy in Mary's acceptance of his wisdom. His courtesy to women includes the liberty of the whole of the personality, the use of all the gifts with which God has endowed her. The parable of the talents is for her equally with man.[11]

The man who made women feel special

We are not sure who the woman was who poured the equivalent of a bottle of Chanel No 5 all over Jesus' feet and wiped them with her hair, but it was an extraordinary thing to do, especially in the home of a Pharisee, of all people. One thing is sure – whoever she was, only a prostitute would tend to let down her hair outside the privacy of her own bedroom. Had she met Jesus before? Was she carried away by an overwhelming sense of gratitude at his acceptance? Was this an opportunity to say thank you to the man who had redeemed the mess her life had become, a determined attempt to show her appreciation at any cost, especially when Simon, the Pharisee, had so singularly failed to do so? How many clients had it taken to pay for such a quantity of precious perfume?

Or perhaps it was an opportunity for the abused to show the abuser that she was no longer in his power. Bethany was a small place, and in that room there could well have been men whose embarrassment was down to the fact that they had seen her do what she was now doing in an entirely different context.

It may well be an uncomfortable situation for Simon and his guests, but Jesus is comfortable enough with his own sexuality not to be disturbed by it.

'Do you see this woman?' he asks Simon.

Silly question – of course Simon can see her. But actually, he can't *see* her. He doesn't wonder how she was reduced to selling her body – whether she was an illegitimate child with no prospect of marriage, a widow struggling to survive, abandoned by her man and left with no support. He doesn't ask what it cost her to do what she did, or why she's making such a display of herself here in his home. But Jesus sees the intention behind the gesture, and accepts it as an expression of the purest love. There is an intimacy here, yet it is utterly safe, because he *sees* and respects the woman she is. He welcomes the tears and kisses, the warm, physical display of emotion, and tells Simon he only wishes men could respond to him as freely.

All of Jesus' relationships with women are characterised by that same easy, loving acceptance and rejection of stereotypes. He called a girl of twelve his 'little darling' when he tenderly took her hand

and brought her back to life; he singled out and healed a bent and broken old lady, crippled with osteoporosis or rheumatoid arthritis, to whom no one gave the time of day; he didn't shy away from an excluded, anaemic woman who had suffered with menstrual problems for years and who made him unclean simply by reaching out and touching the tassels of his *tzitzit*, or prayer vest. Instead he cut through the taboos and commended her for her faith.

And then there was that extraordinary encounter with the Samaritan woman at the well (John 4), remarkable not because she was a woman, but because she was a member of a clan treated like the untouchables in India. A Jewish proverb at the time of Jesus claimed, 'the daughters of the Samaritans are menstruants from the cradle'. But Jesus does the unthinkable and shares her drinking cup. He sits and talks to her as if it's the most normal thing in the world for a Jewish man to do, leaving his disciples in a state of shock. She rushes back to her people and says, 'Come and see a man who told me everything I ever did.' All he told her was that she has had five partners and isn't married to her current man. 'Everything I ever did' didn't really amount to much. But the seventh man in her life gives her meaning, wholeness and purpose – and she passes it on to the village that listens to her story of transformation. So the first real apostle, missionary or 'sent one' in the Bible is a woman.

Jesus makes no gender distinction when he says, 'Whoever does God's will is my brother and sister and mother' (Mark 3:35). A large number of women disciples were his travelling companions, including Mary Magdalene, who had been healed of evil spirits, which meant she had probably shown signs of severe mental health distress and been an object of ridicule and abuse for years. And, what's more, when they provided the basic financial support for his mission (Luke 8:2–3), possibly on the proceeds of their cottage industries, he didn't say, 'Just a minute girls, the men need to be the breadwinners round here.'

Jesus doesn't only raise the status of women. He raises the status of all human beings by enabling them to be what God intended them to be. The pouring out of the Holy Spirit on men and women alike at Pentecost was the natural and logical conclusion of his earthly ministry. It is hardly surprising, then, that women played a key part in the early church.

Prophets, apostles, elders, deacons and fellow workhorses

The Old Testament prophecy in the book of Joel, that 'your sons and daughters will prophesy', was more than adequately fulfilled in the Apostle Philip's household. His four single daughters were all prophets (Acts 21:9). That must have kept Daddy on his toes, especially when they were all at home together. Whenever he went on a mission, he had four potential assistants. No wonder their reputation went before them.

The Apostle Paul immensely valued this new dimension of women's gifting. The final chapter of his letter to the Romans must have one of the longest PSs of any letter ever published. Paul records, one by one – no doubt to a flagging amanuensis – all the friends and colleagues he wants to greet. Ten of the twenty-nine people in his 'roll-call' of the great and good are women. Dick France points out that four of them – Mary, Tryphena, Tryphosa and Persis – are described as having 'worked hard' for the kingdom of God, a translation of the verb *kopiao,* which Paul uses to describe his own and his other male colleagues' ministry in evangelism and church building.[12]

Like those two embattled dears in Philippi – Euodia and Syntyche – Tryphena and Tryphosa in Rome and Priscilla of Corinth are all referred to as *synergos* or co-workers. In other words, Paul regards them as having the same ministry as Timothy, Titus, Mark, Luke and Philemon – the big male guns in his apostolic mission.

The most interesting name on Paul's list in Romans belongs to his fellow prisoner, Junia, 'outstanding among [or esteemed by] the apostles, and . . . in Christ before I was' (Rom. 16:7). Many translations of the Bible call her Junias, though no such male version of the name ever existed in Roman times. Aegidius of Rome in the thirteenth century was the first commentator to describe her as a man. Jerome, the foremost fifth-century Christian scholar, speaks about this 'leader among the apostles' as if she were a woman. Was she an apostle? Even if she was simply 'esteemed by' the apostles, she was quite a force to be reckoned with.

To give some Bible translators the benefit of the doubt, the appearance of that definitive little 's' on the end of her name might have been unintentional, since the mediaeval scribes simply couldn't conceive of a female apostle in the male-dominated Church of the time. On the other hand, they may have added it deliberately, because they wanted the church to stay that way. Either way, mediaeval scribes were notoriously inaccurate.

Professor Richard Bauckham of St Andrew's University thinks it possible Junia may have been Joanna, the well-to-do wife of Herod's influential steward, Chuza, who is described in Luke's Gospel as providing for Jesus out of her income, and was later one of the first at the tomb.[13] The defection of such a powerful courtier to the new religious movement must have sent shock waves through the society in which she lived, which may be why she took on a Latin version of her Hebrew name, to give her greater clout in spreading the Word in the Romanised culture of her home town, Tiberias.[14]

It is a woman, Phoebe, who is entrusted to take Paul's precious letter to the church in Rome – the letter which more than any other sets out his understanding of God's cosmic faithfulness in keeping his covenant with Abraham, so that Jew and Gentile together would inherit God's promise.

He refers to her as a *diakonos,* the same word used for a male deacon, and a 'helper to many' (Rom. 1:1–2). 'Helper' here is a translation of *proistatis* from the verb *proistemi,* 'to preside over or care for'. In other words, she was a supervisor, protector, benefactor and patron, someone who stands by their protégé when they get into a scrape, as Paul had. She was obviously wealthy, and Paul would therefore have had a relatively subordinate social position. She had a prominent role in the church at Cenchreae in Corinth. She may even have hosted it and led it in her home.

As well as acting as postwoman for Paul's letter, Phoebe appears to have been key to his grand scheme for an eventual mission in Spain, seen by the Romans as 'the ends of the earth' – certainly not the safest, or most civilised, of places. What Paul asks of the Romans indicates the esteem in which he holds this woman. 'I ask you to receive her in the Lord in a way worthy of his people and to give her any help she may need from you' (Rom. 16:2).

Priscilla and her husband, Aquila, joint leaders of a church in their home in Corinth, leave it behind to accompany Paul on his missionary journeys. Priscilla is no back up for her man, at his side though slightly behind him, making sure he goes out to preach in clean underwear and matching socks. Nothing suggests that when they share a pulpit, he is the meat and two vegetables while she is the dessert. In fact, she, it seems, takes the lead in correcting the doctrine of the formidable Apollos, who would become one of Paul's regular sidekicks. She manifestly has an outstanding and authoritative ministry in her own right. Contrary to even contemporary tradition, when Paul mentions the couple, he often puts Priscilla's name first. It is believed that their powerful ministry comes to an end in AD 98, when they are both beheaded.

One thing is sure – Jewish or Roman, the first Christian women were not confined to domestic roles. Lydia was a successful businesswoman of Philippi who owned a large house and had her own slaves (Acts 16:14). Damaris, converted in Athens when she heard Paul preach at the Areopagus, was an educated woman in a public role, possibly as a philosopher (Acts 17:34).

In fact, many well-heeled Roman matrons, such as Chloe in Corinth and Nympha in Colossae, used their wealth and standing in society to preach the gospel and lead groups or churches in their own homes, enabling Christianity to gain a foothold in the well-heeled, educated strata of Roman society.

My friends in the French Free Evangelical Church dispute that women can be pastors or elders because of the verse in I Timothy 3 that says that an elder or overseer must be the 'husband of only one wife', or 'faithful to his wife', as the newer versions translate it. But that would mean that no single, widowed or divorced man could be a leader. However, the Greek words mean, literally, 'a one-woman man', so single men are not disqualified, but then, neither are women. In a culture where the men are frequently tempted toward unfaithfulness, Paul is simply saying a married elder must be loyal to his woman and to her alone. The character requirements for the job – warm-heartedness, patience, kindness, gentleness, graciousness, humility and self-control, attributes not always valued in the leaders of today – are used of widows in 1 Timothy 5.

In the letter to Titus (2:3–5) there is a very similar reference to the qualities needed for church leadership, but this time not only for presbytes, the masculine word for elders, but also for *presbytis*, the female equivalent. Some assume this refers to the wives of elders, but why would it, since the man might be single or widowed? The word *presbytis* was actually used in early Christian literature for female elders.

At the crucifixion women were able to come and go without fear of the authorities, which is why they, rather than the men, were allowed to remain throughout. They were not seen as a threat. But when persecution arose against the early church, women were targeted equally alongside the men. In the Acts of the Apostles, Saul of Tarsus was going to Damascus to haul men and women off to prison (Acts 9:2). Why were the women dangerous now? Only if they had become influential figures and leaders.

And the irrefutable argument against the exclusivity of male leadership of the Church is that at the Council of Laodicea in the fourth century, women were banned from these roles. The hierarchical male culture of the Church forbade it. It stands to reason that up to that moment they must have been pastors and elders – though already in a limited capacity.

Martyrs, missionaries and Montanists

By the middle of the second century the persecution of Christians had begun in earnest. But though women suffered alongside the men – hung up by their hair and drowned, raped and ravaged, burned, beheaded, beaten, gored to death for sport by wild beasts – though they were forced to watch their children being killed for their refusal to sacrifice to the Roman gods, they were denied any leadership of the faith that had cost their sisters' lives.

For the first hundred years they had been teachers, administrators, evangelists and prophets, but then the creeping tide of institutionalism pushed them from the centre to the periphery of church life, as the numerous house churches, spread across the great cities, were subjected to centralised control. The new structures were based on the secular, hierarchical model of Roman civic government – in other words, a male, clerical ruling class and a subservient people of God. No communion service could take place unless a male bishop was present to officiate. Anyone who dared to challenge the system was denied access to fellowship. As women's power drained away, the life was slowly stifled out of the Church.

Then, in the latter half of the second century, revival broke out for the first time. Led by a man called Montanus and two women, Maximilla and Prisca, it spread like wildfire through the churches of Asia Minor. Deadening institutionalism lifted as believers in the pews began to participate in services once again. Women preached and prophesied with powerful results, and were restored to key leadership roles.

The official Church hierarchy, terrified that they appeared to be losing control, denounced Montanus as a pagan heretic, though his style was very similar to the ministry in the Vineyard Churches today. However, the major criticism was allowing women such prominence. Maximilla and Prisca were accused of leaving their husbands, of prophesying for financial gain and of being possessed by demons. Attempts were made to exorcise them. Two centuries later, the ministry of women was completely banned, and the Western Church has yet to fully recover.

The masters of misogyny

Man is active, full of movement, creative in politics, business and culture. The male shapes and moulds society and the world. Woman, on the other hand, is passive. She stays at home, as is her nature. She is matter waiting to be formed by the active male principle. Of course, the active elements are always higher on any scale and more divine. Man consequently plays a major part in reproduction; the woman is merely the passive incubator of his seed.[15]

It is evident that Aristotle, who wrote these astonishing words, had never been pregnant! Yet though he lived more than three hundred years before Jesus Christ, though he had no knowledge of the Hebrew Scriptures, his views on women did more to shape the thinking of Church culture than anything Jesus did or said, because of their influence on its founding fathers.

The early church fathers, who lived between the third and fifth centuries, became the authority on Christian belief, but appear to have worn mental, emotional and spiritual blinkers when it came to the place of women. Hostile to Hebraic thinking because the Jews had killed their Christ, steeped in the classical, Greco-Roman mind-set, and beset by struggles to come to terms with their own carefully controlled sexuality, their writings are a sorry catalogue of anti-female rhetoric. Yet these views seeped their way into the Church's conscious and subconscious thinking and influenced biblical exegesis for many centuries to come.

Tertullian (AD 160–240), the Father of Latin theology, who referred to woman as 'the devil's gateway' a siren who lured the poor, unsuspecting male into sin – was the first to use 'let the women keep silence' from the letter to the Corinthians (1 Cor. 14:34) as a justification to turn churchgoing women into dummies. They were not to be allowed to pray, teach or even sing. The outbreak of Montanism modified his views somewhat, but the established Church chose to ignore what it regarded as his later aberration and clung instead to his pre-charismatic misogyny.

Clement of Alexandria (150–220 BC) insisted that women should wear an early Christian version of the burqa, lest they be a source of temptation to men.

Origen (185–254 BC) claimed that God couldn't even lower himself to look at women. For the sake of reproduction they were a necessary evil. Origen castrated himself.

Saint Cyril, Patriarch of Alexandria (died 444 BC), was so adamant that women were inferior and were not to teach men in any capacity, that when a local woman, Hypatia, dared to contradict him and went on teaching astronomy, maths and philosophy to her male students, he incited his monks to murder her and burn her flesh as they hacked it off the bone.

Saint Augustine (354–430 BC), hailed as greatest of all the church fathers, started out as a real Jack the Lad, freely indulging the pleasures of the flesh. After his conversion and entry into the monastic life, the memory of it haunted him and filled him with shame, while titillating his imagination at the same time. He couldn't understand why he wasn't more holy, and projected the blame for his sexual temptations on to the objects of his fantasies. His self-disgust is disguised by a thin veneer of hatred for woman: 'Only man is fully created in the image of God. The female state is a deformity.' Augustine referred to Eve, and every woman who followed her, as the great deceiver and seducer. Even sex within marriage was a necessary evil, to be avoided if possible by any male who wanted to remain pure.

Saint Jerome (340–420 BC) referred to women as 'miserable, sin-ridden wenches', and popularised the idea of Mary's perpetual virginity, despite the New Testament references to Jesus' (half) brothers and sisters. John Chrysostom (347–407 BC), the greatest preacher of the Greek Church, said, 'God maintained the order of each sex by dividing the business of human life into two parts and assigned the necessary and more beneficial aspects to the man, and the less important, inferior matters to the woman.'[16] Some might be tempted to say that not a lot changed in the Church in the sixteen centuries that followed Chrysostom's preaching.

The early centuries of the Church were not entirely bleak for Christian women. It would take more than the jaundiced pronouncements of its founding fathers, even if they were the spiritual intelligentsia, to curb women's spirits and force them into subservience. Reluctantly, the Church had to recognise that, whatever the theory of the leaders, in practice women's capacity for holy living and godly service was as great as any man's. A truly spiritual woman was encouraged to pursue the monastic life, presumably because if she took a vow of celibacy, she was no longer 'available' and a source of temptation. Though evidence suggests this wasn't always the case, and as religious communities were mixed-gender, women often became fair game for male predators. Still, an exceptional woman was given the chance to exercise her leadership gifts – particularly in Celtic Britain.

Celtic warrior women

While the women of the Roman Empire belonged to their husbands, along with any property they brought into the marriage, the lives of Celtic women followed a more Hebraic model. They were highly respected matriarchal figures with a great deal of freedom in their close-knit communities. Like Boudicca in AD 60, a woman could become a tribal chief, or even a military commander leading her people into battle. The only drawback was that in an era when Britain was divided into many hostile, warring kingdoms, tribal lords seemed to have an unfortunate habit of marrying off virginal daughters, nieces and wards to suit their own expansionist urges.

For a Christian young woman, entering a religious community was one way of escaping the clutches of some powerful heathen brute. Not much of a choice, really, but if she became an abbess, she could do whatever she wanted with her land, exercise considerable organisational and managerial skills, and maintain a measure of independence. She had authority over men, taught them the Scriptures and trained them for ministry. According to the edicts from the traditionalist Church in Rome, the only things she was not allowed to do were become a bishop or officiate at a communion service. Nonetheless, Brigid of Ireland managed to get herself consecrated bishop rather than abbess. No one knew for sure whether it was because the officiating Bishop of Kildare was so overwhelmed by the evident power of the Holy Spirit upon her, or because he fell asleep during the service and didn't notice she was a woman.

The innate equality of men and women in Celtic society meant that leading churchmen such as Saint Patrick of Ireland were not threatened by a powerful or clever member of the opposite sex. Since a religious community would require daily communion, every abbess appropriated her own bishop, though there was never any question about who had the ultimate authority over the order. It generated many close, extremely fruitful partnerships – like Brigid and Conleth, who demonstrated the possibility of single men and women working hand in glove without sex getting in the way.

The most outstanding female Celtic Church leader after Saint Brigid was Hilda of Whitby (AD 614–80). On a windswept peninsula high over the North Sea, at Streanaeshalch, now Whitby, Hilda presided over one of the most exceptional communities of all time. Every member was committed to a disciplined life of study and prayer, and to working in whatever way they could to bring justice, mercy and peace to the world outside. Drawn by its reputation, like moths to the light, a motley group came to Whitby from miles around and every walk of life, for spiritual direction, counselling, support and prayer, to learn the creative arts such as poetry, music, writing and graphics, or to study the Scriptures. Whoever they were, clerical or lay, noble or poor, they were shown the same attention and care. Caedmon, the first popular British poet, moved in permanently. Five of Hilda's students became bishops, including John of Beverley, and Wilfred, who would cause her the most painful searching of heart.

While the Whitby community flourished, the Church in Britain was becoming ever more deeply divided between the free-spirited Celtic form of worship and the more formal Roman style. On a visit to Rome, Wilfred was completely seduced by the power, pomp, riches and ceremony of the church hierarchy there, and was sent back to Britain with a commission to bring the Celtic Church to heel. The growing tensions came to a head in AD 664 at a national consultation on the future of the Church, held at Whitby, with Hilda in the chair.

It is hard to imagine what she felt. The famous Synod must have been extremely difficult for her. She revered and respected the great Cuthbert, defender of the Celtic Church, with its commitment to equality, community and helping the poor. That was where her own inclination lay. But Wilfred had been a bright and brilliant student and she was extremely fond of him. She must have used all her conciliatory powers to preserve the unity and integrity of the Church she loved. But in the end, conflict was contrary to Cuthbert's nature and she watched him capitulate to Wilfred without a fight.

It must have broken Hilda's heart to witness the defeat of a way of life that was her very raison d'être, and by a past student she thought she knew and trusted, but had manifestly gone astray. She may well have wondered how different things might have been had she abandoned her impartiality and offered Cuthbert more support. But in the end, the Roman Church was always powerful and wealthy enough to impose its dominance of the smaller, poorer Celtic Church. Hilda and Cuthbert would only have postponed that eventuality for a while longer, though they might have preserved some of the culture they loved, had she encouraged Cuthbert to stand firm. She must have known that her attempt to compromise was bought at far too high a price, for, as far as female leadership was concerned, she had effectively 'pulled up the ladder' behind her.

Churchwomen mediaeval and modern

In the centuries that followed, the attitude of most church leaders to women could be summarised in the words of the mediaeval monk and theologian Thomas Aquinas (1225–74). Woman, he wrote, was 'defective and misbegotten . . . biologically, spiritually and intellectually inferior'. As a concession he added, 'A necessary object, a woman, needed to preserve the species and provide food and drink.' This is about as far from God's intention at creation as it is possible to get – more Taliban than true Christianity.

But, true to form, there arose from time to time a woman to prove him wrong – like Julian of Norwich, born around 1342, a great mystic, writer and counsellor, whose spiritual insights attracted visitors from miles around. A recluse, Mother Julian lived a life of prayer and self-denial in her hermit's cell, and was given no leadership of the church to which she was attached. Even so, she must have expected criticism, for she wrote in her *Revelations of Divine Love*, 'Because I am a woman, ought I therefore to believe that I should not tell you of the goodness of God, although I saw that it is His will that it be known?'[17]

For Mother Julian, if God is total and complete he must be male and female, mother as well as father. Her distinctively obstetric language to describe the process of rebirth is still fairly shocking today. Jesus carries us within himself in love, and as pregnancy leads to childbirth, so the pains of his death are really labour pains that bear us 'to joy and eternal life'. And then, just as a mother puts her child tenderly to her breast, 'our beloved Mother, Jesus, feeds us with himself', by his body and his blood. Not surprisingly, her writings were seen as too esoteric and fanciful for the early Protestants and fell from favour at the Reformation. Perhaps the imagery was just a little too hard to stomach.

The great Spanish mystic, Teresa of Ávila (1515–82), was the first woman to be declared a doctor of the Church – but not until 1970. She founded and reformed Carmelite convents all over Spain, and gently, but firmly, challenged the established male authority of her time in its attitude to women. If the Spanish king could exalt and honour whoever he chose, without being constrained by any lower official, so, she claimed, the King of Kings could bypass the hierarchical structures of the Church and give special gifts to women, if he so chose. Even so, she envied men their freedom to come and go and 'spread the news abroad about who this great God of hosts is'.

In the nineteenth century, women began to reappropriate that freedom in the name of social justice, as the revivalist power of the holiness movement gave them the courage to weather opposition and preach in public once more. The doors to ministry overseas swung wide open and they proved on other continents what they might have been capable of doing at home, had they been given the chance.

In foreign lands, where out of sight was out of mind as far as the Western Church hierarchy was concerned, they laid the foundations of churches that thrive today in Africa, China and Asia. They challenged, with surprising success, the cultural attitudes that denied women and children their basic rights. They built hospitals and clinics, opened schools and developed cottage industries. And as they took the message of Jesus' love for women to countries where women knew only oppression and abuse, as they proclaimed the freedom of the gospel, they received a new freedom for themselves in leading, preaching and establishing small communities.

Amy Carmichael, restoring Hilda's vision – in India

At the turn of the nineteenth century, Amy Carmichael (1867–1951), a remarkable combination of Irish Protestant and mystic, was a thorn in the side of some Western missionaries in India with her outspoken refusal to submit to either imperialist tradition or the rigid caste system. Wearing a sari, she lived simply for many years with a band of local women, trying to rescue little girls sold as cult prostitutes to the Hindu temples. As it became evident that the girls needed shelter and education, she founded a community of both men and women at Dohnavur. Amma, or 'Mother', as Amy was known, watched over a growing 'family', not unlike Hilda of Whitby's community – a kind of model village, with schools, workshops, weaving sheds, sewing-rooms, hospital, chapel, farm and fruit and vegetable gardens. Amy's vision was to demonstrate God's love by serving the local area and beyond. Like Whitby, Dohnavur became an oasis, not just for the rescued girls, but also for many travellers seeking spiritual truth, comfort and hope.

It is a tribute to the way she implemented that vision that Dohnavur still exists. Today, Indian nationals lead projects designed primarily to support the poor, in child development, education, healthcare, community development and the conservation of nature. But it nearly wasn't so. Amy's decision to include men in her community caused major disruption and threatened its very survival. One particular Englishman, Stephen Neill, went out to India as a young man, ostensibly to see her work and support her, but later, as a bishop, decried her reputation and challenged her authority – much as Bishop Wilfred had done to his spiritual director, Hilda of Whitby. Stephen and a few of his young male, largely public school compatriots couldn't cope with what they saw as her distinctively female, and therefore inadequate, style of leadership. Her collaborative, rather than authoritarian, approach to her team made them uncomfortable.

Yet it was the emphasis Amy placed on the quality of communal relationships that made Dohnavur unique. In her eyes, it was incompatible with Christ's sacrificial love that the older missionaries in India were forever arguing, criticising and then ignoring one another. Any alternative required a firm discipline. Every member of the community was required to sign up to a life of self-denial, mercy and forgiveness that would always put the other first. Her demanding rules for life, which she lived to her last, bedridden years, flew in the face of every contemporary notion of achievement and success. Amy was no ascetic. Children loved her. They recognised the Irish mischief in her eyes. But within the team there would be no excuses for self-centeredness or aggrandisement. And, unlike Hilda of Whitby, she succeeded in preserving the way of life that underpinned all she believed.

Amy never went back to Ireland, but in the twentieth century, female missionaries who did return home, albeit temporarily, 'on furlough' – to raise financial support – often presented a problem for the Church. These women, who were great church founders and leaders abroad, were often denied access to the pulpit. It was perfectly acceptable for natives, both male and female, to be the beneficiaries of their ministry, but not so-called 'civilised' congregations. To get around these difficulties, missionary meetings were often held in an unconsecrated building, preaching was called 'speaking', and a sermon referred to as 'an address'.

As Lavinia Byrne put it,[18] having challenged a world which had been established by men for the convenience and servicing of men, missionary women suddenly discovered that the Church was found as wanting as Islam, Hinduism and the African religions. It failed to offer them the freedoms of the Christianity they were preaching abroad. They suddenly came face to face with the fact that, at home, their very success was a threat to the establishment. And this was an irony because they had seen first-hand that raising the status of women did not diminish men; rather, it raised men's status too.

Despite the fact that she finally managed to persuade the Indian government to ban the abuse of children in their temples, Bishop Stephen Neill, in his 'definitive history' of missions written in the 1960s,[19] barely mentions the extraordinary achievements of Amy Carmichael, or the many other remarkable women who substantially improved the quality of life of the people they loved and served. Nor was there any recognition of the wives of the great pioneers, who either laboured at their husband's side or let them go and lived on alone, raising the children at home, and laying down their lives – literally or metaphorically – for the gospel. These women simply didn't count. But then, after almost nineteen centuries of being overlooked, attitudes to pioneering women were not going to change overnight.

'It is extraordinary,' writes Hyam Maccoby, scholar on first-century Judaism, 'that it has so often been believed that in Pharisee law women had no rights, and that it was only the advent of Christianity that raised women to the status of legal personages. The historical fact is that the abolition of Pharisee law by the church led to the loss of much humane legislation and to a tragic lowering of the status of women.'[20]

How was that possible? Many would lay the blame squarely at the feet of the Apostle Paul – but perhaps history has done him a great injustice.

Chapter 5
The Silent Woman?

I brought up my children to believe there was nothing a woman couldn't do. Seeing my ineptitude at handling anything vaguely mechanical, Joel had one or two doubts about that in his boyhood, happily dispelled when he realised that his female classmates were not tyrannised by gadgetry and machinery the way his mother was. The new generation, like his sister, could change a plug, hang cupboards and shelves, and change a flat tyre without the ignominy of having to flag down a male passer-by. In fact, at university she was known as 'DIY Barbie'.

Joel's egalitarian convictions remained unchallenged until he arrived at Oxford University. In his first term he was helping arrange a special event for Jewish students on behalf of the Christian Union. There were problems in finding a suitable speaker.

'I suppose if we were really stuck, my mum could do it.'

The suggestion was greeted with an uncomfortable silence.

'Well, I know she's my mum, but that's not a problem, is it?'

'The fact that she's your mum isn't a problem,' one of the students explained. 'The fact that she's a woman is.'

Joel refrained from a sarcastic comment to the effect that he had noticed his mother was a woman. In many ways he was too staggered to respond at all. To cancel such an opportunity because of rigid adherence to dogma – dubious dogma at that – was beyond the realms of both his experience and his comprehension.

He soon discovered that no woman was allowed to become the President of the Christian Union or to speak at their main evening meetings. Notions of equality which, like most of his generation, he had taken for granted, were being challenged in this microcosm of the Church, not by a brigade of traditional old boys, but by the so-called cream of society's bright-eyed, bushy-tailed intelligentsia. And all because of two verses in the Bible – one in the book of Corinthians that said women should keep silent, and one in the book of Timothy that said they shouldn't teach.

Joel tried to encourage his fellow students to see that in the not-too-distant future many would have female bosses with the authority to hire and fire them, so why impose a set of culturally alien rules upon themselves that might cause them a struggle later. But in vain. The gaping chasm between the secular and sacred worlds in which they moved was no paradox. It simply didn't exist. They clung to their one interpretation of the verses, blissfully unaware that by inference, their message to Western society was that the Bible was out-of-date and irrelevant. Since that simply isn't the case, it's time to tackle some of those tricky texts head on here.

Wrestling with the text

Anyone studying a passage of Scripture has to ask themselves four basic questions. What did it mean in its original context? What do the words actually mean? How does it fit with other texts on the same or similar issues? What is its meaning for today? All traditions accept that this is a necessary process in biblical exegesis.

Among Christians there seems to be a deep-seated fear that to look at a passage in its cultural context must somehow reduce its relevance, and contradict Paul's teaching that 'All Scripture is God-breathed and is useful for teaching, rebuking, correcting and training in righteousness' (2 Tim. 3:16). So, unlike the Jewish people, they often have a remedial knowledge of their history and no sense of where they have come from or how they got here. There seems an assumption that the Church simply landed from heaven in its present form one day, like a flying saucer from Mars.

But far from reducing Paul's teaching, understanding the back-drop to his letters makes it more accessible and expands the potential breadth of its application. Once upon a time, when I arrived at Paul's letters in my daily readings, I would feel the muscles in my stomach knot. How could such a great and godly man be so dismissive of half the human race? Gradually, I developed a feeling for the world in which he lived and now understand why he said what he did, and I can face him with equanimity and excitement, and positively dispute any suggestion that he was a misogynist. It is often our ignorance that has earned him such a bad press.

Delving into the original meaning of the words used in the text, matching them with the same or similar words used elsewhere and analysing the choice of language can be a fun piece of detective work. Is the translation accurate? Does the grammatical construction of the sentence have any significance? The use of different words in different translations for the original Hebrew or Greek can even produce conflicting interpretations of the text.

Being Jewish does not make me an expert in ancient Hebrew. Despite years of instruction – two hours of classes every Sunday morning and one hour after school three days a week – my Hebrew is fairly rudimentary. I was taught to read Hebrew fluently so that I wouldn't look silly in the synagogue on Sabbath or festivals, but translation was a painful process that left me cold. We simply learned the Torah by rote, and it was so painfully slow that by the time my education was deemed complete, the Children of Israel still hadn't managed to get out of the desert. But it gave me a basic knowledge of how words were put together, the difference made to the root by adding suffixes and prefixes, and those mysterious hieroglyphics that are the vowels.

If the Bible is inspired, which of the many translations over the past 2,000 years is the most inspired, and how might the variations affect our perceptions? We have already seen how two contrasting translations of the word *tsachaq* can completely alter our opinion of Sarah and our interpretation of her actions. What about the subtleties surrounding Priscilla in the story in Acts 18 where she and her husband put Apollos straight? In the original Greek Priscilla is named before her husband, which suggests that, on this occasion at least, she took the lead in the partnership (verse 26). In the English translation authorised by King James I in 1611, however, the order is reversed and Aquila is mentioned first, a sign that the translators still felt it necessary to show traditional deference to the male.

Or take another example. In the original Greek, Paul's closest buddies, Timothy, Epaphras, Tychicus, Apollos and Phoebe are all referred to in various letters as *diakonos*, translated as 'minister' in the King James' version of the Bible – with one exception. The only woman *diakonos*, Phoebe, is called a 'servant'.[1]

Is it pure coincidence that, despite commissioning an English Bible, King James I was one of the most misogynist monarchs ever to mount the British throne? He refused to allow the improvement of education for women on the grounds that 'to make women learned and foxes tame has the same effect: to make them more cunning'.[2] He believed women were all like Eve – highly susceptible to demonic influence. Witchcraft was punishable by hanging. Guilt could be established on hearsay without recourse to the normal system of justice. Anyone who disliked or resented a female neighbour, or found her just a little bit strange, could report her to the authorities, and they did. It's likely that the rather bigoted culture of the time could well have coloured translations of the first Bible in the English language.[3]

Comparing texts on any one issue, taking the whole range together, gives an overall perspective which extracting lone verses out of context can never do. In fact, lone verses can lead us up blind alleys. For example, 'The blessing of the Lord makes us rich and he adds no sorrow with it' (Prov. 10:22, paraphrased), has been used to justify health and wealth as a sign of God's blessing, even if the reality of life in developing countries fails to support that interpretation. Jesus, in fact, extolled and lived a life of poverty, but that's a harder path to follow.

The power on the platform

Whether we justify our position from the texts or, like the Catholic wing of the Church, from history, the status of women is such an emotive issue that it almost always reaches us in a pre-packaged state. We come to it with a host of preconceived ideas, wearing sunglasses tinted by our background, culture, personal preferences and negative or positive experiences of women in authority – including mothers and teachers – that filter out whatever we find uncomfortable.

Male fear of losing this one last, safe bastion of supremacy can be very real, and that's understandable, but it isn't only men who are opposed to women preachers or leaders. Women can be equally vehement in their objections, which is more surprising. But in her study of the differing communication styles between men and women, Professor of Linguistics at Georgetown University, Deborah Tannen, explains that 'men and women who do not conform to the expectations for their own gender may not be liked', particularly by members of their own gender.[4] Women can fear that when some of our species break rank and behave in a way that is deemed unfeminine, we will all forfeit male approval, and our *teshuqah,* that instinctive need for an affirming male, wants to prevent that happening at any cost.

Whatever the arguments for and against female leadership in the Church, they are often far less rational and far more emotional than they may first appear. There was a student in our church called Chris who came from a background where the very idea of a woman speaking from the pew let alone the pulpit was anathema. He struggled with the way women were allowed to preach in our church, especially Ruth, our young people's worker. His real difficulty was that he admired and respected her, and was forced to admit that there were few people from whom he had learned more about what it meant to be a disciple.

'So what's the difference between my sitting next to you here in a pew, sharing something I think I've learned from the Bible, and my sharing it with the entire congregation from the front?' Ruth asked one Sunday night, exasperated by the inconsistency of his arguments and in fighting mood.

'That's different!' he insisted.

'Only geography. You have no objections to my teaching strapping great teenage lads in the Sunday School.'

My husband Peter watched the interaction with some trepidation, and not a little admiration for Ruth's assertive powers.

'Look,' she said to Chris, when she saw he was refusing to give an inch, 'why don't you use your imagination and try to think your way into how God feels when he sees me up there. What does he say? "How dare she! Doesn't she know she's only a woman?"

'No,' Chris admitted reluctantly, 'I suppose he thinks it's great.'

Instinctively, Ruth felt the issue was about power, the perception of the person who stood six inches up on the raised platform.

'Then I tell you what,' she said, taking the kind of risk that Peter admitted later he would never have taken himself, 'you go away this week and think about it, and if you really believe that it's a sin for me to preach, it is your Christian duty to tell me so and I will resign my job.'

'You can't do that,' Chris stammered, shrinking a little from the petite, almost delicate-looking woman who had held his gaze throughout. 'You're such an amazing person.'

'Yes, and I've felt called to teach the Bible since I was a child.'

Chris looked completely bewildered. It had never occurred to him that a woman might have such a sense of calling.

'So if I've been wrong all these years, it's your responsibility to tell me, and I will resign.'

What Chris and many others would like are black and white answers, which are so much easier than facing up to the apparent contradictions in the text, and between the text and reality. Yet we cannot escape them. Our knowledge of remarkable female church leaders forces us to confront the issue head on. Some would say, of course, that we cannot base Church doctrine on experience. But the Church wasn't born with a guide to early development. Its doctrine evolved by reflecting on experience and known theological principles. Gentiles were only accepted into membership because they had been filled with the Holy Spirit as the Jewish Christians were. Such had been his mindset against that possibility that the Apostle Peter had needed a special revelation to convince him that non-Jews could be kosher.

So would the Apostle Paul really have disapproved of female preachers and teachers? What would he have made of Corrie Ten Boom, the elderly Dutch woman imprisoned in Ravensbruck concentration camp for rescuing Jews, who, after her release, travelled the world with the message, 'There is no pit so deep, that God's love is not deeper still', words spoken by her sister Betsie, just before she died in the camp. Or Kathryn Kuhlman with her dramatic gift of healing, who drew thousands to her evangelistic crusades in the

1950s and 1960s? Or Jackie Pullinger, the Englishwoman who has given her life to working among the triads and drug gangs of Hong Kong and whose unique success earned her the financial backing of the Hong Kong government? It hardly seems likely.

How did Paul really relate to women?

> The letters of Paul say three things: love God, love your neighbour, and you women caused all the trouble in the world, so just sit still and keep quiet.
>
> The Reduced Shakespeare Company in *The Reduced Bible*

The notion of the equality of men and women may no longer be disputed in Western society, but the fact that the secular world believes the Bible has a down on women is. When the Reduced Shakespeare Company toured the country with its 90-minute version of the Word of God, its three-point summary of Paul's letters raised many a knowing laugh. Yet throughout his descriptions of his adventures and escapades, there is never any suggestion that the Apostle had an aversion to females or their ministry, or that he deliberately steered clear of their company. On the contrary, he appears to have positively welcomed their partnership in his work, and even targeted them in his evangelistic strategy.

Luke, the doctor, an eyewitness to the events of Pentecost and, of all the New Testament writers, most sensitive to the key role women had to play, describes how he and Paul went down to the river on the Sabbath to find a place of prayer, and sat among the women who had gathered there (Acts 16:13), confirming that Jewish women already had a part to play in religious life. If Paul were opposed to women's freedom, it seems more likely he would have criticised them, rather than seeking to enhance what they were already enjoying. In fact, Lydia, who is converted there and then, persuades Paul to use her home as his base whenever he is in Philippi.

Not only does Paul refer to women as full colleagues, patrons and friends, but also, when he describes the sacrifice his missionary travels entail, says rather wistfully, 'Don't we have the right to take a believing wife along with us, as do the other apostles and the Lord's brothers and Cephas?' (1 Cor. 9:5). There were obviously moments when he would have loved to have one special woman in his life. This is no woman-hater. Since he was a Pharisee, and Pharisees always married, he could well have been a widower.

Paul's most all-encompassing statement of egalitarianism is in his letter to the Galatians, a predominantly Jewish church, where he says that once a person belongs to Jesus Christ there is no Jew nor Greek, slave nor free, male nor female (Gal. 3:28). In the gospel there is no room for superiority, posturing or domination. Admittedly, the context is salvation, but Paul is saying that all the old man-made distinctions created by race, status and gender have been broken down by the cross and resurrection. Hierarchy has been dismantled; exclusion is not an option. A new order has come into being, and the proof of it is Pentecost. The Holy Spirit was not and is not discriminatory. So no need for Jewish men to thank God they're not a woman.

When Paul talks about gifts and ministries of the Holy Spirit (1 Cor. 12) he does not say evangelism is for the men, tea-making is for the women; teaching is for men, typing is for the women; prophecy is for the men, praying at home is for the women; leading is for the men, sitting in silent support is for the women. 'All the gifts are produced by one and the same Spirit. He gives them to each person, just as he decides' (1 Cor. 12:11). So why would he then urge women to keep silence in services? It doesn't appear to make sense.

Let the women keep silent

> Women should remain silent in the churches. They are not allowed to speak, but must be in submission, as the law says. If they want to enquire about something, they should ask their own husbands at home; for it is disgraceful for a woman to speak in the church.
>
> (1 Cor. 14:34–5)

Taken at face value, these verses appear to condemn women to sit through every act of worship like fibreglass mannequinn, unable to read a lesson or join in the singing, let alone pray or preach. I did hear recently of a church where women were not allowed to ask a question or make a comment in a Bible study, but had to write it down and hand it to the nearest male. That really is extreme, for only slightly earlier in the same letter, speaking about propriety in worship, Paul says that any woman who prays or prophesies in public must cover her head (1 Cor. 11:5). There will be more on head covering, but for the moment it appears we are left with a complete contradiction. If a prophetic ministry was an essential vehicle for encouraging and empowering congregations, a means of sharing a vision for God's wider plans and intentions, if it was a call to integrity, authenticity and radical lifestyle, it must have involved a measure of preaching, and required a certain amount of authority. So in what situation should a woman be silent and submissive? Why might her speaking be a disgrace?

I have five possible interpretations of these two verses, but there are probably many more.

(1) The respectful worshipper theory

Predominantly Greek and Gentile, the Christians in Corinth were a remarkable collection of trophies. 'Do not be deceived,' Paul reminds them, 'neither the sexually immoral nor idolater, nor adulterers nor men who have sex with men nor thieves nor the greedy nor drunkards . . . will inherit the kingdom of God. And that is what some of you were' (1 Cor. 6:9). There was certainly a history of 'sexual irregularities', as Dr Stephen Travis, formerly Vice-Principal of St John's Theological College in Nottingham, so delicately put it, when he explained the background to me.

Orgies and gorge-ies had once been the order of the day, and the Corinthians were not finding it easy to change the habits of a lifetime. 'The Lord's Supper', which included a full meal, had descended into an undignified, disorderly bun fight. Participants tucked in on a first come, first served basis. Some, predominantly the poor who couldn't afford to bring food, were left without any, while others stuffed their faces or were rolling drunk.

There was also disruptive behaviour during worship – women leaving their hair uncovered like prostitutes, people speaking out in tongues without waiting for an interpretation, others competing to get their prophecy heard.

Paul tells them in no uncertain terms that 'God is not a God of disorder but of peace' (1 Cor. 14:33). He is at pains that outsiders shouldn't be tempted to think that Christianity is just another pagan cult with the followers in a permanent state of inebriation, sexual licence or spiritual ecstasy. Instead, it must be obvious from the way they live that they care for each other.

This is the context for the greatest treatise on love ever written. 1 Corinthians 13, so often read at weddings, is actually about 'agape' – an extraordinary quality that should be the hallmark of any Christian community. Without it, the spiritual gifts are little more than a cacophony of discordant sounds. Love isn't rude, pushy or self-seeking. It puts the other person first. In other words, whether applied to a male or female, it actively chooses to be submissive.

According to Dwight Pryor of the Center for Judaic-Christian Studies in Dayton, Ohio, the ex-prostitutes in the congregation had a particular little call they used to attract the men, which would have no doubt added to the general din and disturbance of meetings. The Greek word translated as 'silent' is *sigeo*. It can mean to be quiet when someone else is speaking, to behave or to pay attention. It is possible that these women are being told to stop disrupting the services and to show submission, or courtesy – not just to the prophet or preacher, but also to God himself.

Putting these verses into their historical context might give them increased contemporary relevance. In almost all of our churches, when Peter gave the invitation to receive the bread and wine at Communion and members began to move out of their seats, it appeared to be some kind of signal for a general hullabaloo. No quiet reflection – the bladder and the urge for chatter took over. Whenever he challenged the congregation about it, they blamed the arrival of the children from their groups. But actually, it was the adults, not the children, who made the most din. And much as it sticks in my throat to admit it, the women were the most susceptible.

(2) The respectful partner theory

A second possible interpretation revolves around the Greek word *gyne* which can mean 'woman' or 'wife' – a source of some confusion in many texts. Paul has just finished speaking about prophecy, concluding, 'Those who prophesy can take it in turns. Others should then decide if what they are saying is true.' If 'women' in fact means 'wives' in this context, then Paul could be telling the wives of any men who have just prophesied that they should refrain from evaluating, criticising or challenging their husbands in public. They can wait until they get home instead. After all, it is a common courtesy, and especially in a marriage.

Although Paul was radical for his time, if social structures were not in conflict with Christian teaching, he didn't set out to challenge them. The Greco-Roman household, classically defined by the philosopher Aristotle, was the basic unit of the state. Civic order required a Roman man to have absolute power in his home. Well-to-do Roman matrons often remained out of sight at the rear of the house and were not encouraged to meet with guests unless they were specifically invited to do so. They were certainly not 'gadabouts' as some of the new Christian women were accused of being.

The non-Jewish women in the church at Corinth appear to have been excited by the new freedoms Christianity bestowed, particularly full participation in worship, and were throwing off many traditional restraints and conventions, such as covering their heads. Paul seems to be anxious that a husband's authority isn't undermined simply for the sake of it, throwing home life into disarray and causing disorder in the church community.

I have seen many women reduce their husbands to the size of a flea. The male ego may well be rather fragile, but that does not give women a licence to flatten it with a few well-chosen words. It doesn't encourage respect for either of them.

I didn't agree with every decision my husband made in his capacity as a church minister. In fact, I often gave him a hard time when he got home. But it would never have been appropriate for me to do so in public. That would have been humiliating, as well as embarrassing – for all concerned. Peter and I still remember the excruciating, hot-under-the-collar feeling of witnessing a minister's wife challenge her husband's decision at a full church meeting. It silenced any debate, and I decided that even if I drew blood, I would bite my lip rather than put him in that position. Effectively, then, I was the only church member gagged at annual general meetings, and no matter how hard it was at times to keep my thoughts to myself, that was only right and proper.

(3) The respectful disciple theory

The third possible interpretation follows on from the second. Debate was central to the rabbinic teaching method of the time – known as *remez*. It would often involve asking apposite questions, a technique Jesus used to great effect when he was under siege from the Pharisees, or when he refused to let the disciples off the hook. 'Who do men say that I am? But who do you say that I am?' It was part of an ongoing, deepening teaching process.

In first-century synagogues it was traditional to follow the reading of the Scriptures with a lesson or sermon that basically consisted of a question and answer session. Prophecy, it seems, was to be subject to the same discussion. The late Professor Safrai of the Hebrew University of Jerusalem, an expert on Judaism at the time of Christ, said it was considered indecorous for a woman to question a man in public, though she could do so at home.[5] She was also allowed to debate the Scriptures in a women-only study group, of which there were many at the time. It may simply be that Paul was re-emphasising the accepted behaviour of the time, though he must have known that Jesus never castigated, and actually affirmed, Mary for sitting at his feet in the traditional position of a student or disciple.

(4) The repeat of the question theory

Some of Paul's letter to the Corinthian church is a reply to questions they have been put to him. Some are obvious. Paul helpfully repeats them, for example, 'Now, about what you were asking on the subject of staying single . . .' Others require readers to make an informed guess. The Corinthians are still terribly confused about sexual ethics, and want to know if a Greek man needs to be circumcised, and whether they should eat food offered to idols. Given both the Greek and Jewish traditions of members of the congregation it is highly likely there are some who would prefer women to stay silent in the public meetings. One interpretation of these verses is that Paul is merely repeating something the Corinthians have written to him, so that he can then quash it completely with his explosion of exasperation in verse 36: 'Did the word of God originate with you? Or are you the only people it has reached?' In other words, are you arrogant enough to think that you alone have a monopoly on correct dogma?

(5) The naughty scribe theory

The most controversial, but thought-provoking, interpretation belongs to American Pentecostal theologian Gordon Fee.[6] He claims there are many strange features about these two particular verses, the opening phrase, 'As in all the churches . . .' for a start. We know now that women were not silent in all the churches. From the time of Pentecost at least, they took an active part in worship. Then there are the words, 'as the law says . . .' But the Torah, or written law, never suggested a woman should be silent in services. According to the historian Josephus, oral tradition stated that, 'The woman, as the law says, is in all things, inferior to the man', but never, in any of his letters elsewhere does Paul give any weight to the Jewish oral law. Furthermore, when Paul does expound the Torah, he normally gives text and verse. Not here.

Fee also makes the point that the sentiments of the two verses do not fit in with Paul's overall attitude to the role of women, particularly since he describes so many of them as his fellow workers, and claims to the Galatians that the distinction between male and female has been done away with by the cross.

Fee therefore comes to the conclusion that some rogue scribe – a traditionalist who was unhappy with the new freedoms given to women – took his chance and added the verses at some later date. Furthermore, the whole passage reads more easily and makes a great deal more sense without the interpolation of these two odd verses in the middle.

Some may find Fee hard to swallow on this particular point and wonder how many more texts he explains away. He is in fact entirely orthodox in his approach to Scripture, and knowing what we now know – that key texts were occasionally tampered with to support a writer's prejudice[7] – means he has a very convincing argument.

In the end, we have to admit we do not know exactly what Paul meant, and can take our pick from a host of possibilities. In his commentary on 1 Corinthians, William Barclay says, 'In all likelihood what was uppermost in Paul's mind was the lax moral state of Corinth, and the feeling that nothing, absolutely nothing, must be done which would bring upon the infant church the faintest suspicion of immodesty. It would certainly be very wrong to take these words of Paul out of the context for which they were written.'[8]

But if women were not banned from taking part in worship, what about the vexing issue of authority?

I do not permit a woman to teach

A woman should learn in quietness and full submission. I do not permit a woman to teach or to assume authority over a man; she must be quiet. For Adam was formed first, then Eve. And Adam was not the one deceived; it was the woman who was deceived and became a sinner. But women will be saved through childbearing – if they continue in faith, love and holiness with propriety.

(1 Tim. 2:11–15)

After I had spoken in Cape Town, urging women to go out and conquer the world for Christ, I was approached by an attractive young ordinand, who told me with immense pain in her eyes that her fellow students, all men, regularly hit her over the head with these verses, and informed her that her place was in the kitchen, not at theological college. She knew her calling was to the pulpit, but to gain any headway she desperately needed to be able to stand her theological ground. At the time I didn't know how to help her. I hadn't taken the verses seriously enough or studied them in any depth. Now I have and I'm so sorry that I let her down.

In fact, I think that for many years I was an ostrich, shutting out what I didn't want to face. Paul's first letter to young Timothy always left me feeling put down, patronised and very confused. How, having worked so closely with women, could he suddenly be two-faced enough to forbid them a teaching role?

Once I began to dig into the text with the help of impressive theologians and Greek scholars like Richard and Catherine Clark Kroeger, who wrote an entire book on these few difficult verses,[9] and once I began to align them with the Paul that I knew cared deeply for all the Church, I began to grasp their meaning. Paul was no chauvinist. He was a father figure, as concerned for the integrity of the church in Ephesus as he was for the church in Corinth, and even more concerned for Timothy, the young man he has mentored as if he were his own son, and sent into such a hotbed of sexual hi-jinks.

Timothy was raised and taught the faith by two women – Eunice, his mother, and Lois, his grandmother. He served his apprenticeship as an evangelist at Corinth, where Paul was ministering in partnership with Priscilla and Aquila. Priscilla and Aquila had also accompanied Paul to Ephesus. Without doubt the young Timothy had seen formidable Christian women in action, in two very different settings and at a very formative time in his ministry. No doubt he learned a great deal from these fearless, feisty women. So it seems highly unlikely that his rabbi would suddenly instruct this young minister to deny his upbringing and adopt a universal prohibition on women preachers.

It must be context here that is crucial to any real understanding of the text.

The sex symbols of Ephesus

Ephesus was a thriving trade port. Carved into the pavement down in the docks was the figure of a woman with a sign across her chest which read 'follow me', and next to it a foot pointing the men to the local brothel as they left the ships. In this lively, bustling Gentile metropolis, where there were many converts from paganism, some, it appears, were loath to let go of their more libertine traditions. Paul had left Timothy in Ephesus expressly to put a stop to syncretism – a confusion of Greek mythology and the gospel he had preached to them. He knew that left unchecked, false teaching would destroy the infant church.

When I was at primary school we had one rather eccentric, elderly teacher called Miss Davies, so in love with the myths of the Greeks and the Romans that she neglected arithmetic and spelling. I didn't mind; I was fascinated by her stories. I knew the names of all the gods and goddesses, major and minor, in both Greek and Latin, and their specific roles and preoccupations – Zeus or Jupiter, temperamental father of them all, teasing mortals and sending ineffectual thunderbolts from heaven to bring them into line; Aphrodite or Venus, charming yet cruel, enticing humans into hopeless, amorous entanglements. And then of course there was Artemis or Diana, patron of archery and hunting, stalking the countryside in search of sport, a strong, macho goddess.

For years I never appreciated the benefits of this precocious wisdom. After all, I was Jewish. It wasn't my history or my culture, and it wasn't even real. Now the realisation hit me that this was the backdrop of the Church, the context in which it was born and grew – the key to understanding Paul's epistles. Thank you, Miss Davies.

The most important deities in Asia Minor were often female, direct descendants of their ancient pagan counterparts. 'The Great Mother', as she was known, had different names at different times and in different places. In the Old Testament she was the idol Ashtoreth. Elsewhere she was Demeter or Cybele but, whatever her name, this goddess had one universal attribute – she was the initiator of existence. All life came from and returned to her womb. She could reproduce without needing a male.

Ephesus housed the most famous shrine ever built to the great earth mother and it did wonders for the tourist trade. She was known there as Artemis and every day her magnificent temple attracted thousands of worshippers from miles around. Supported on a hundred massive columns, it was one of the Seven Wonders of the World. I saw the remains of some of those columns on a day trip to Ephesus as part of a package tour to Turkey, a welcome relief from lying on a beach in rows with hundreds of other British tourists. Judging by the massive bits and pieces still remaining, the temple must have been breathtaking – a vast, ornate building that seemed to reach up to the heavens. But, to be honest, my main memory of Ephesus is of the ancient toilets, a long public bench with holes gouged out at regular intervals, where men would sit in rows and chat or read while they did the necessary. A whistle would signal the end of the session and an opportunity for the women to take their turn. Heaven knows what happened to those with constipation, or an upset stomach.

Halfway up the main street we stopped outside a small terraced property, and our Muslim guide pointed out a fish symbol carved into the pavement. It was almost invisible, a sign only to the initiated that this was the home of the new Christian cult. I saw at once how oppressively overpowering the dominant Greco-Roman culture must have felt to the people who slipped in and out, dwarfed by the magnificent buildings that surrounded the house, symbols of prosperity and worldly success – particularly the Temple of Artemis with its endless procession of visitors tramping past the door.

Inside the temple stood a huge statue of the goddess. She wore a high crown, representing the walls of a city, built by her benevolence. The top half of her body was covered in multiple egg-shaped breasts. Three rows of stags were attached to her skirt from waist to feet. Reliefs of bees, rams, bulls, crabs and griffins covered the rest of her, to highlight her responsibility for all fertility, in both animals and humans. In cities other than Ephesus her devotees praised her perpetual chastity. In Ephesus they worshipped her for her surrender to love without restraint – a more attractive option for pilgrims? Sexual ecstasy was the means of establishing direct contact with the deity herself.

This, then, was the Blackpool of Asia Minor. Trippers came from far and wide looking for a good time. Unlike Blackpool, however, Ephesus' tourist industry and healthy economy enabled it to become the richest province in the Roman Empire, a banking centre for the whole of Asia. Inevitably, Ephesian dignitaries were hardly pleased when the Apostle Paul preached the gospel with such power that some of the locals burned their magic books. Christianity was not good for business. The silversmiths who made high-class, tourist tat – miniature statues for personal use, so that Artemis could be worshipped in living rooms and bedrooms everywhere – instigated a riot. For two solid hours a frenzied crowd screamed, 'Great is Artemis of the Ephesians!' (Acts 19:28, 34). If the silversmiths lost their business, the pharmacists must have done a decent trade in throat lozenges.

In challenging the whole idea of the goddess mother, Paul had undermined the very economical and social ideologies that were at the heart of Ephesus' reputation and success. Without Artemis, what would Ephesus have left? And after all, a fertility goddess represented a great deal of easily available, lucrative rumpy-pumpy. Its champions, like today's perpetrators of accessible hard-core porn, were not going to allow any incursion into their liberties without a fight.

Seduction slips into the Church

It is easy to see how, living in such an eroticised culture, some church members might have confused or even wilfully combined the life-giving Artemis with Mother Eve, ancient mythology with Christian doctrine. It seems clear in Paul's letter to Timothy that this heresy was being preached by none other than the church leaders or teachers (1 Tim. 1:3, 7). And their greatest following consisted of a number of women who had not only welcomed them into their homes, but were now also actively engaged in propagating their ideas. Presumably this particular group included a number of vulnerable young widows. In 1 Timothy chapter 5, it might appear that Paul is implying that all young widows are universally lazy, wanton gadabouts, muck-rakers and mischief-makers. But it's hardly likely that he thought all young widows everywhere were morally suspect. A look at the adjectives used to describe them – 'idlers' and 'busybodies' – reveals the problem (1 Tim. 5:13).

The Greek for 'gossips', *phlyaroi*, actually has nothing to do with passing on tasty titbits of information. It means to talk nonsense or untruthfulness. And the Greek word for 'busybodies', or *periergoi*, is 'workers of magic'. In other words, he describes these particular widows in the same terms as false teachers – full of meaningless [foolish or empty-headed] talk' (1 Tim. 1:6) and who 'follow deceiving spirits and things taught by demons' (1 Tim. 4:1). They had been seduced by an early form of gnostic heresy that turned Christian truth on its head. They claimed that the Creator, the God of the Old Testament, was evil. Having made the material world, he kept human beings imprisoned in it, determined to bar their way to the spirit world that lay beyond. The false teachers believed the Serpent could release human beings, with the help of Eve, who exposed this secret knowledge when she ate from the forbidden tree. She was the mediator between humans and Satan. Sexual licence was religious freedom, a way of connecting human flesh with Eve, the divine mother. Hardly surprising Paul is so outspoken in his letter to the young pastor he has so carefully mentored. The new church must not be infected with such poisonous stuff.

Authentein, the word translated as 'authority' in, 'I do not permit a woman to assume authority over a man' (1 Tim. 2:12) is not used anywhere else in the entire New Testament, so there is no biblical way of cross-checking to find out what Paul had in mind. The word carried no suggestion of usurping authority until the third or fourth century.

In their intensive word study, Richard and Catherine Clark Kroeger were forced to turn to Greek drama for clues on its original meaning. They discovered that, in its literal sense, *authentein* was in fact an extremely rare verb, meaning, 'to thrust', presumably with a sword, as it tended to be used by Greek dramatists to refer to murder or suicide.[10] In Greek mythology there was a close association between sex and death. Death was often the consequence for the poor, benighted human who dared to mate with a goddess. The sword was also a phallic symbol, so, at the time, *authentein* had a popular slang meaning. It was a rather coarse word for sexual relations. Now why would a nice former rabbi, a preacher of the gospel like Paul, resort to such strong language? Only if he deplored what was happening in Ephesus. It would appear that a group of women were using their sexual charms to ensnare susceptible men and entice them in as their new followers. This was more than just erroneous. It was downright destructive. It was evil.

'For Adam was formed first, then Eve', Paul continues. 'And Adam was not the one deceived; it was the woman who was deceived and became a sinner' (1 Tim 2:13). This has nothing whatsoever to do with superior male intellect or moral judgement. Nor is Paul suggesting that woman is more vulnerable or susceptible to sin. In fact, in his letter to the Corinthian church, Paul lays the blame for the fall firmly at Adam's door: 'For as in Adam all die, so in Christ all will be made alive' (1 Cor.15:22). Nor is Paul establishing a hierarchical order in creation. That would be a denial of the God-given equality of all human beings, irrespective of race or gender. Rather, Paul is confronting the way certain women in Ephesus were manipulating the Genesis story for their own ends. Eve was not the earth goddess. She could not reproduce alone, without a relationship with Adam. At creation men were not given authority over women, nor were women given authority over men. Women were never intended to use their sexuality to control, subvert, manipulate or dominate men. Paul was setting the record absolutely straight. It is hardly surprising therefore that he told Timothy to silence this pernicious little group.

According to theologian Gordon Fee, the Greek present tense, 'I do not permit', may be more accurately translated in this context: 'I am not permitting here and now', supporting the view that the verb is specific to the situation rather than a generalisation. Instead she is to 'learn in silence', which Fee says doesn't mean 'not speaking', for then no woman would ever be allowed to participate in worship at all, but 'with a quiet demeanour'.[11]

Carefully translated in context, the verse begins to look like this: 'I am not permitting these women to teach while they seduce men and claim they are the author of man. Instead they are to learn with humility, for Adam was created first, then Eve.' In other words, they were not to be given a platform until they could prove they had learned the basics of true Christian doctrine and were disabused of their subversive, dangerous ideas. There would be no more revealing clothes, no more eyeing up anything in a toga, no more flirting or suggestive behaviour, all positively encouraged from the pulpit, and all condemned by Paul in the strongest possible terms (1 Tim. 2:9). Instead, they would submit to learning a greater wisdom and truth.

Saved through childbearing?

But how will Timothy know for certain that these women have undergone a genuine transformation? 'They will be saved through childbearing,' says Paul (1 Tim. 2:15). Does he mean there is an alternative to salvation through the blood of Christ and his death on the cross? That surely cannot be reconciled with the rest of his theology. Does he mean their life will be spared in childbirth, as some theologians suggest? From the beginning of time Christian women have died in childbirth, like any others – many still today in developing countries where there is no access to basic healthcare. Is Paul suggesting that mothering is the highest role for a woman, and has some kind of redemptive function – easy for a busy man who has no children himself? If that were the case, why in his letter to the Corinthian church does he spell out the advantages of staying single?

The key here is the Greek word for 'saved', *sozo*, which can also mean 'restored'. These Ephesian women will demonstrate their restoration from deception only when they become godly women, bringing up children, running a home and doing good in the community, the domestic model Paul would have known for Gentile women. Even then, only when this new life of 'faith, love and holiness with propriety' is ongoing, can Timothy be sure that their redemption is complete.

In marked contrast to the women denounced here as false teachers are the deaconesses or women ministers whose attributes Paul goes on to describe in the next chapter of his letter to Timothy (1 Tim. 3:11). Because of the confusion caused by that little word *gyne,* some translations suggest he is referring to the wives of deacons, but Fee and others think he would have said *their* wives, and not 'the women', if that were the case. It is more likely he was speaking about genuine women ministers, who are to earn respect by being reliable, not malicious, nor partial to a drink or two too many. In other words, they will have the same qualities he commends for any male leader.

Does it all matter?

At the end of the day, what difference does it make whether women are allowed to preach or not? Shouldn't we be prepared to give up our right to the pulpit since it's so contentious, for the sake of love and unity? In our French church I have had to, though it seems downright barmy, in a country where human resources are very limited, not to use the gifting that is under their very noses. But we also run a larger group in our own home where I preach freely, and the four church leaders have all been subjected to it – without complaint. It would be a denial of an essential part of God's good news for all people if we simply succumbed without a fight.

For the majority of young people in the West the equality between men and women is so much the norm that the alternative is a shock to their system. When they see overt sexism operating in the Church, it's small wonder they caricature Christians as reactionary, out-of-touch fuddy-duddies, and turn away from the very truths we want to share.

Surely the gospel spells freedom, not restrictions, for all men and women. Perhaps this should be our guide in those tricky issues that cause such conflict – what is going to be the most challenging and liberating message for the society in which we live?

Conservative Christians have always feared that 'if our herme-neutical principles can lead us so clearly to discard the plain injunctions of Scripture on this one issue, we are bound also to approve homosexual practice, since the same principles apply'.[12] Dick France, a leading evangelical New Testament scholar and a former principal of Wycliffe Hall Theological College in Oxford, wrote a short essay called *A Slippery Slope?* to address this argument, which still causes bother some twenty years later. France, who was originally opposed to women's ministry, tried to explain that it was the last chapter of Romans that had convinced him that Paul regarded female co-work-ers as equal, over and against the apparently conflicting verses. In other words, since there are arguments for both views, Christians are free to make up their own minds about this issue. But moral issues, he says, such as sexual relations, are a different matter, and he sees why those who support women's leadership in the church may still struggle with gay marriage.

However, where there is room for a variety of opinions and views – on issues such as Sabbath observance, for example – Christians should not be guided either by contemporary or church culture, but by what seems most in keeping with the spirit of the gospel. 'The history of biblical interpretation is the story of new insights discovered often under the pressure of changing circumstances and of cultural shift – the eventual abolition of slavery is a celebrated example.'[13]

For people like my husband, Peter, who had always thought he was egalitarian but who slipped unconsciously from time to time into the superior male mode of his childhood upbringing, it was a revelation to discover that to live in denial of the equality and compatibility between men and women, forfeited so soon after creation, was to live without the redemption Christ paid for at the cross. The message of equality is a message of vibrant new life and freedom for a world where sexual exploitation is still rife, and women can be valued so much less than their male counterparts. To deny women the chance to share in every aspect of ministry alongside the men is a negation of the liberating, life-giving message of the gospel.

When women have a voice

Throughout Christian history, times of spiritual awakening have been characterised by the appearance of powerful women in the pulpit.

In the seventeenth century, Quakerism produced some outstanding women preachers. On my first visit to our local castle in Lancaster I was very struck by the life-size dummy of a woman wearing an extraordinary contraption over her head and face – a sort of cap made of iron bars, which covered her mouth and forced a piece of metal into it. Apparently, the 'scold's bridle' was the standard form of punishment for any woman accused of being the village gossip, or even a shrewish, nagging wife. The bridle was locked onto her head, then she would be led out into the square and fastened into the stocks, where she was pelted with rotten fruit or more dangerous missiles that could do a great deal of damage.

I questioned whether that could happen to any woman, and our guide asked us to notice that she was wearing Quaker dress. The Quakers, he said, were a 'fundamentalist Christian sect', who believed in the Bible, the work of the Holy Spirit and, worse, the equality of men and women. For that they were regarded as enemies of the state and many, including the outspoken local preacher, Margaret Fell, who later married the Quaker leader, George Fox himself, were imprisoned in the castle. A Quaker woman could find herself incarcerated in a dungeon or locked into the scold's bridle for no greater sin than leading the equivalent of an Alpha course – sharing the gospel with her neighbours – for that was regarded as a hideously unfeminine thing to do. Yet, despite the possible consequences of their actions, Quaker women refused to be gagged and went on preaching both in private and in public.

As I stood looking at her, it made me wonder what I would have done in her place. Do I sometimes put myself into a gag because I don't want to appear strident or unwomanly, or because I'm afraid of the consequences? One of the perks of the aging process is the freedom to be outspoken, because I care much less now about what people think of me.

Between 1761 and 1791 John Wesley appointed many women as local preachers and itinerant ministers. His approval of their ministry, though with some reluctance, paved the way for the Wesleyan Holiness movement to thrust a host of remarkable non-conformist women into the limelight.

Phoebe Palmer (1807–74), an American evangelist and preacher, became a major force behind the great American revival of 1858, and was the first to preach a baptism of the Holy Spirit in the United Kingdom. She was in such demand and away from home so often that her husband eventually retired from medicine so that he could support her ministry. The four years she spent in Great Britain laid the foundation of the Pentecostal and Charismatic movements that would impact the Church for the next 150 years. Phoebe justified a woman's right to preach on the experience of Pentecost. If the Holy Spirit had fallen on women and men indiscriminately then, what was to stop him anointing women for ministry today?

It was on Pentecost Sunday morning in 1860 that Catherine Booth (1829–90) first rose from her pew and walked up into the pulpit of her husband's church to 'share a few thoughts'. The impact on the congregation was so great that her husband announced, 'My wife will complete her sermon at the evening service.'

The wife of William Booth, founder of the Salvation Army, had never felt any inclination to preach. Catherine simply wanted to be a pastor's wife. Her William, she was sure, would see hundreds turn to Christ wherever and whenever he preached, and she would be right behind him, supporting him all the way. Sure enough, when William preached hundreds were converted, but when she began to preach, thousands responded.

Neither Phoebe Palmer nor Catherine Booth had sought the limelight. In fact, both were reluctant to take up a calling that would expose them to verbal and physical attack, public criticism and allegations of being unwomanly and even ungodly. But in the end, both felt that was a small price to pay for doing what God had asked of them. When breast cancer brought her remarkable ministry to a premature end, Catherine Booth whispered as she lay dying, 'What would I have said to my maker if I had not been faithful to the heavenly vision? What would I have said to him for all that wasted fruit?'

Phoebe Palmer was convinced that it was simply a matter of time before the Church gave women preachers its blessing. Catherine agreed. Inequality was 'a remarkable device of the devil'. Her husband, William Booth, famously asked how any army could go to war with half its forces chained to the kitchen sink. Her close friend, the campaigner Josephine Butler, wrote in 1892, 'Women themselves have been very slavish. It is humiliating to see a gifted woman, with dignity enough for a Bishop or Prime Minister, putting herself willingly under the guidance of some inexperienced, not gifted clergy-boy.'[14] Nineteenth-century Christian women felt it was time to stop colluding with those who held them back, and to prepare themselves for the host of new opportunities about to open up before them. It was as well they didn't know then just how long they would have to wait for the fulfilment of those dreams.

In 1901 Florence Barclay, whose novel *The Rosary* sold more than a million copies, began a weekly women's Bible class in the Victoria

Room in Leyton that attracted around five hundred women. Once a year, on Good Friday, the Bible reading was thrown open to men, and more than a thousand people packed the hall. But with Florrie Barclay the acceptance of high-profile, evangelical women preachers was coming to an end – in Britain at least. In the USA it continued sporadically through the twentieth century with women such as Maria Woodworth Etter, Aimee Semple McPherson and Katherine Kuhlman, all holding huge campaigns with high drama, mass conversions and miraculous healings. Yet even they operated alone, despite, rather than with, the support of the Pentecostal tradition from which they came. Susan Hyatt concludes, 'As the Pentecostal Revival spread and diversified, equality waned', and in their desire for acceptance – the old *teshuqah* – 'women tended to return to their socially acceptable place as subordinate partner. As the Holy Spirit's presence withdrew, the hierarchical social patterns of institutionalism snuffed out the egalitarianism that had characterised the early revival period.'[15]

In post-First World War Britain, a new cynicism and disillusionment put paid to evangelical certainty, and there appeared instead a succession of remarkable, Anglican laywomen in the gentler, more mystical tradition of Hilda of Whitby and Julian of Norwich.

Evelyn Underhill was the first woman to lecture in religion at Oxford University and to lead retreats in the Church of England. She didn't become a committed Anglican until later life, yet Michael Ramsey, a previous Archbishop of Canterbury, is reputed to have said that she, more than anyone else, was responsible for keeping spirituality alive and well in the Anglican Church in the period between the wars.

Like Mother Julian, she established a reputation as a spiritual counsellor and hundreds of people, both ordained and lay, flocked to the retreats she led at the Anglican Retreat Centre in Pleshey in Essex. Although the Anglo-Catholic clergy were opposed to the ordination of women, none seemed unduly averse to allowing her to instruct them in how to keep their spiritual life in good working order, when the very pressures of clerical life mitigated against it. In diocesan lectures she regularly challenged them to maintain a disciplined life of holiness and prayer, whatever the distractions, however great the demands of their congregation.

Evelyn Underhill never campaigned for women to become ministers of the Church, but many of her gifted Anglican colleagues did, including Maude Royden (1876–1956), who worked among the poor in Liverpool and became a fearsome campaigner for women's suffrage and the rights of the socially oppressed. In 1917, though she knew she had a call to minister in the Anglican Church, she accepted the offer instead of a post as assistant minister at the City Temple, a Congregationalist Church. She wrote, 'The church will never believe that women have a religious message until some of them get, and take, the opportunity to prove that they have. My taking it in a non-conformist church will ultimately lead, I believe, to other women being given it in the Church of England.'[16] In the 1920s and 1930s people travelled miles to hear her preach at the Guildhouse in Kensington.

Maude Royden, Dorothy Sayers, and a host of other outspoken Anglican women preachers and broadcasters who often used the equivalent of the BBC's *Thought for the Day* as an opportunity to express their demands for equality, would have been horrified to see an advert in the Church of England Newspaper in the first year of the next century. A church that had passed Resolution B (exempting them from having a woman vicar), was looking for 'a mature, dedicated, prayerful, Bible-based evangelical Christian. The focus will be teaching the Bible amongst women.' In other words, she would not be allowed to preach to the men.

Women and authority

Women who are called to the pulpit face some difficult decisions. If they preach confidently and boldly they can run the risk of being called abrasive or even aggressive. They may find themselves a threat to men and a pariah to other women. But if they preach hesitantly and uncertainly, apologising for their very existence, they are not likely to be asked again.

Our expectations for how a person in authority should behave are at odds with our expectations for how a woman should behave. If a woman talks in ways expected of women, she is more likely to be liked than respected. If she talks in ways expected of men, she is more likely to be respected than liked. It is particularly ironic that the risk of losing likeability is greater for women in authority, since evidence indicates that so many women care so much about whether or not they are liked.[17]

The old *teshuqah* clutches at our hearts again. When I first started preaching I had so few female role models it was hard to know how. I faced the same struggles and criticisms as Phoebe Palmer, Catherine Booth and Josephine Butler – a hundred years later. I think that respecting the congregation is the best clue. In the end every woman must find her own voice and unique way of preaching with authority, confidence and love. Today, a woman in the pulpit is the norm, but I still hear one or two who seem to me to be fulfilling expectations, or emulating other women, or men, they admire.

Lavinia Abrol, a well-known speaker in Northern Ireland, where the Church can still be rigidly traditional, told me how one Mother's Day she had been invited to preach at a rural church some miles out of Belfast. During her sermon she told the story of how she had lost her lovely baby daughter. Afterwards the church treasurer came to her in the vestry, weeping. He had lost his son only a year before. 'Why is it when a man preaches,' he said to her through his tears, 'he never seems to touch another man's pain?'

Like Catherine Booth, Michelle Obama began her speaking career as her husband's other half, but it soon became apparent she was so much more than a foil for the man. She has an exceptional gifting in her own right, the ability to express her emotions, to move her audience, to make them feel she knows and understands them, to challenge and inspire both men and women.

I have to admit I cannot think of any good reason why God would deny a woman the chance to teach or lead. When I spoke on women and authority at our church, a wonderful 95-year-old saint rose to his feet and said he couldn't understand why people got so het up about the subject of women in leadership. What was their problem? Had not God foreseen the freedoms women in the West would have today? Had it caught him unawares? Even if it were true that Paul in his time had not really approved of women in the pulpit, had not God, who knew and saw all from the beginning to the end of time, reserved for himself the right to change his mind? It was unthinkable his Word would ever be irrelevant or inappropriate for contemporary society. And anyway, what was lost if women did preach? 'Surely,' he said, with all the godly wisdom of his age and experience, 'there would be more to lose if they didn't, and a great deal to be gained if they did.'

Chapter 6

The Submissive Woman?

There were three experienced ministers' wives on the panel that evening – one who would later become a bishop's wife – as we, rather nervous, soon-to-be-in-their-shoes young women, who had accompanied our husbands to theological college, waited in anticipation for the glimmers of wisdom that would light our way into an unknown and daunting future. Each of the three pieces of advice was the same in essence: 'Don't worry your husbands with your minor problems to do with running the home and the children. He is doing God's work. Release him to fulfil his ministry.'

It took me a while to register what they were saying, but at the third similar answer to our questions I was up, almost involuntarily, and on my feet. 'I didn't know we were called to be parish doormats,' I heard myself say in the uncomfortable hush. 'I thought marriage was about each releasing the other to fulfil our God-given calling and potential.' I can't exactly recall the panel's rather embarrassed response, only the dismissive reaction of the other student wives: 'We always knew you were a radical and a feminist.'

I wasn't consciously either of those things. Two years' experience as a detached youth worker before my marriage had certainly opened my eyes to the demoralising effects of social deprivation, and left me with an intolerance of the prospering of one human being at the cost of another. Otherwise, I was fairly conservative, the educated daughter of a traditional, fairly well-heeled Jewish family with no real aspirations to a career at that stage, and two pre-schoolers at home. Even the stringencies of living on a clergy stipend hadn't really crossed my mind.

As for women's rights, in those heady days of the early eighties they exercised the minds of many of the female students fighting for the right to be ordained, and my instinctive sense of fair play put me in their camp, but I hadn't been sufficiently engaged or had the time to study the theology. In fact, I was a lazy thinker who had simply passed from middle-class Jewish assumptions to the accepted conservative evangelical views of the time. Once, newly married, I held forth at a women's group about the virtues of the stay-at-home wife, completely demolishing one of my closest friends, mother of three small boys and a brilliant science teacher. How could I have been so opinionated, so oblivious?

But if the college wives thought I was out of order that night, several of the single women students cheered me on. I had wondered why they had turned up at a wives' meeting, but learned later that it was to gain some insight into how they, as female curates, might handle the possible competition – she who could be a threatened, destructive force in their ministry. They were deeply concerned that so many of the wives felt 'called' to ministry along with their husbands, even though he, not she, would have the training, the job, the pay packet and the predominance. If the wife saw herself as the key partner in ministry and not just marriage, there was a great danger that her nose would be put out of joint by an employed female assistant.

Even now, so many years later, in certain parts of the Church, the idea of husband-wife ministry teams seems more embedded than ever, though there is barely any model for it in the New Testament. No married partnerships are mentioned other than Priscilla and Aquila. The Apostle Peter had a wife who accompanied him, but we know nothing about her, not even her name. Little is said about the marital status of any of the early disciples, apostles and church leaders. They ministered as individuals and in partnerships, mainly with someone of the same gender, but not necessarily with their spouse.

It is a concept that seems to have been absorbed from American culture, where it was initially a means of permitting women to minister while ensuring the man remained top dog – though, in fact, depending on the giftings of the pair, that wasn't always the reality on the ground. On that evening in theological college I had unintentionally questioned an accepted status quo and threatened some of the student wives by challenging their perceptions of the role they hoped to play. It was only later I learned that two of the women on the panel virtually ran their husbands' churches. Yet a doctor's wife wouldn't expect to play a major part in her husband's professional life, any more than a plumber's wife would pick up his toolbag and respond to an emergency call to mend a leak. Why should a minister's marriage be any different?

To be fair, in the past, few husbands encouraged their women to explore and follow their own calling, in the Church or anywhere else. It was culturally acceptable for a wife to be backup, support, substitute and understudy, rather than a key player. As late as 1959, in his study of the wife with the 'meek and quiet spirit' in I Peter, the great Bible teacher Alan Stibbs says:

> Meek describes the way in which such a wife submits to her husband's demands and intrusions by docile and gentle cooperation. Quiet describes her complementary and constant attitude, and the character of her action or reaction towards her husband and towards life in general. She shows no sign of rebellion or resentment, fuss or flurry. [1]

I looked up 'docile' in the dictionary. It says, 'domesticated' or 'easy to manage', rather like the family pet. No flurry is all very well for a woman who is naturally phlegmatic, but when you are as sanguine as I am, it may not be easy to live up to Stibbs' rather passive ideal, which seems more like the sharia Muslim view of marriage. Fortunately, the former isn't acceptable any longer in Western culture. But it was supported for centuries by two New Testament concepts which were used as a mandate for the subordination of women in general, and not just wives: headship and submission.

Of hats and head coverings

> I want you to realise that the head of every man is Christ, and the head of the woman is man, and the head of Christ is God. Every man who prays or prophesies with his head covered dishonours his head. But every woman who prays or prophesies with her

head uncovered dishonours her head – it is the same as having her head shaved. For if a woman does not cover her head, she might as well have her hair cut off.

(1 Cor. 11:3–6)

On 6 November 1942, the Church of England relaxed the convention that women must wear hats in church. No, it wasn't a sudden revelation that Anglican women had been lumbered for years with a cultural anachronism. Hats had been de rigueur in polite society for well over a century and, generally speaking, women who could afford the fancier models loved them and had a wardrobe full, unlike their socially inferior sisters who owned one in cheap, serviceable felt that had to serve every occasion. The Archbishops of Canterbury and York were simply responding to a wartime 'request' from the Board of Trade that in a time of financial exigence women be discouraged from spending the country's hard-earned cash on unnecessary fripperies.

Hat-wearing, however, owed as much to biblical as social convention. It was a statement about the place of women – which was under the authority, or so-called 'headship', of men – and it was based on a rather tortuous argument the Apostle Paul uses in his letter to the new, unruly Corinthian church. In the entire New Testament, there is no such word as 'headship', and only two references to man as 'head' in his letters – one to the Corinthians and one to the Ephesians (Eph. 5:23). Both letters were written to predominantly Gentile churches about order and decency, rather than about salvation.

In the church in Corinth, where women were enjoying the new freedom to participate in worship, some appeared to want to go too far too fast. It was customary at that time for a woman to wear a loose covering over her head when she was out in public. (For a man, covering his head was a traditional sign of mourning.) Only temple prostitutes walked out with their hair hanging loose over their shoulders. St John Damascene, writing in the fifth century, was shocked at the impropriety he witnessed in the city of Constantinople. It was 'the setting of dances and jests . . . as well as of taverns, baths and brothels. Women went about with uncovered heads and moved their limbs in a provocative and deliberately sensuous way. Young men grew effeminate and let their hair grow long.'[2]

Similarly, Paul was obviously taken aback by the gung-ho attitude in the Corinthian church to the normal cultural mores of decency. How could a Christian woman let herself be mistaken for a prostitute? What did it say to outsiders if her appearance suggested that the same kind of sexually induced religious ecstasy that went on in the pagan temples was taking place in the church? They might be forgiven for assuming Christianity was simply another pagan cult. So Paul argues first and foremost that for the sake of decency a woman should cover her head – and if she won't, then cut off all her hair. That didn't leave her with much of a choice. In the tradition of the Roman oppressors, only women of questionable sexuality wore their hair short. Long hair on a man also blurred gender distinctions, and Paul wanted to pre-empt any allegations of impropriety. With both Romans and Jews the reputation of the Church hung on a cliff edge. For the sake of the gospel Paul submitted to many of the social conventions of the day, even having his young associate, Timothy, circumcised, so that the Jews couldn't dismiss his message on the grounds that he wasn't strictly kosher. Becoming a Christian did not give women licence to overturn the rules of propriety. The delicate balance and inter-dependency of relationships between the sexes was not to be sacrificed for the sake of individual freedom.

In our society, where a head covering for a woman has more to do with the weather than her sexual mores, it no longer has any relevance in religious observance. In fact, when I see a woman in church with a scarf draped over her head, I'm tempted to tap her on the shoulder and tell her she honestly won't be taken for a sex worker if she takes it off.

And of hats and heads

A man ought not to cover his head, since he is the image and glory of God; but woman is the glory of man. For man did not come from woman, but woman from man; neither was man created for woman, but woman for man. It is for this reason that a woman ought to have authority over her own head, because of the angels. Nevertheless, in the Lord woman is not independent of man, nor is man independent of woman. For as woman came from man, so also man is born of woman. But everything comes from God.

(1 Cor. 11:7–11)

But Paul also argues that women should cover their heads, not simply because it was proper behaviour, but also from the creation story, and that gave rise to the tricky notion of 'headship'.

'The head of woman is man, the head of man is Christ and the head of Christ is God.' (1 Cor. 11:3, paraphrased).

So what, first and foremost, does it mean for God to be the head of Christ? Is there a divine chain of command? The traditional Christian theology of the Trinity maintains that the three members of the godhead are co-equal. To suggest from this verse that God is somehow superior to Christ or has authority over Christ erodes his divinity and is a heresy known as subordinationism. There cannot therefore be any suggestion of a divine hierarchy in the text.

Immediately after discussing head covering, Paul moves on to use the metaphor of the human body to describe the essential relationship of members of the church (1 Cor. 12:12–27). And Christ is its head. '. . . a body, though one, has many parts, but all its many parts form one body . . . and those parts that seem to be weaker are indispensable' (1 Cor. 12:12, 22). But a disembodied head cannot function, any more than the rest of the body. So the whole picture is one of inter-dependency and unity, rather than authority.

A metaphor is a picture, a clever way of conveying a difficult, abstract concept in accessible, everyday language. In other words, it's a 'this is kind of what it's like', and therefore cannot be applied rigidly or made into doctrine, because ultimately a metaphor is not a reality, and breaks down. The problem once again is our contemporary cultural mindset, our Western tendency to think in structural pyramids and orders of importance. Today, the word 'head' denotes authority, as in headteacher, or the head of a company. But the Greek word used here for head is *kephale*, and does not mean boss or chief. It can refer to the human head. Salome asks for the *kephale* of John the Baptist, knowing it won't be much use to her, just as the rest of his body won't be much use to him without it.

Dr Katharine Bushnell, a missionary in developing countries, whose experiences of the appalling abuses of women made her determined to build a case for the equality of women, believed that the idea that Christ was head of the Church is a back reference to verse 22 in Psalm 118, which says, 'the stone the builders rejected is the head of the corner'. The cornerstone gives support to a building, so Christ supports his Church and holds its members together in a cohesive unity.[3]

Since *kephale* usually means source of a river, or even of life, Paul's view of Christ in his letter to the Colossians reflects Katharine Bushnell's interpretation. He says Christ is 'before all things, and in him all things hold together . . . he is the head of the body, the church; he is the beginning . . .' (Col. 1:17–18). In the next chapter he warns believers not to be diverted by strange teachings that would cut them off from their head, their source of life, 'from whom the whole body, supported and held together by its ligaments and sinews, grows as God causes it to grow' (Col. 2:19). Ultimately, this indivisible interdependency between Christ and his followers allows spiritual life to flow through the veins of the Church.

And so, in his instructions to the Corinthians on head covering, Paul concludes that man is born of woman, in other words, though man was the source of woman in creation, woman is the source of man in procreation, and Christ, who came from God, is the source of life for both of them.[4] The picture Paul has in mind is of a circle, not a pyramid.

When the Apostle wants to convey a sense of hierarchy he doesn't use the word *kephale*, he uses *archon*, which means 'chief' or 'ruler'. And his word for authority is *exousia* (Rom. 13:1–2). The Septuagint, or Greek, translation of the Hebrew Scriptures, completed before the time of Christ, can be a useful dictionary of the meaning of many New Testament words used by Jewish writers like Paul. A scholar called S. Bedale pointed out in 1954 that the Hebrew word for 'head', *ro'sh*, appears 180 times in the Old Testament and is translated as *archon*, rather than *kephale*. In fact, it appears the translators actually avoided the word *kephale* if there was any sense of authority in the text.[5]

Up to the 1960s most theologians believed that the 'headship' did imply some kind of female subordination to male authority – all except a theologian called S. T. Lowrie who, as early as 1921, wrote what must have been a very controversial article defending the idea that women should be appointed as ruling elders in the church.[6] For centuries, marriage had brought such benefits to men that there was no reason for them to question whether long-established patterns of behaviour were actually biblical.

Changes in the status of women in the West, however, made a re-examination of the Scriptures imperative. Later theologians, including F. F. Bruce[7] and Gordon Fee, felt there was nothing in the passage to suggest any sense of hierarchy. The word 'authority' (exousia) is used only once in the passage on head covering, and refers to a woman's authority 'over her own head'.[8] Paul is so anxious that 'at first blush', as Fee puts it, these verses might look as if they indicate subordination, that he adds a rider at the end of his argument. Man is born of woman and therefore as dependent on her as she is on him.

Paul's concern in 1 Corinthians is not with hierarchies, but with relationships. Men and women come from each other and were made for each other. To support his argument he goes back to the book of Genesis where man is created for 'God's glory', and exists to bring his maker praise and honour. But woman is God's crowning glory, for man is incomplete without her. She came from his side and is the one companion suitable for him. Nothing must be allowed to blur the boundaries between the genders, spoil that special relationship or bring it into public disrepute. That was why head covering was an important gesture at the time. As the great commentator Matthew Henry puts it in his own inimitable way:

> Man being the last of the creatures as the best and most excellent of all, puts an honour upon that sex as the glory of God. If man is the head, woman is the crown, a crown for her husband, the crown of visible creation. The man was dust refined, but the woman was dust double-refined, she was one step further removed from the earth.[9]

No woman could have put it better! It is hard to know exactly what Paul means when he says a woman should have 'authority over her own head, because of the angels', but perhaps he means an uncovered head is a distraction, not only for the congregation but even for the angels,[10] who participate in worship, because it's an expression of the glory of man rather than God. So the covering is not a symbol of woman's subjection to man's authority, or of her need for his protection. It was rather a sign of her authority to minister.

So does 'headship', as it became known, have any place in a male-female relationship, and if it does, what is it? Women had always released and resourced their men; that was how it had always been. But now Paul, in his own inimitable way, while demanding order and decency from the women, has managed to present the male with a new challenge. If man is a source of life rather than a dominant force, he has a particular responsibility to resource, release and empower a woman, rather than the other way round. 'Headship' is more about accountability than authority. So what might that mean for the great institution of marriage?

What on earth is submission?

Submit to one another out of reverence for Christ.

Wives, submit yourselves to your own husbands as you do to the Lord. For the husband is the head of the wife as Christ is the head of the church, his body, of which he is the Saviour. Now as the church submits to Christ, so also wives should submit to their husbands in everything.

Husbands, love your wives, just as Christ loved the church and gave himself up for her . . . In this same way, husbands ought to love their wives as their own bodies.

(Eph. 5:21–5, 28)

Wives, submit to your husbands, as is fitting in the Lord.

Husbands, love your wives and do not be harsh with them [embittered with them].

(Col. 3:18–19)

Holy women of the past . . . submitted themselves to their own husbands, like Sarah, who obeyed Abraham and called him her lord.

(1 Peter 3:5–6)

Although many have tried over the years, there is no way these verses on submission can be stretched to apply outside the marriage relationship. That is the only context here.

Marriage, in the pagan world of Paul, wasn't exactly a picnic for the wife. It had little in common with Jewish culture where love was the expectation, and monogamy the order of the day. Roman marriage was primarily contractual. A Roman woman had status in society, but little guaranteed affection in the home. She had a right to property, but not to her husband's fidelity.

In the fourth century BC, the popular Greek statesman and orator Demosthenes declared, 'We have mistresses for pleasure, concubines to care for our daily body's needs and wives to bear us legitimate children and to be faithful guardians of our households.'[11] Once childbearing was done with, a wife seeking sexual fulfilment would probably have to find it outside the home.

Plato, the Greek philosopher, student of Socrates and teacher of Aristotle, a key figure in the development of Western, let alone classical culture, claimed that only a lesser mortal would bother wasting his affection on a woman at all. The truly noble soul was masculine and would seek another male as the object of its love.[12] Leading a debate shortly after the New Testament was written, Demosthenes judged that the obligation to marry should be universal, 'but let the love of boys be reserved only for the wise, because perfect virtue flourishes least of all among women.'[13]

Aristotle, the philosopher and founding father of much Western thought, claimed that a man was intended by nature to rule as husband, father and master, and that to dispense with such a natural order would be a disaster, not just for the family, but also for the entire state. In other words, proper household management was a political issue. Any hint of overturning the accepted social hierarchy would be a threat to the harmony of society as a whole. If religious groups like 'The Way', as the early Christian church was called, which had begun to attract large numbers of women, allowed them to question the status quo, they would be deemed subversive and subjected to closer scrutiny.

It is no surprise, then, that for the sake of the reputation of the infant Church, Paul appears to submit to the view of the acceptable household structure – but there is a major difference. Marriage, he tells the Ephesians, is akin to the sacred relationship between Christ and the Church, for salvation has brought a new reality of grace into every relationship. So Paul is now investing marriage with a status it has never had in the Roman world, and issues men with a new challenge which must have left them reeling – but we shall come to that.

The Greek word used for 'submission' is *hypotasso*, which has several possible interpretations. First and foremost it means 'to behave in a responsible manner', in other words, to show respect and common courtesy. There is no suggestion in the text that the husband should make all the key decisions, or the ultimate decision in an impasse, while the wife simply says, 'Yes, darling. You're always right, darling. Whatever you say, darling.' I once took part in a TV debate on submission with the wife of the founder of one of the newer church networks, who said she had always practised submission and that her husband had only been wrong three times. Who's counting? I certainly can't, as Peter and I make decisions together. It's the only way to live, without my hitting him over the head with the handy rolling pin of blame.

Besides, Paul tells the Christians in Ephesus to submit to one another, and how could we let every other church member tell us what to do? We'd end up in pieces, pulled apart in countless different directions. Since *hypotasso* can also be translated as 'to unite one person with another', it could, therefore, in the context of both marriage and the church community, actually refer to living in harmony, peace and oneness with one another.

Hypotasso can also mean 'to remain in another's sphere of influence'. In chapter 2 of his Gospel, Luke tells how, unknown to his parents, the twelve-year-old Jesus stayed behind in the Temple in Jerusalem to study Scripture with the rabbis. When his parents eventually caught up with him, they took him back to Nazareth, where he was 'subject to them'. From his bar mitzvah, at the age of twelve, a Jewish boy is regarded as an adult spiritually and is responsible to God for his own good deeds or failures. Even so, from that moment on, Jesus did not necessarily do everything his parents said, but he lived happily within their sphere of influence and showed them the respect to which they were entitled.

In my dictionary, 'respect' is defined as 'an attitude of deference, admiration, or esteem'. Personally, I don't find the idea of admiring or esteeming my husband all that difficult – but then, I married a man of great faith, and I can't remember him ever persisting in anything that would seriously diminish my good opinion of him. But to judge by the success of Laura Doyle's book, *The Surrendered Wife*[14] which took America by storm in 2001 and is still selling some twenty years later, it would appear that in this age of self-fulfilment and expression, respect in marriage is not intrinsic, nor courtesy all that common. It should be noted, however, that this former marriage guru lived in Los Angeles where a marriage lasts as long as a computer, and self-development is the only antidote for self-loathing. One of the three women who agreed to take part in her therapy group filmed for television was a committed Christian, on to her third husband, and she wasn't too keen on him since he had put on a great deal of weight. It was imperative she learn to accept him and value him for who he was – but it didn't come naturally.

However much Laura Doyle may have claimed a new revelation for herself, some aspects of her concept of surrender have a biblical ring to them. 'People often say submissive wife instead of surrendered wife,' she said on the television programme, 'but submissive has the sub word in it which means below, so that word doesn't fit with me'. Surrender, on the other hand, she says, means to relinquish voluntarily.

Here it is again, raising its ugly head – the old *teshuqah*, the need to control and manipulate, in order for my wishes, needs and desires, my fulfilment to be delivered upon a plate. *Hypotasso* strikes at the heart of it, urging us instead to let go, give way and value our partner's opinion as much as our own. It has nothing to do with becoming a creeping Uriah Heep, but making a positive decision to acknowledge, appreciate and even embrace another person's perspective. That respect, maintains Paul, should be the hallmark of every Christian relationship. And don't he and I therefore both have 'relinquishing' to do at times?

I asked a group of friends one evening if they practised submitting to one another. Ruth, our youth worker, reflected, 'Well, there was that night we all went for an Indian when I really wanted a Chinese.' She meant it for a laugh, but as we unpacked it, her words began to appear less trite. Friends who love and trust each other submit to each other almost without thinking most of the time. When we don't, it is probably an indication of how shallow our relationships really are.

I tested out some of Laura Doyle's ideas against my own experience of marriage to see whether it worked. The surrendered wife, she says, relinquishes control ('I asked you to buy cabbage and you came back with chocolate biscuits? Well, what a lovely surprise, dearest!'); respects her man (better not to say over Sunday lunch, 'You lost it at the end of that sermon, my dear', and certainly not when guests are present); receives his gifts graciously (What gifts? He says he doesn't know what to buy); expresses vulnerability ('I really would appreciate your help in the kitchen, darling, when you can drag yourself away from your work'); admits when she needs help ('There's no need to lose your rag just because I've lost the word-processor toolbar – again!'); and takes good care of herself (I watch television cycling on an exercise bike, does that count?).

Some wins, some fails, but overall not a bad score, or so I thought, until I asked my daughter, Abby, whether she thought I was the archetypal surrendered wife and she laughed in my face. 'It doesn't need to work for you,' she explained, 'because your relationship doesn't depend on instructions. When you love someone, respect and kindness is instinctive.'

Encouraged, I asked her what she thought of Doyle's, 'For the greatest intimacy, agree with your husband's ideas even when it scares you.'

'That woman needs shooting,' she snapped back, and this was before her own marriage, when she happily rejected the notion that a surrendered wife should rely on her husband to handle the household finances. In their case, that would have been more than a scary prospect, and her husband was more than happy to bow to her better budgeting.

My spouse also found some of Laura Doyle's suggestions belittling. 'I married you because I knew you would stand up to me,' he said. True that when we first married I was disconcerted to find there was a right way for everything – even the arrangement of knives, forks and spoons in the cutlery drawer. I thought I must have a disordered mind and tended to accept everything my clever, highly organised husband said – until I realised his rationale was to do things exactly the way his mother always had.

'The worm finally turned,' my mother said, watching me with amusement when, along with reorganising the kitchen drawers and cupboards to suit my convenience, I began to challenge a number of his ideas.

It is unbelievably patronising to suggest the male ego is so fragile that disagreement of any kind will cause it to crumble into so many pieces that we won't be able to sit Humpty Dumpty back on his wall. Submission is not relinquishing responsibility. If I took that idea to its logical conclusion I'd never get a decent night's sleep. I had better explain. One of the greatest areas of disparity of preference in our marriage is over the sleeping arrangements. For some years I put up with a continental quilt, when the truth is, I hate them. It's probably because of some profound emotional damage done in babyhood, but I prefer being swaddled as tightly as possible in sheet and blankets. We have finally reached a not very satisfactory compromise – we have a sheet and a quilt. A far better idea might be single beds, but I cannot somehow yield to that symbol of a sexless, truly English marriage. My friend Pat says she cannot understand the way two entirely different activities have become so confused. 'Sleeping is one thing, and love-making entirely another.' She has a point, but it is in fact much harder to let the sun go down on your anger when your bodies are forced into contact, albeit by the tangles in the sheet, than if you have the means of preserving a glacial separateness. Touch speaks louder than so many words.

One night I found him in bed with his iPad. My surrender was admirable. 'If that thing can do for you what I can, then I shall take the hint and sleep elsewhere.' It went and I stayed, though it manages to wander back in from time to time – accompanied now by headphones.

To be fair, friends plagued by the temptation to dominate and manipulate their men, as Sarah and the matriarchs did, tell me they have been grateful for Laura Doyle. After all, the Apostle Peter says Sarah called Abraham 'lord', and holds her up as an example of godly obedience for women with non-Christian husbands. Sarah, obedient? Since God resigned himself to telling Abraham to do whatever his wife suggested, it looks very much as if the shoe were on the other foot.

In fact, the Greek word for 'obey' used by Peter in his letter means 'to listen carefully, or attentively', as Sarah does when she complies with Abraham's request to pose as his sister. But when King Abimelech makes off with her, God warns him, 'You are as good as dead because of the woman you have taken; she is a married woman' (Gen. 20:3). The normal Hebrew word for wife is *ishah*, but for once in the whole of the Old Testament, the root word translated here as wife is *ba'al,* or lord and master. So Sarah, on this occasion, is the mistress or woman-in-charge of Abraham's household and wellbeing.

The Greek word Peter uses for lord is *kurios*, which also means 'sir' or 'master'. In New Testament times this was a common form of address, for example the equivalent of today's 'Dear Sir' at the top of a letter. In other words, the term was a simple courtesy. As we have already seen, for good or ill, there were a number of attempts at mutual control in this marriage, causing near havoc.

What struck me about the three women in Laura Doyle's televised therapy group was that they were not kind to their men. They nagged and criticised them for not being what they wanted them to be, basically because they weren't satisfied with themselves. It is to the Ephesians that Paul also says, 'Be kind and compassionate to one another, forgiving each other, just as in Christ God forgave you' (Eph. 4:32). The measure of forgiveness we receive should be the measure we give and, however hard it can be, a partner is not exempt. There is little as liberating for any human being than to be totally accepted by someone who knows us exactly as we are, warts and pimples, foibles and failures. That is marriage for you – a lifetime of sharing your dirty laundry and bad habits, and a lifetime of living with it.

Sadly, however, down through the years, a number of men have not been averse to using the teachings of Paul to justify behaviour he would find totally unacceptable. No woman is required to surrender to or put up with any form of violence in the home. In fact, evidence suggests that removing herself from the situation altogether may be the only means to convince her husband to get the help and therapy he so badly needs.

Paul says a wife has as much control over her husband's body as he has over hers – and that truly was a revolutionary concept in Roman society. She, like he, is entitled to regular, satisfactory and exclusive sexual relations. 'The wife's body does not belong to her alone, but also to her husband; in the same way, the husband's body does not belong to him alone, but also to his wife' (1 Cor. 7:4, paraphrased). This is the only suggestion of authority or control in the marriage relationship, and it is mutual – a yielding in love of the most intimate part of one's being to the other.

And now for the men

A wife is lower than a slave, for a slave at least can be freed.

Aquinas

It is obvious from the writings of St Thomas Aquinas, the Dominican monk and great teacher of a theology owing a great deal more to Aristotle than biblical principles, that Roman thinking on marriage was alive and well in the mediaeval Church.

But subjugation is a pagan, not a Christian concept. Paul himself tells the Philippians that Jesus chose to become a servant. He washed his disciples' feet. He told them not to lord it over one another, and said that a child was greatest in the kingdom. This is the context for Paul's teaching on all relationships. His master was radical, and when it comes to marriage, so is Paul.

Imagine the faces of the Ephesians as his letter is read out. 'Wives, submit to your husbands.' The men nod in self-righteous approval, and look at their women knowingly. There has to be a limit to these newfangled liberties their wives are now taking. But in the next breath, 'Husbands, love your wives as Christ loved the Church and gave himself up for her,' and the smile is wiped off their faces. There is probably a stunned silence while the information is absorbed, then a gasp as the implications sink in. Paul is addressing a culture where men expect to wield the power. He is demanding a self-sacrifice of Christian men, unparalleled in Roman or even Jewish society. He is rejecting all the accepted stereotypes. Women are not the problem, which is how the text has been traditionally interpreted. The men are. And this is radical stuff.[15]

Christ laid down his life to liberate and release his Church. He nourishes, feeds, enables and resources it. He is *kephale* – its source of life. This clarifies the concept of headship and puts it into a league of its own. Theologian Colin Brown puts it this way:

> The headship and lordship of Christ does not consist in authoritarianism. Rather it is expressed precisely in self-giving. Likewise, the husband's headship is to be exercised in the same self-giving in which he lives out his new nature in Christ. The headship consists in a renunciation of all authoritarianism; the only subjection that it is to demand is self-subjection for love of the wife.[16]

How could Paul intend a man to have absolute power over his wife, when the Apostle has now disempowered the husband so completely? A man cannot be domineering, for he is no better than his master, and Christ modelled a radical new life of service.

I asked Peter how he understood headship and he said, 'I felt it was my religious duty to chaplain my children – to read the Scriptures and pray with them – and also to ensure that you felt fulfilled, whether you chose to work in or out of the home. I still feel I am the breadwinner, but that's probably just the accepted stereotype I was brought up with, and there is no personal crisis in the times you have earned more than me.'

Peter's role in helping our children develop their own relationship with Christ filled me with awe. I was always the sleeping partner. I just cannot wake up in the morning, and took the stories and the prayers in our big double bed lying down. But when we discussed his concept of 'chaplaincy' of his family, we both could see that it was based on a feeling of accountability to God for us, rather than any theology of 'headship', for nowhere does Paul actually refer to a man as the head of the family or home. That was an American 1960s idea, promoted by Larry Christenson in books like *The Christian Family*, a conservative backlash to the new phenomenon of women going out to work. I found it interesting that Peter still saw himself as the breadwinner. I did eventually earn quite a lot more than him, (that's not difficult when you're married to a clergyman!), though his job was more secure than mine and we lived in the tied house that came with it. He accepted the situation manfully – and enjoyed the benefits, which contributed to our buying a retirement summer home in France.

We once watched a couple ride a tandem swiftly and gracefully up a steep, narrow, cobbled hill.

'Wow,' I said to Peter, mind-blown with admiration, 'isn't that a great picture of marriage?'

'No good for you,' he said dismissively.

'Why not?'

'You'd hate always being on the back.'

Now why should he assume I would always be on the back, and not on the front? The old cultural traditions are alive and well in most of us, but it is dangerous not to see them for what they are, and to use the Bible to back them up. In today's society many men are not the major breadwinner; they may be unemployed. Nor is every woman called to be a mother. Many are single or cannot have children.

I just have to take my hat off to Paul. His teaching on marriage is an example of how timelessly apposite the Bible can be, and how all-encompassing and relevant Paul's vision was. It is woman, the natural communicator, with the skills to reduce a man to pulp with a few well-chosen words, who is told to respect, while man, warned at the Fall that his instinct will be to rule over women, is told to love, nurture and cherish. One must relinquish control, the other must relinquish power.

Yet despite the fact that Paul entrusts the role of sacrificial self-giving to the man, in almost every age since it has been seen as the woman's prerogative. It has been her job to release him, not just to be the hunter-gatherer, but to find self-fulfilment too, even if it reduced her to being a golf or football widow, or the skivvy in the family. Throughout history, marriage has rarely been as good for women as it has been for men, and even now, when I look at some of the marriages I know, on the whole the wife makes most of the compromises. Men are so single-minded and focussed – whether it be on their career, hobbies or sport – that they often unwittingly put themselves first. And how sad that, almost invariably, the Church has supported the cultural stereotype, rather than the radical message of redemption.

One hot afternoon in Ibiza, during the ritual afternoon tea with my parents-in-law under the shady pine trees of their lovely retirement home, my mother-in-law began to speak of her misery when my father-in-law left his job in Geneva and took a parish in Ashton-under-Lyne. They exchanged a flat overlooking Lac Léman for a monstrous Gothic vicarage that leaked every iota of heat their pockets could pour into it. 'Paul was always busy,' she said, 'the children unhappy. I never saw him. At one point I became suicidal.' This was a shattering revelation for my father-in-law, as much as it was for us. There was a long, awkward silence, until he suddenly interjected defensively, 'I had my work.' I'm not sure that after all these years, this was any comfort to her.

Social attitudes have changed. While the Church has been struggling to catch up with new attitudes to the role of women, society has been redefining what it means to be a man. Woman's new independence catapulted men into an identity crisis. Relinquishing power could in fact provide an unprecedented opportunity to lay down the burden of macho-ism and alpha-male-ism, the pressure of playing the omni-competent leader and breadwinner. Instead, they could be free to live in partnership with women, expressing their real fears and needs, sharing in the joys of raising the children. But I fear they have been conditioned to keep their emotions in check for so many generations, long before feminism threatened their social isolation, that it may be a while yet before all are fully coaxed out of the cage. However, COVID-19, with shared home-working, home-schooling, home-running, may just be the catalyst to a new order

– for those who enjoyed it. Unless they revert with a sigh of relief to the old ways. Or rush to the solicitor for divorce papers. On the other hand, there seems to be some evidence, certainly from young women I have met, that the coronavirus may have stalled their careers, as the major burden of childcare, home-schooling and domestic duties landed, as ever, on their shoulders.

A survey published in the first week of July 2001, still the biggest study into 23.1 million British men,[17] and borne out by virtually every survey since (though COVID-19 might have broken the mould), showed that the new man was a figment of the imagination. Men still weren't sharing in the cooking and cleaning, or looking after the children. Personally, I think watching a family picnic on the beach provides all the research we need. Who heaves the food hamper around, organises the plastic plates and sandwiches, feeds the dog, wipes the children's noses and towels them down when they come out of the sea? Who has remembered a change of trunks and swimsuit? Where's Dad? Half a mile away playing frisbee or organising beach cricket. So which of the genders is the more organised, logical and rational?

Marriage is a challenge for men. It can demand a great deal of women. But our very differences make it an adventure. Paul stresses that Christian marriage is very special. It must be distinctive – to challenge the lifestyle of those around us, to protect fidelity and loyalty, to prove that this is the best, the most wholesome way to live. That's why he also warns those of us who have been entrusted with such a gift, that it is our duty and our calling, insofar as we are able, to make it last.

Till death do us part

Marriage should be honoured by all, and the marriage bed kept pure, for God will judge the adulterer and all the sexually immoral.

(Heb. 13:4)

Society is obsessed with the notion that monogamy means monotony, and would like to believe that the trade-in of a tired relationship carries no consequences, but Paul couldn't be clearer about our responsibilities if he tried.

We once laid on a Valentine's Day dance and buffet at our church to celebrate romance in marriage.

'If ever there was an oxymoron, that must be it,' said the journalist from the BBC local radio station. 'What do those two words have in common?'

It was a night to remember all the same – and that from folk who rarely darkened our door.

Generation X-ers, a term used to describe anyone born between 1960 and 1985, have a tendency to dispose of what no longer meets their needs. A Generation X Lifestyle survey revealed that 84 per cent of non-Christian young people, and 97 per cent of their Christian counterparts, thought marriage should be for life.[18] So far so good. But then 68 per cent of non-Christians and 32 per cent of Christians agreed that it should only last as long as a couple loved each other, and that divorce was a perfectly acceptable way out, demonstrating, once again, the wide chasm that exists between our ideologies and the reality of living them out. This looks a lot like consumer marriage. The relationship is expendable, to be crumpled up and flushed away when it becomes dull or difficult, or a better offer appears on the scene.

But then, many Generation-Xers haven't had a model of a happy long-term relationship. And that can make it hard to understand how good marriage can be, and why it might be worth every ounce of dedication a human being can muster.

Among Christians, the divorce rate is as high as it is in the rest of society. And the Church is far from immune to adultery. There's an old Jewish saying: 'A sin repeated seems permitted.' Society's self-indulgence whittles away our resistance. On several occasions my husband has been shocked to hear the perpetrator see no reason why he shouldn't bring a new partner to church, in full view of the deserted spouse and children. Writing in *The Times*, journalist Libby Purves said:

This British willingness to ditch relationships, once they cease to feel good all day long, is linked to the juvenile romantic idea that sexual desire is 'bigger than both of us' and inevitably leads to the arrival of a removal van. This creed is rarely a source of happiness ... And with the new religion of 'non-judgementalism', there is no social punishment for prising a parent from the family hearth.[19]

And there is no way any of us can sit in judgement. 'Pride comes before a fall', and all the other proverbs and truisms we know so well and ignore at our peril, have a terrible way of wreaking vengeance on those of us too arrogant to believe it could ever happen to us. On the other hand, those who suggest that couples who survive have some kind of innate luck and have never known temptation are living on another planet. I have crawled to the edge of that yawning abyss and peeped over, but God, in his great mercy, got hold of me by the scruff of the neck and yanked me back – just as he had to drag Lot unceremoniously out of Sodom and Gomorrah. And have I been thankful for it over the years.

Peter and I have made it a principle to tell each other when we're finding someone else attractive. It seems the most effective way of killing temptation quickly. The first time I dared mention it, Peter simply said, 'I thought you'd been a bit distracted. Don't worry. I know you love me.' And immediately I thought, 'Of course I love this wonderful man, now and forever. Who wouldn't? What an idiot I am.' How could I hurt beyond reason a man who has only ever sought my best, or the children who expect my best, or the community to which I belong and which would be destroyed by any betrayal?

The Hebrew word for marriage is *kiddushim*, a plural variation of the word *kaddosh* or 'holy'. 'Holy' for the Jew does not mean 'put on a pedestal', or in a glass box, removed from the nitty-gritty of everyday life. On the contrary, 'holy' means special, a unique gift of God to be enjoyed and appreciated to the maximum by those to whom it is given. A marriage is not to be shared by anyone but the couple. Intruders tread on holy ground at their peril, and that includes parents and children, as well as work colleagues, neighbours, and that acquaintance on the number 42 bus.

It is a closeness that can feel claustrophobic at times, though. While women usually have a wide selection of female friends who meet a variety of their different emotional and social needs, men tend to rely solely on a wife for friendship and intimacy. Particularly since Peter's retirement, I find myself longing for my own space – just for a while. A week or even two might be nice, as long as I know it is temporary. There are times when marriage seems to interfere with my freedom to do as I want when I want and the sacrifice feels hard.

I gave up a full-time career in the media when we moved to Lancaster, where there was no media being made, and found myself instead, for a number of weeks, stripping wallpaper, polyfilling and painting almost twenty-four hours a day. Our large vicarage with its high ceilings had been rewired, but left undecorated, it was a dank, dark shell of torn wallpaper and bare plaster. 'And we don't even own the blinking house,' I exploded one night, hurling my brush across the room. My hands were rougher than sandpaper, my nails broken off, there were bits of paint in my hair and wallpaper in my mouth. 'I've had enough,' I yelled. 'I'm going.'

'Where?' asked Peter.

'Home,' I said.

'Where's that?' he asked, as I made for the door.

At that point, I realised, feeling stupid, that I didn't know where home was any more. I had nowhere to go. So I sat instead in the middle of the floor, wondering what to do. I had never felt so miserable in my life, so certain I wanted out – of marriage, motherhood and ministry. What had any of them done for me? One or two ideas of possible boltholes formed in my mind, friends who would have me for a week, or two, perhaps longer.

I was on my way to the phone when I remembered the children sleeping upstairs. We had only just moved. They were disoriented too, adjusting to new schools, while living on a building site. They needed me. So did Peter, even if he needed a painter and decorator more at that precise moment. I couldn't simply walk out on my responsibilities. Good, old-fashioned words like loyalty, perseverance, for better for worse, flooded into my mind, blow them, apparently from nowhere, and demanded acquiescence, even though it was through gritted teeth. I had the power to bring love, life and peace to this little household – or I could smash it apart. So reluctantly I went in search of the turps. I still have a patch of hair, about the size of a penny, that turned white overnight with the stress of those few weeks. But in the end, I was glad I hadn't run away. Real faith is so often about the will, and not just the emotions, what we do rather than what we feel, and the rewards are often immeasurable. Home for me was wherever Peter and the children were.

One of the most helpful things ever said to me was that we fall in and out of love many times in a marriage. On occasions the spark may seem too feeble to survive, then suddenly, in the right environment, it bursts into flame all over again. Woe betide any outsider who wilfully sets out to extinguish that spark when it may be at its most fragile. For when a partner of more than twenty, thirty, forty years still has the power to induce the most mind-blowing, stomach-lurching passion, then marriage is as God intended it – the most liberating, joyful relationship ever given to human beings.

I am thankful I chose a truly monogamous man. I could never have trusted a womaniser and flirt, a man who needed the adulation of the opposite sex to fill a deep hole at his centre, and who subjected his wife to the whispered sympathy and pity of all their acquaintances. Instead I have been given a man who truly tries to live out the Apostle Paul's encouragement to love, nurture and encourage his wife as Christ loves the Church, who silently puts up with the dints and scratches on the back bumper of the car, valiantly corrects my manuscripts, graciously polishes my scuffed-looking boots, and endlessly sorts out my messes on the computer.

At our wedding, in the middle of his sermon, Alex Buchanan, the preacher, well known in those days for his extraordinary gift of prophecy, said, 'Partings there will be when the way of the cross demands it.' In the car, on our way to our honeymoon, I said to Peter, 'So, you're going to travel a lot.'

'No,' he said, and we promptly forgot all about it.

No one could have been more surprised than I was when, after writing a book or two, I began to get invitations to speak all over the country. So much for darning his socks and ironing his shirts. I was away from home almost every week. It wasn't easy for either of us. I took the babies with me and fed them in some very odd places. When they were too big to take, I left them behind with Dad, who, they complained, fed them some very odd food. I hated leaving Peter to look after them and missed them terribly. I was consumed with guilt at times. Not only the prophecy, but also the words spoken so unthinkingly that evening at St John's Theological College certainly came true in our experience. At different times our different ministries took priority. We were called to release each other. But as we did, an almost perverse law came into operation. The more we let go, the more we had to give. Our different worlds each enriched the other.

What we do for love

I know very little about a certain missionary wife called Mme Coillard, except this wonderful story that seems to capture the essence of what marital love can be. The Coillards were missionaries in South Africa in the middle of the nineteenth century, and had apparently witnessed scenes of shocking barbarity during the first Boer War. Their ministry required they work apart for a great deal of the time, so any time together was a joyous, precious gift.

One particular year they agreed to meet up to celebrate their wedding anniversary at a little hut in Leribe. Meanwhile, she was at Harrismith negotiating wood for the mission buildings, while he was on a speaking tour. Between them ran the treacherous waters of the River Caledon.

When she reached the stream, the waters were in high flood. She was told that her husband had been swept away and drowned as he tried to cross to her. This was likely to be true, since drownings were a frequent occurrence. But when she discovered he was still alive, she made up her mind to get across to him, whatever it took, and off she strode into the heaving waves. Two powerful Zulus ran after her, took one arm each and carried her, while several swam in front of and behind her, to hold her up if the others tired or failed. Silently and resolutely, the little band pressed on, fighting against the current. From the opposite bank her husband could only stand and watch in amazement and terror, as only the head and shoulders of his wife appeared above the flood. At last they all reached the shallows and

Mme Coillard lifted her skirts and ran out to him, drenched and exhausted, but triumphant. She thanked and blessed each of the Zulus, changed into a riding habit and rode with her husband to their little turf hut at Leribe.[20]

This must surely go down in history as one of the bravest, most determined attempts to celebrate a wedding anniversary, and I have no doubt it was worth it. If Mme Coillard is the practical embodiment of something resembling positive, wifely submission, I think I could live with it.

Part 3

The Contemporary Woman – Living with the Legacy

Chapter 7

The Sexual Woman

If, in biblical terms, woman's inheritance is the privilege of speaking life into her world, how do we live it out in our contemporary corner of the globe, in our homes, roles, relationships, and workplaces? First, we have to come to terms with one of our fiercest critics – ourselves. We have to make peace with our bodies, and that can be very difficult when we feel constantly judged and found wanting.

Sexy or asexual?

Probably no man has ever troubled to imagine how strange his life would appear to himself if it were unrelentingly assessed in terms of his maleness; if everything he wore, said or did had to be justified by reference to female approval; if he were compelled to regard himself, day in day out, not as a member of society, but merely as a virile member of society. If the centre of his dress-consciousness were the codpiece, his education directed to making him a spirited lover and meek paterfamilias; his interests held to be natural only in so far as they were sexual. If from school and lecture room, press and pulpit, he heard the persistent outpouring of a shrill and scolding voice, bidding him remember his biological function. If he were vexed by continual advice on how to add a rough male touch to his typing, how to be learned without losing his masculine appeal, how to combine chemical research with seduction, how to play bridge without incurring the suspicion of impotence. If, instead of allowing with a smile that 'women prefer cavemen', he felt the unrelenting pressure of a whole social structure forcing him to order all his goings in conformity with that pronouncement.[1]

Dorothy Sayers, plea in the 1940s for women to be treated by the same standards as men, rather than by their sexual attractions, certainly had a contemporary ring to it for many years to come. After all, it was only in the 1980s, during the debate in the Church of England Synod on the ordination of women, that one churchman argued, 'Women, unlike men, radiate sex and their temperament is inappropriate in church ... Their ordination would introduce distractions and earthiness into worship.'[2]

A long-retired bishop told Sue Lawley on Radio 4 that he was very afraid that if he saw a woman ministering the sacrament, he would be tempted to take her into his arms. His own particular fancy appeared to be dangly earrings, but he could just as well have said fishnet tights and suspenders. Or perhaps he was using the old temptress argument for the occasional exposé of one of his clergy in the tabloids. At least he didn't make any pretence of a theological foundation for his arguments. It didn't seem to occur to him he was demeaning most of his own sex, who are not so overcome by the presence of women in the workplace that they make unacceptable advances to their colleagues several times a day. Nor that some women have also found the man in the dog collar attractive, but deal with it appropriately.

A few days after the first women were ordained, the *Daily Mail* ran a feature on the Rev. Joy Carroll, the inspiration for the Vicar of Dibley, complete with a large photograph of her in miniskirt, dark hair tumbling over her shoulders – and the inevitable, large swinging earrings. Her mail for the following few days was full, not of offers, but of complaints – from both men and women. The reasons for their objections were not very clear. Like the early church fathers, they simply reflected the 2,000-year-old discomfort with any mix of body and spirit, secular and sacred. This schizoid division, known as dualism, was the legacy of Platonic philosophy, not New Testament theology, and it did women a great deal of damage. Here is Tertullian (AD 160–240), an early Christian writer from Carthage in the Roman-dominated province of Africa:

And do you not know that you are Eve? The sentence of God on this sex of yours lives in this age: the guilt must of necessity live too. You are the devil's gateway: you are the unsealer of that tree: you are the first deserter of the divine law: you are she who persuaded him whom the devil was not so valiant enough to attack. You destroyed so easily God's image, man. On account of your desert – that is, death – even the Son of God had to die. And yet you think of nothing but covering your gowns in jewellery? You should always go about in mourning and in rags.

Beset by temptation, Tertullian and his fellow fathers of the faith felt revulsion for their sexual fantasies, and projected their anger on to the object of their desire. The early fathers persuaded themselves that a women's sexuality gave her magic powers and that the male was her helpless victim. Woman is temptress, seductress and sorceress, responsible for all the misery in the world. Man, noble, good and pure, alone created in God's image, has been deprived of his greatness, not through his own sin, but through the sin of woman. He is tainted, demeaned and reduced merely by contact with her. By the third century, Augustine spoke with disgust of the shame that attends all sexual intercourse. Saint Jerome believed marriage was not only detrimental, but also harmful.

This negativity towards sexual feelings continued throughout the history of the Church. Today, many male ministers continue to disguise their sexuality in black and grey, badly fitting suits, unfortunate socks and shaggy haircut. That same pressure seems to have transferred itself by some kind of osmosis to an army of older women ministers, who hide any hint of femininity behind an asexual tweed jacket and brogues. But then, they are damned if they are sexy, and damned for being unfeminine if they are not, so they can't win.

Certainly in the 1980s and 1990s, before women were ordained, I sat on a number of diocesan committees, the only woman in a room full of dog-collared males, and was treated as if I wasn't there. Women were invisible, and it felt as if the Church had lost a limb. It was certainly disabled. Decisions were never as effective without a feminine perspective.

It is hardly surprising, then, that their bodily existence is where women are most vulnerable, most subject to abuse, most easily stripped of their confidence. Over the centuries their sexuality has been used in myriad ways to deny them equality and keep them from crashing through the glass ceiling – in misconceptions and fears about periods, incessant pregnancies, the menopause, restrictive fashions and accusations of either physical weakness or unfeminine, unattractive behaviour.

Male leaders of institutions, in industry, government, education, the NHS or even the Church, have sometimes handled their fear of the opposite sex, or even of their own sexual feelings, by openly denying women access to leadership roles, or by flirting with them to undermine their authority. To desexualise or over-sexualise a woman has the same effect. It devalues and dehumanises her. And when women resort to female wiles to achieve their own ends, they devalue themselves. There is a certain amount of innocent flirtation and play in most creative male-female relationships, but when sex becomes a weapon, the game is over. So, how do we find our way through the bewildering mixed messages that bombard us on every side, and rejoice in our sexual selves?

Marie Stopes and the bizarre road to freedom

When Marie Stopes opened the first birth control clinic in March 1921, little did she guess at the freedoms contraception would eventually give to millions of ordinary women. Initially, the clinics were intended for married women only. Stopes had written her guide to 'Married Love' in 1918 and it included a chapter on birth control. It was so controversial that no publisher would touch it, but when her husband-to-be paid to have it published it went into five editions in the first year.

She founded the Society for Constructive Birth Control and Racial Progress in the same year. Its aims were to counteract 'the steady evil . . . of the reduction of the birth rate on the part of the thrifty, wise, well-contented, and generally sound members of our community', and to prevent 'the reckless breeding from the C.3 end, and the semi-feebleminded, the careless, who are proportionately increasing in our community', because of the slowing birth rate at the other end of the social scale. Its methods were the 'racial' cervical cap, advice on coitus interruptus and spermicides of soap and olive oil, and they proved to be surprisingly effective.[3]

There was, it seems, a side to this heroine of women's liberty that was completely unacceptable. Stopes was a eugenicist. She believed in a superior white race, and that the ignorant, the diseased and the feckless poor should be stopped from procreating because of the degenerate children they were bound to produce. Ideally, she would have liked the sterilisation of women who were prone to drunkenness and of bad character, 'the feeble minded and insane', Jews and half-castes. This was largely why her clinics, which faced sustained opposition, were opened in areas of high urban deprivation and poverty.

She tried to win over the bishops of the Church of England to her cause, calling herself a prophet. They, in turn, passed a resolution against 'the deliberate cultivation of sexual union' and against 'the open or secret sale of contraceptives'. The Catholic Church was even more opposed to her work, and fought her for the rest of her life.

But in the end, God had the last laugh. It was contraception that paved the way for those most denied opportunity because of their reproductive system to benefit most from her work.

When I started my first job as a detached youth worker on the streets of Manchester in the 1970s, becoming pregnant was the only way most teenage black women could find attention, status, a council flat and something to love and be truly loved by – even if that meant throwing education out of the window. Some twenty-five years later, when I became the local communications lead for Blackpool with the national campaign to reduce teenage pregnancy by 50 per cent, young women, particularly black young women, were seriously taking up the offer of free contraception, as they were discovering that education offered a passage to a much more influential future, and ambition was the best form of contraception. Ironic that a eugenicist and supporter of Hitler was the pioneer who pushed open the door.

All the evidence shows that giving young people information actually delays their first sexual encounter, yet the myth persisted, often propagated by religious groups, that educating them will encourage promiscuity. In fact, not all under-seventeens have a sexual relationship, or want it. Many of the girls I met in Blackpool, given a rare opportunity to talk honestly, admitted there wasn't much pleasure in being bounced against a wall like a rag doll for however long it took for a young man to find satisfaction – fortunately, not very long. In areas of social exclusion, where teenage pregnancy rates were the highest, sex was the cheapest form of entertainment – unless it led to infection, HIV or an unwanted baby. But when they acknowledge that it isn't quite the fun it is made out to be, who will tell these young women about pleasure as God intended it?

Sex-obsessed or silent?

I was never so aware of the need to answer this question as when I had a daughter, and wanted her to grow up without the guilt, shame and disgust I saw in so many women of my mother's generation; who tried to pass it on to mine. Desire was rarely acknowledged – except that it got you into trouble. All I was told about the facts of life was that an unwanted pregnancy was the worst that could happen to you, or rather, the family's reputation. A lack of accurate information, unrealistic expectations and fear led to disappointment. For some of my contemporaries, sex became something to be endured rather than enjoyed and ended abruptly at the menopause or even sooner – possibly because it never brought any pleasure in the first place, largely because women were taught not to say what it was they wanted. Morecambe and Wise were once asked on radio the secret of their relationship. 'It's just like a typical British marriage, without the sex,' Eric Morecambe said. There was a pause. 'In fact, it's just like a typical British marriage.'

When I worked for the NHS, the Psychosexual Counselling Service opened and, once some bright spark was inspired to remove the sign from the door, attracted a large clientele. In fact, judging from the demand, we are not as sexually educated and liberated as we think we are. If Virginia Nicholson is right,[4] that the pill led many men to believe women were as up for sex as they were and that they could have what they wanted when they wanted it, then it might well have been a mixed blessing. Why work at being a creative, imaginative, intelligent lover if sex was available without effort or skill? No need to sharpen up their technique.

The media portrays couples bonking almost on acquaintance. They achieve simultaneous orgasm in five seconds. They have to. Programme makers have one aim – to stop us switching channels or reaching for the off button, and they know that if we were to be subjected to the realistic length of time decent foreplay takes, boredom would drive us to channel hop before the heavy breathing even begins. And yet young people swallow most of what the media tells them.

A previous Archbishop of Canterbury, George Carey, claimed that society was obsessed with sex. Society might be, but the Church certainly isn't. Even today, apart from one or two delicate references in the marriage service, sex is rarely mentioned in sermons or youth teaching programmes, and young people are left to assume they were found under the nearest gooseberry bush, or if there was a moment of passion that led to their sitting in the pew, it was an unfortunate incident over and done with a long time ago. We expect them to pick up Christian morality and values by osmosis, but what they actually pick up tend to be our negative vibes. A Lancaster student once said to us, 'You tell us to wait, but never tell us if it's worth waiting for.' He was right – and we do young people a great disservice.

If sex is merely recreational, it becomes non-relational. The Greco-Roman-based Western tradition is that feelings, mind and body are three distinct parts of the human being and function separately. Emotion is often disengaged from the sex act altogether today. Love has little or no part to play in the giving of the body. It means the participant can become a spectator. How does he/she compare with all the others I've had? Was he/she worth the effort? Do I ever want us to meet up again, and how would I feel if we did? No awareness here of the commitment, the work, the practice necessary to make the earth really move.

And the mind can be the body's greatest critic, not its greatest fan. Mine keeps reminding me that I'm getting old, that the sags, folds and broken veins make me look like a page in a road atlas. Then it whispers that my man couldn't possibly still fancy me. He's probably fantasising he's with some delicious, leggy young blonde. And I lament the youthful body I have lost, until he tells me that however much a gorgeous young woman in a tiny miniskirt might almost blow his fuses, he only truly desires me – and shows it. And little else does a woman's sense of wellbeing as much good as that. Viva long-term relationships! We should be singing their praises from the rafters, while recognising at the same time that not everyone is given such a great gift.

Many people are not in a sexual relationship. And some are more at ease with their sexuality than their married friends, who have a cover for not facing up to a negative self-image. The very nature of celibacy forces them to confront who they are, how they feel about their bodies and how they relate to the opposite sex. One of my great heroes on the subject of sexuality was the Roman Catholic priest Jean Vanier, who founded L'Arche communities for people with special needs. In *Man and Woman, He Made Them*, he described the wonder and healing of both the sexual love between two people with special needs and the platonic love between celibate individuals living in a close community. He believed society's unhealthy emphasis on what he calls 'genital sexuality' is a result of the disappearance of community life and the ties of true friendship.

In 2020 the late Father Vanier was accused of sexually abusing six women. His theology transformed the hearts and minds of multitudes. His ideal was to provide loving, joyful, colourful, committed communities where women and men, able-bodied and those with special needs could come together as male and female and celebrate their sexuality in its widest sense. And it was a wonderful vision – for if sexuality is about self-acceptance at its deepest level, integrating our body with the rest of our being, enjoying the many sensations of pleasure it can yield, if it means loving ourselves so that we can love others, then Christianity has a great deal to offer. Yet I fear his vision may have died with the man because of his foolish, destructive, abusive inability to live out the dream. And so the dourness, coldness and silence of the Church's history on the subject lives on. And young people find little panacea there for their alienation, isolation and self-doubt, and turn elsewhere for what looks like a better offer. I didn't want that for my daughter. And I shall let her have her say.

Me and my body

Our real obsession – to the point of neurosis – is with body image. Society whittles sex down to its lowest common denominator – whether we get it or not, and defines sexuality as the way in which we get it, but sexuality in its broadest sense is about how comfortable we feel in the skin God has created for us. And the truth is, we don't always like, let alone enjoy, what we are. That is the real reason why the subject is so loaded.

Our deep ambivalence about sexuality is reflected in the change in woman's image in the last seventy years. Before 1960 the media portrayed the ideal woman as homely and non-sexual, in pinny and slippers, a competent housewife, a brilliant cook, a devoted wife and mother. After 1960 and the advent of the contraceptive pill, there was a complete reversal of standards. Today, in every magazine, on every billboard, women are young and gorgeous, free from blemish and flab. Men can be middle-aged icons, if they still have hair, no beer belly and look like George Clooney, but it is only now, in the twenty-first century, after years of the aging vanishing trick, that women too can have a longer shelf life.

Our daughter, Abby, grew up in a fairly traditional family unit, though not as nuclear as some, for a vicarage child also belongs to the church, and has the benefit – and the pressure – of being part of a fairly close-knit community with a great deal of peer support and a host of positive adult role models. But was that enough to help her make wise choices? From the moment she was born, I was determined she would grow up free from the negativity about her body that seems to pursue most human beings, but especially young women. Instinct told me that the better her body image, the less the impetus to share it around. Only a girl who needed to prove her attraction to herself would give it away without deep heart-searching first.

I used every tool known to a mother to keep the demons of self-loathing at bay. Throughout her childhood I told her repeatedly that she was beautiful, and I didn't have to lie. She was. And it wasn't simply a matter of looks. She was instinctively thoughtful, loving and giving, naturally joyful and vivacious. She didn't need to improve on nature, knock her body into shape or conform to any expectations.

I didn't realise that dissatisfaction with a newly emerging body was a highly contagious teenage disease, for which there is as yet no effective vaccination – not until I read this poem she wrote at a creative writing event at school.

Pleasure or Pain?

Waxing, bleaching, crying, screeching.
Pleasure or pain?
Needles and pins to cover our skins,
Rods and rings through different things.
Pleasure or pain?
Sugaring and shaving, dieting, craving,
Nature waning, money draining.
Pleasure or pain?
Gimmicks and creams to fill us with dreams,
Struggling for beauty beyond calls of duty.
Puffing and panting, raving and ranting,
Desperate to meet the standard, but find that you're stranded
Between pleasure and pain.
Highlights or lowlights? Lemon? Or egg-whites?
Curly or straight: heated debate
Or rollers.
Spot cream and nail file, perfume and hair style,
Pleasure or pain?
Skin cream and make-up as soon as we wake up.
Lipstick for pride, at least on the outside.
Teeth straight and white, reflecting the light,
A dazzling smile for an insecure child
Hiding.
Pleasure? Or pain.

Abby Guinness, aged 17

For teenagers, every extraneous pimple or blemish is a major disaster. So had I lost the battle? Where had 'Pleasure or pain' come from? Abby continued,

I was struck by inspiration one night as I sat with mud on my face, grease on my hair and streaky tan on my legs. The ooze of my situation made me wonder if it really deserved the title of 'pampering'. It seemed more a kind of masochism that all females must ritually indulge in.

. I was fully qualified in titivation by the time I was seventeen, and realised it must have been inspired by my mother. Who else? She was the queen of make-up, and her publicity photograph for BBC radio was fondly known as 'The Jewellery Advert' – a real Jewish Mama, and I wouldn't have her any other way.

Hair removal, filing my nails, make-up: I learnt them all from her. But copying her wasn't always straightforward. When I was nine she marched me to the bathroom and before I was allowed to leave the house, made me scrub off the make-up I had put on. I was only allowed to pierce my ears when I was twelve. I pierced my belly button when I was sixteen – without her permission.

It was Mum who first plucked my eyebrows while I lay on her bed, straining to keep my eyes open and feeling hot tears roll into my ears. She demanded that we follow 'the natural line of the brow'. When I gathered the courage to do it myself I found it hurt less and was satisfying, until I was baring uneven and ridiculous eyebrows. They grew back and the next time I followed 'the natural line of the brow'.

The poem born on that night felt like frustration with men, who demand such perfection of us. On further reflection, I don't believe they do. Some have categorically told me they don't and were surprised I should think so. It seems that women competitively encourage it in each other. Or maybe it was just my own frustration at striving to be like my mother.

Happily, Abby's awareness of that particular frustration helped her to ditch it and my silly vanities, and become her own person. All the same, it goes to show that we can never take anyone further than we have been ourselves – especially our children, for, unlike other acquaintances, they have access to our hidden side, and an unfortunate tendency to inherit our neuroses as well as our allergies. But if we dump our weaknesses and failures on our daughters, rather than own up to them honestly and openly, they can do more long-term damage.

My mother openly told friends and acquaintances that I was the least attractive of her three children. I still remember her telling me to 'put a bit of lippy' on before we went out, in case an eligible man just happened to cross our path. Unfortunately, she sighed, I had inherited my father's looks. And I was a plump and plain teenager with frizzy hair and a sallow complexion. I felt unattractive, especially after one of the boys at my brother's school shouted 'Ugly Yid' at me. Ugly words – how they mess with our heads. And how vital to reject their negative consequences if we are not to pass them on to the next generation.

My obsession with 'putzing', as the Jews call it in Yiddish, was, I suspect, an attempt to surprise my mother. And some of the unpleasant little boys at the Grammar School. The German means 'to brush or preen'. The Oxford English Dictionary describes it as 'to engage in inconsequential or unproductive activity', and that's a great translation of the Yiddish word for the hours spent in front of the mirror trying to improve on nature. On the other hand, when my mother's Aunt Rae began to register my existence with a 'Greatly Improved' every time she saw me, it was a source of great satisfaction – even if it was the best of backhanded compliments.

I am delighted that as Abby threw off her teenage years she also threw off the pressurising Jewish Mama gene and became her own woman. Yes, it was a huge surprise, but a necessary and wonderful one. But then, even as an adolescent, she seemed aware of the challenges and consequences of an obsession with image. So perhaps some of the spoken wisdom did get through after all.

I don't want my Mum or anyone else to think I am scarred by negative body image. Despite the pressures of society with its constant debate about the effect of waif-like models in fashion and advertising, I feel positive about my body. I admit a great deal of it is luck. I do have a good figure, thanks to my genes and a healthy lifestyle. I worry much more about an unpredictable complexion and Neanderthal hairiness than I do about fighting flab.

During my teenage years the worries about my appearance were very real and very time-consuming.

I had a friend at school who was crushed and almost seriously damaged by a boyfriend who told her that she should lose weight. She started to take diet pills and have highly erratic eating habits. There was nothing that I or my other friends could say or do to redeem the situation. His opinion was worth ten of ours.

Another friend in the same group was crippled by low self-esteem and constantly miserable, until eventually a few blokes showed an interest. Most of them treated her abysmally, but the seeds were sown; she knew she wasn't repulsive and a transformation occurred.

I spoke recently to a young teenager mortified by her appearance because the boys she liked weren't interested in her. But however much I spouted my past experience and told her to wait because the time would come, it didn't help. All she needed was a man to tell her she was attractive. And that isn't always going to happen at fourteen.

It has to be true that having faith in a God who loves you unconditionally is the basis of self-worth. I hated reading *Bridget Jones's Diary*, because the ultimate conclusion seems to be that getting a man is the only way to find personal fulfilment. But just as Mum admits that when you have a husband you rely less on God, knowing that God loves you will not give you the same rush of pride that you get from a wolf-whistle or someone calling you beautiful. So, much as I hate to admit it, and as adamant as I am that relationships should only be attempted when both parties are able to stand alone, men and women are co-dependent because they find their self-confidence in each other.

Although I had never explained it to her, it seems the old *teshuqah,* that need to appeal to a man, simply will not leave a girl alone, even though Abby recognised early on that there is no accounting for taste or chemistry, that handsome men don't necessarily marry pretty women, and pretty women don't necessarily marry handsome men, and that the most gorgeous people may not be in a relationship. But in today's celebrity-conscious world, it's a hard truth to convey – despite the fact that the heir to the British throne preferred an older, plainer model to the very beautiful woman he had married.

When Peter went into the local comprehensive school to do a marriage seminar, he thought that after two hours he had managed to convey the superiority of character over charisma. But when he asked the pupils to list what they were looking for in a life partner, 'good looks' was still top of the list.

Body and soul

Advice to Daughters

Beware the men who seek
the soft and changing tone
and overlook the bleak
white armature of bone.

He is a fool who loves
only the dimpled face.
It is the bone that moves
ungainly, or with grace
to fill a singing space.

And time will come and hone
his sharp and eager beak
upon the flesh alone,
and then the bone will speak.[5]

Evangeline Paterson

The only person in the Bible to win anything because of their physical attractiveness is Esther. Her reward for winning a beauty competition may be a Persian king, and though it enables her to save thousands of lives, it's a booby prize if ever there was one. Leah, with the squint, becomes a great matriarch. The prophet Isaiah says of the Messiah, 'He had no beauty or majesty to attract us to him', and that there was 'nothing in his appearance that we should desire him' (Isaiah 53:2). In other words, no matter how he has been portrayed, Jesus came with no Hollywood appeal to make us fancy or follow him.

The Bible goes out of its way to make the point that looks count for nothing, so they obviously exerted a similar influence centuries ago as they do today. When Samuel goes to the house of Jesse to pick a king for Israel, he is automatically drawn to the tall, fashionably dark, macho older boys, not the little red-headed runt of the pack who is out minding the sheep. 'Don't let physical appearance be your guide,' God says to Jesse. 'I don't look at what people value most. They look at the outside. But I look at what is in the heart' (1 Sam. 16:7, paraphrased). God always did love King David's heart, for he was filled with humility and grace, and remained loyal and true to the very end. Whatever his looks, those qualities made him a very attractive human being.

It is this real 'me' that outlives the body, which, however gorgeous, slowly falls apart. At 75, Hugh Hefner, founder of the *Playboy* magazine empire, kept a harem of seven, almost identical, live Barbie dolls. To remain with him they had to stay exactly as they were and never grow old.

'And what will you do when age gets the better of you?' Ruby Wax asks them in a TV documentary.[5]

'It won't happen for ages,' they mew.

'But it will,' she pushes.

'Not with plastic surgery,' they insist.

The Apostle Paul's recipe for eternal beauty is much less surgical, though it can be radical and costly. It involves remaining God-focussed throughout our life. We become more, not less, attractive as the years go by, transformed on the inside from one degree of glory to another, until, eventually, we become the very image of him (2 Cor. 3:18). 'She's the image of her father,' they used to say of me when I was a little girl. I liked it because I loved my dad.

It is an illusion to think that eventually we will become disembodied spirits floating through the ether. The New Testament is clear that we will have new, perfect, identifiable bodies. So coming to terms with our bodily identity is more important than simply enabling us to function better in the here and now.

Adam and Eve didn't have a body image problem. God was pleased with his design, and they were merrily naked. But after the Fall, when women came to be valued for their reproductive capacity, physical attraction inevitably began to matter. Enter the fear of rejection. It is almost as if a gene is passed through the generations that urges us to mistrust, not enjoy, what God has made. Instead of filling us with a sense of delight and wonder, our bodies have become a source of embarrassment and shame.

I still get angry with the gynaecologist who left me with a long horizontal scar across my lower middle many moons ago. Why didn't he offer me other ways to treat fibroids rather than the hysterectomy that created a long dint just above the pubic bone with flesh hanging over it? It left me feeling self-conscious in bathing costume and bikini, not to mention with the inevitable irritable bowel syndrome that blights most women after their innards are yanked out and stuffed back in again, and causes embarrassing, unladylike farting. What really makes me angry is that it never once occurred to him that I would mind the savaging of my figure and femininity. Like a plumber, he dealt purely and simply with a malfunction of the system and thought I ought to be grateful.

And if that's how I feel about a hysterectomy scar, how must it be for the women who endure the trauma of breast cancer, or even face or mouth cancer? Many years ago I made a television programme about a woman minister who had had a large cancerous tumour removed from her face. As I went to meet her for the first time, I wondered how I would feel. It was typical of me to focus on my response, rather than her ordeal of facing the camera. As I got out of the car, a tall and lovely young woman walked towards me with her hand out in welcome, and to my embarrassment I found myself asking if it was her. Of course it was. She had a patch across the upper half of one side of her face, but the inner life radiating out of the other half was so attractive that I registered only that.

Model Katie Piper, who was subjected to a horrendous acid attack by a former boyfriend, has done so much to challenge society's narrow concept of beauty, but for both her and the woman minister I filmed, it hasn't come without a long struggle to come to terms with, and even to embrace, the body they now have. And for both, being loved and accepted and desired (mostly by the men in their lives) for who they are has played the largest part in the healing process.

If only all surgeons realised they deal not just with bodies but with emotions as well, and that the two are inextricable. For body image is about feeling, not fact. It is totally irrational. That's why parental reassurances do little to comfort a teenager whose face has erupted into a tiny spot just before an important date. That's why some couples I know who dearly love each other and have been together for years still make love with the light off, missing out on vital visual stimulus. Women can tell themselves until they are blue in the face that, despite the fashion for gaunt, skinny, boyish bodies, many men prefer lush softness and curves and somewhere they can lose themselves.

And it isn't only women who struggle with those feelings. Peter asks me from time to time if I still find him attractive now that he's bald. And I am so reassuring. 'No, darling, I only married you for your full head of hair.'

'There is a wariness and unease in the body language of some Christian men,' said lecturer in theology and television producer Angela Tilby at a Sheffield clergy conference. 'A tendency to sloping shoulders, wringing hands and a bowed head. Not the straight upward gait of Imam and Rabbi. Compare the Christian minister's wife with her Jewish or Muslim counterpart. She is clearly a jolly nice woman; well-scrubbed rather than sexy, whereas Mrs Cohen and Mrs Patel frequently manage to be both.'

I have nothing to wear

I also want the women to dress modestly, with decency and propriety, adorning themselves, not with elaborate hairstyles or gold or pearls or expensive clothes, but with good deeds, appropriate for women who profess to worship God.

(1 Tim. 2:9–10)

Your beauty should not come from outward adornment, such as elaborate hairstyles and the wearing of gold jewellery or fine clothes. Rather, it should be that of your inner self, the unfading beauty of a gentle and quiet spirit, which is of great worth in God' sight. For this is the way the holy women of the past who put their hope in God used to adorn themselves.

(1 Peter 3:3–5)

Our most obvious expression of sexuality is in what we wear. Clothes are never simply functional. They say something about who we are and what we feel about ourselves. The French Lieutenant's Woman would probably never have become disastrously embroiled with the French Lieutenant had she gone out that fateful night in a sensible brown anorak, rather than shrouded in a mysterious black cape.

I have always struggled with the idea of a gentle and quiet spirit, feeling somehow that 'mouth on legs' was more my style. A quiet spirit and 'appropriate deeds' seem a very dull alternative to Jewish flamboyance. There's a story about Hymie Goldberg, who is walking along the street when a flying saucer lands in front of him. Out of it climbs a Martian in a shimmering, golden lurex suit. 'Oh,' he says, as the strange being shimmers towards him, 'Love the bling. Does everyone on Mars wear clothes like that?'

'No,' says the Martian, 'only we Jews.'

It was a shock when I first became a Christian to find that in the rather repressive evangelicalism of the seventies I was considered 'fast' because I wore very short skirts and make-up. I had a bright red sleeveless dress, bought for me by my mother for a bar mitzvah that was cut away at the shoulders and had two rings of white stitching on the front in a very interesting place. I had no idea it was causing problems in the university Christian Union, until I was told off for being provocative by a female friend. But then, she had been brought up in the Brethren, and, to my total incredulity, insisted on wearing an old-fashioned brown felt hat to church because that was what her mother would have wanted.

I went to my first university ball with pearl buttons threaded through my hair and struggled with my conscience all night. Should Christian women give gold and pearls, highlights and lowlights, indeed all 'adornment' a wide birth and, as Tertullian suggested, go about 'in rags', as if we were 'in mourning', covering up our latent sexuality with dull colours and drab, unlovely clothes? In the seventies, it was still a sign of piety to be terribly 'mish', like a missionary on furlough, out of touch with the latest styles, hiding any sexual charms behind a dated hairstyle, tweedy skirts, and thick, lisle stockings.

My husband is forever lamenting the fact that I can't be a man for a day. How else could a woman appreciate the struggle they face when that testosterone is tickled by billboards, hoardings, iPad, film and newsagents shelves – not to mention the flash of flesh on the pavement? Perhaps I should have a little more sympathy for the early church fathers. For a man, 'I need you to admire me, but not touch me,' can be a mixed message. How easily we underestimate the impact of what we wear.

On the other hand, we cannot be terrified or tyrannised into denying what makes us uniquely feminine. A friend of mine who was a nurse in Morocco told me that though the women there wore full burqa when they went to the mosque, the men would line up outside and ogle their feet as they came out. Male desire cannot be curbed simply by imposing restrictions and covering the body up. From neckline to hemline, shoes to earrings, there are as many possibilities of turn-on for a man as there are varieties of the species.

Fashion has changed dramatically over the centuries. The Romans admired thinness, but in mediaeval times plump was erotic. Necklines were cut so low, a woman could fully bare her breasts, but revealing an ankle was too daring by far. In the nineteenth century a lady had a corseted waist and was delicate, frail and pure, while a good-time girl was heavy, blousy and robust. Only half a century ago the idea of women wearing trousers was greeted with shock and dismay, as Dorothy Sayers makes clear when she talks about the issue being 'so distressing to bishops'.

We are asked: 'Why do you want to go about in trousers? They are extremely unbecoming to most of you. You only do it to copy the men.' To this we may properly reply: 'It is true that they are unbecoming. Even on men they are remarkably unattractive. But, as you men have discovered for yourselves, they are comfortable, they do not get in the way of ones activities like skirts and they protect the wearer from draughts. If the trousers do not attract you, so much the worse; for the moment I do not want to attract you. I want to enjoy myself as a human being, and why not? As for copying you, certainly you thought of trousers first and to that extent we must copy you. But we are not such abandoned copy-cats as to attach these useful garments to our bodies with braces. There we draw the line. These machines of leather and elastic are unnecessary and unsuited to the female form. They are, moreover, hideous beyond description. And as for decency – of which you sometimes accuse the trousers – we at least can take our coats off without becoming the half-undressed, bedroom spectacle that a man presents in his shirt and braces.'[6]

Ankle-length or miniskirts, platform or stiletto heels, ruffled cuffs or false nails – it is amazing how many fashions and beauty rituals, so often designed with men in mind, inhibit a woman's freedom and reduce her competence. Western foibles are tame compared with neck stretching, foot-binding or genital mutilation, deadly traditions all of them, performed in the name of female desirability.

When the Apostle Peter calls on women to be 'gentle and quiet', he is addressing women whose husbands have resisted conversion, urging them not to rise to their partner's taunts and arguments. Instead, they should be patient and let the transformation in their lifes speak for itself. Don't spend his money on the fripperies you once spent it on – the designer labels, expensive hairdos and other status symbols in Roman society. That, says Peter, will make your men really sit up and think – an idea attibuted, erroneously some suggest, by St Francis years later when he wrote, 'Preach the gospel at all times. When necessary, use words . . .'

Nothing captures for me the intention of the Apostle Peter quite like the story Naomi Gryn tells of her grandmother, Bella. In her introduction to the autobiography of her father, Rabbi Hugo Gryn, who spent some of his teenage years in Auschwitz, she writes that when the Nazis invaded the little Hungarian town, Bella buried in the garden her Sabbath candles, kiddush cup, eight-branched chanukiah used at the Feast of Lights, and Hugo's excellent school report of that year. They were still there, just as she had left them, when she returned from Auschwitz, and she eventually managed to smuggle them out to Hugo, who had settled in England. 'For my father,' writes Naomi, 'that these family treasures had survived the war, was a powerful parable about the values that his mother cherished most: not her furs and jewellery, but the symbols of a Jewish home.'[7]

Even Jesus tackled the subject of clothes. Perhaps he overheard one of his female followers complaining she had nothing to wear. 'See how the flowers of the field grow. They do not labour or spin. Yet I tell you that not even Solomon in all his splendour was dressed like one of these . . . will he not much more clothe you . . . ?' (Matt. 6:28–30). The flowers of the field are not grey or beige. They are a riot of colour. Nor did King Solomon appear in public in washed-out tracksuit bottoms. He dressed to impress – even if he didn't resort to charity shops for recycled bargains, as I often do. It is fine to look a schmuck from time to time – a nice Yiddish word meaning a slob – but if dressing up at all, even for an occasion, makes us feel uncomfortable, it may be an interesting reflection on our feelings about our sexuality.

First impressions are important. In my work in public relations I dressed to represent the company. In promoting the kingdom of God, I represent my Maker. There are times when it is important, not so much to power dress, but to look and feel efficient and in control. It worries me when Abby says, 'You're not going out like that!' because she is my best barometer of fashion. Does she mean I would be embarrassed if I went out 'like that', or she would be embarrassed if I went out 'like that'? Either way, when she speaks, I listen. I would advise every woman to find a younger shopping accomplice, for while it is important to be ourselves, no one can dispense with a little honest advice. The following, penned by Abby, was inspired by my arrival home one day from Marks and Spencer with a pair of gold moccasins with tassels on them.

Somehow, mothers magically forget their own days in the spot-light of fashion and follow the unwritten dowdiness rule for over-forties. If parents could bear to look at photographs of themselves as teenagers, they would doubtless notice how remarkably similar they look to their children (apart from the disastrous haircuts of the seventies). My Dad had Buddy Holly glasses. As for Mum's flared trousers and platform shoes . . . enough said.

Haven't parents noticed that most teenagers quickly grow out of the gothic era, the ripped jeans trend or the 'Is it a skirt or is it a belt?' phase? Why do they spend so much time fretting over it when it is a normal and predictable part of growing up? Why can't we give teenage girls a break? If they're not embarrassed, why should we all be embarrassed for them? It's probably the only time they'll ever want to experiment wildly with their image; extreme self-consciousness soon overcomes them, and after the necessary student years a daughter will settle into a highly acceptable wardrobe.

A mother, however, is far more difficult to tackle. They have a habit of festering in a Bon Marché-dominated world, and daughters can forget any hopes of them 'growing out of it'. Who started the notion that once you have children nobody cares what you look like? Remember, once your children are old enough to notice, they will be more embarrassed by you than you ever are by them.

Mothers and daughters have a mutual duty to dress each other well. This works in both their interests when they need a wardrobe to raid. The first key to a successful shopping relationship is tactful honesty. A deferential comment about too much cleavage and people getting the wrong idea is usually better received than, 'You're not my daughter if you go out looking like a tart!' The stronger the maternal reaction, the stronger the filial defiance, the greater the cleavage. The second and vital rule is never try and dress the other in what you would wear yourself.

What does a girl need to know?

Information really is power. One of the main aims of the teenage pregnancy campaign was to encourage parents to talk to their children about sex and relationships. An acquaintance of mine was amazed to hear that her student daughter had been traumatised when she was admitted to hospital with a suspected ovarian cyst. She thought she only had one ovary and might lose the possibility of having children.

Abby was totally mystified by a male student friend who had to go out of the room whenever the girls mentioned periods. His mother never told him about the female reproductive system and now it is such a mystery it scares him rigid. Who thought old-fashioned attitudes to sexuality disappeared with gaslights and gramophones?

My grandmother, like many young flappers in the Roaring Twenties, knew nothing of the facts of life on her wedding night, and was so horrified at her rude enlightenment that she ran home to her mother. She was sent promptly back and told to get on with it. (Not put up with it – Jewish women are much more earthy than that.)

My mother never bothered to tell me the facts of life. She assumed I knew – at what age, I'm not sure. Since I was about sixteen when she first broached the subject, it would have been strange if I hadn't found out for myself by then, so I learned about it in the usual sniggering, giggling manner girls do, which isn't the best.

Abby thinks I was the one to explain the facts of life to her – so I may have got something right – courtesy of Nick Butterworth and Mick Inkpen who produced a wonderful book called *Who Made Me?* with graphic illustrations of mischievous little sperms chasing a serene-looking ovum, and Mum and Dad wriggling around having a great deal of fun in the process.

Why the fuss over women breastfeeding in public? It's a sure giveaway of a deep discomfort with the body. Peter and I felt it was important to have a relaxed approach to nudity with the children. It is natural and neutral outside a sexual context – though I did draw the line when the children were in their teens and my heading for the bathroom seemed to be an unspoken sign that mother was a sitting duck, available for deep heart-to-heart chats. Sorry ducklings, don't follow me. I'm not being prudish, but I do like my private space sometimes.

Many children grow up feeling uncomfortable about their own bodies because the genitals are never mentioned, and they assume that whatever is shrouded in silence must be bad. I once saw a TV documentary on contemporary sexual behaviour where men were invited to push a pin into a large drawing of the female genitalia where they thought the clitoris was. It was a bit like pinning a tail on the donkey blindfolded. Most hadn't a clue where it was, despite the fact it plays an essential part in the female response. This is not usually the case in Orthodox Judaism, where a man is expected to give his wife pleasure on the Sabbath and festivals. A sensitive rabbi preparing a young man for marriage would ensure he knew how to do that. (Nowhere, incidentally, does the Law suggest that a man is entitled to the same.) Judging by the number of women who have come to us over the years in near despair over the lack of sexual pleasure in their lives, I often wonder whether it shouldn't be a compulsory part of church marriage preparation too. We take far too much for granted.

When we went on holiday to my in-laws home in Ibiza, Peter and I regularly went for an afternoon 'siesta'. Then, one year, we realised from the 'we know what you mean' look from the children that our code had been cracked. 'Okay,' we said, 'if you're so clever, you answer the phone and the doorbell, and give us a break.' Teenagers have their uses, and I'm glad they learned that their parents still enjoyed 'siestas'.

I am not advocating that girls need to know all the intimate details of our relationship; simply that we need a more honest, open, joyful approach to a vital part of our lives, so that they will know there is a treasure worth waiting for, worth keeping for the right person. The Song of Songs, a poem full of belly buttons, boobs and other bumps, is one of the most erotic love poems ever written, and it's there in the Bible, a wonderful antidote to the early church fathers' Christianity, for whom sex was the most unfortunate mistake God ever made.

Perhaps one of the saddest things about contemporary attitudes to sexual union is that its familiarity breeds contempt. We no longer celebrate it, as some rural communities did in past centuries where the marriage night was cheered on from outside a door or window. It can't have done much for the couple's enjoyment, but at least it made the point that such a major commitment was public, communal and worthy of a party.

'Smear test time,' I moaned at the girls in the office one day, clattering away at my computer keyboard, without thinking. 'I'm hardly high risk. I've only had one partner.'[8]

There was a sudden silence at the desk opposite.

'One!' Angie said. 'Only ever one?'

Unwittingly, it seemed I had lobbed a grenade across the room.

'Why, how many have you had?'

Angie used her fingers to count. She had to go through the process several times.

'Sssseven, I think . . . at the moment.'

Her most recent relationship had just come to a painful end after seven years.

'Doesn't it get boring? The sex, I mean.'

'No,' I said, 'gourmet sex is like good wine; it takes time to perfect.'

'I envy you,' she said, wistfully. 'Here I am, a bit of a shipwreck really, nearly fifty and no man, no sex, and no chance of any kids now.'

I didn't want Abby to learn the hard way – unlike a student member of our church, raised in a Christian family, who told me that, in desperation to find out what 'it' was like, she had thrown away her virginity at a party one night, and what did it matter who she slept with now? 'And where does it say in the Bible that we shouldn't?' she added aggressively.

I could have shown her, but that wouldn't have helped. Instead, I tried to explain that one stupid encounter shouldn't rob her of forgiveness (either God's or her own), or the chance to start again, but her successive, meaningless relationships were robbing her of any chance of retrieving her self-respect.

The joys of waiting

It is God's will that you should be sanctified: that you should avoid sexual immorality; that each of you should learn to control your own body in a way that is holy and honourable, not in passionate lust like the pagans, who do not know God; and that in this matter no one should wrong or take advantage of a brother or sister.

(1 Thess. 4:3-4)

In this earliest piece of the New Testament, Paul is unequivocal on the subject. Self-control, a major theme in many of his letters and a despised and neglected concept in today's hedonistic society, is the key to empowerment for those who find and keep it. One young woman told her minister how hard it was to resist the pressure at school to give up her virginity. He said to her, 'Just say to your friends, I can become like you in a minute, but you can never again become like me.'

Abby was given the grace to live out the ideals she stated in the following so many years ago. I don't claim responsibility for that. Having older role models as her peers, including a school nurse, to whom she could talk openly and freely certainly helped.

When two people in my year at school had sex, everyone knew about it. We were in Year 10, the fourteen–fifteen age group, and there were probably a few experienced yet silent people dotted around the place, yet for some reason, it suddenly became the most talked about subject for a whole week. Eventually, people came to the conclusion that it was boring and went back to playing football or cricket, or wandering around the school grounds aimlessly passing the lunch break.

The publicity undoubtedly put pressure on the least confident people who began to wonder if something was wrong with them. Those with more self-esteem and maturity (I love saying that, because I was one of them) thought they were foolish and vowed to wait.

By the time we reached the sixth form, one by one my friends succumbed and whispered secretly about their dreadful experiences with the morning-after pill. I have to say, I am sure there were more virgins than ever owned up – probably around 70 per cent – though most of those would be the boys, because the girls were seeing older people out of school.

University is apparently the place to lose your virginity and join your peers in more knowledgeable conversation on the subject. In my first term, a game of truth or dare revealed that seven of the ten of us there were virgins. I've been told that by the end of our three years there will only be me left, but I don't believe that's true. I know a lot of people waiting 'for the right person'. My reasons for not having sex are probably only half God focussed and half plain common sense. The risk of pregnancy, sexually transmitted diseases and cervical cancer to name just three, make it pretty clear that sex is not to be undertaken lightly.

Dad once explained to me that whether or not you think sex is a gift from God, it creates a spiritual bond between a couple and though the couple might split up, that bond can never be broken. I realised how right he was when I witnessed a friend of mine so tangled with her sexual partners that she couldn't extricate herself. There had been three, but when the next one came along she would end up cheating on the old one. She kept trying to decide on just one, but the other two would always be around tempting her back into the intimacy they had shared.

Another of my friends was cheated on by her boyfriend of two years which caused her immense pain, and the third kept getting mixed up with boys from the Navy. In a frank discussion in our common room each said they wished they had waited and they were jealous of my reserve. I was lucky enough to be looking forward to sex, while they were all hurt by it and sick of its consequences. To be fair though, I don't think I really had all that much reserve. I just hadn't met anyone I wanted to sleep with. When you think about it, sex is really quite a strange and undignified thing to do, and I would need to trust my partner and feel at ease before I was able to undertake any sort of intimacy. I didn't want anyone to see the dimple on my bum or the stretch marks on my thighs unless I knew they would take me forever, warts and all, those I have and those I'm going to get.

In the car on our way for a day's shopping, Mum and I discussed why sex has been so misrepresented to my generation. She observed that people now see sex as an entitlement and so Christianity is seen as depriving people of that right. When God created sex, he gave it as a gift in order that a committed couple might have a close bond, enjoyment and the ability to reproduce. It is not a commodity; it is a bonus to make that one relationship special. Humans are the only creatures designed to have intercourse face to face, and among the few who gain pleasure from it. Why then does it cause more heartache than pleasure? Why have we got it wrong? There is nothing exciting about a wedding day if the couple are already sexually active together. Who cares about a bit of legal paperwork? But when two people commit themselves to each other, knowing the reward they're going to get at the end of the day, that's really worth celebrating.

People can be so selfish when it comes to sex. They think, 'It's my decision,' or 'It only affects me.' But if a man leaves his wife because he and his new partner 'deserve to be together', what about his children, his wife and the devastation he leaves behind? What about the example it sets to the next generation that personal happiness is all that matters? What about the friendship groups of the couple? I have seen whole groups of friends shattered by broken relationships. Sex can make people lie; it makes them secretive, guilty and deceitful.

I admit that getting older and meeting more people you find attractive means the urges are stronger. People say they have sex by accident. Can it be an accident? It's not really like crashing a car or dropping a vase. Personally, I can't see how it could just be a whoops-a-daisy and look what we did. Sex is extremely appealing – there isn't any way around it. It can be hard to keep control. Being accountable – to friends, mentors or parents – having someone know about your situation can help. I hold on to the fact that when it is right, it will be a million times better than getting it wrong, and the only sure way of knowing you will be together forever is to agree to get married and work at your relationship. Sex as God intended is, I hope, I'm sure, worth every second of waiting.

Abby's innocent hopes and aspirations contrasted painfully with the bright young graduates, so like her, who worked at that time in the White House, and, seduced by their power, became entangled with much older, married men. Writing in *The Guardian* about the disappearance of White House intern Chandra Levy, who was having an affair with congressman Gary Condit, journalist Sharon Krum asked why so many intelligent young women working in DC, like Monica Lewinsky, fell into this particular trap. She spoke to ex-intern and Washington Post columnist, Sally Quinn. 'We presume that because young women today – beneficiaries of equal opportunity and affirmative action – are able to claim power for themselves, they are immune to a powerful man . . . But Quinn says that feminism only goes so far in DC, and then basic human behaviour trumps ideology.'[9]

The problem is that human behaviour has a tendency to conquer a person's values, in Christianity as much as in any other ideology. Every woman of every age needs to recognise the lure and abuse of power, and have the skills to handle temptation, pressure and seduction – especially now, post-Weinstein.

But it's so much more difficult, when our culture positively encourages young people to treat sex as a commodity, and the great divide between the sex act and relationship is so deep it seems the rift can never be repaired. Young women go out for the evening looking for 'a bonk' – a one-night stand with a man whose name they may not even know and will never see again. Every summer hundreds of these doe-eyed beauties walk the paseo in Ibiza's San Antonio clubbing mecca and, no thanks to booze and drugs or plain naivety, end up the following morning feeling sick and used. But it's also true of most weekends in many Western cities and towns.

A woman who has been or feels abused will find it hard to trust herself to a man again. A rape trial focusses not on, 'Did you know this man?' or, 'Did you like this man?' but, 'Did you consent?' There is no emotional content here. As a society, we have become so accustomed to dividing body, mind and spirit that when it comes to sex, the emotions seem to count for little, when in fact it's the body that is treated as worthless. But we cannot give away our bodies without it affecting the whole. I saw, when I led the youth group just a few years ago that, for the girls, sex wasn't all it was cracked up to be, and they felt they had lost something of worth. In various churches we have been in, older women have shared that their marital bedroom is haunted by the ghosts of previous relationships, regularly parading around the bed. It appears that Abby's comments of twenty years ago stand today.

The joy of making love

When I presented a local radio debate on teenage pregnancy from a sixth form college, one of the female students said, 'At school they gave us the biological facts, but never told me what it would feel like to fall in love.' Emotion, not disembodied desire, is more likely to rob a girl of her common sense. 'Women need a reason to have sex,' says Billy Crystal in the 1991 film *City Slickers*, 'men just need a place.'

A man may spend his entire life in search of the key to female sexual arousal, and it's been dangling in front of him all the time – romance begins to turn the lock. To open the door, and keep it open, requires a great deal of gentleness, patience and imagination. It is an art that can take many years to learn, and that is why it needs long-term commitment and dedication, and it begins, not in the bedroom, but in the kitchen. Women are often so exhausted by running the home, the garden, the children, the dog and the budgie, sometimes on top of a job, that they have little energy left over for grand passion at nightfall.

Popular American sex therapist Dr Archibald Hart said that, given the poor sexual technique of some men, it is hardly surprising that women are not always very interested. 'Men who want a better sex life not only need to learn how to be better lovers, but also how to carry the emotional and physical burden of housework and child-rearing. To put it bluntly: many men only have themselves to blame for their low sexual satisfaction.'[10] What might relationships be like if older men could mentor younger men in this area, talk to their sons and pass on their best tips, as they do in football or computing, but it just isn't as acceptable a subject of conversation.

Women do have a sex drive, but it is easily driven underground by a culmination of minor and sometimes major setbacks. When sex becomes a trial, as it evidently does for some couples, it may mean there are unresolved differences and resentments in the relationship. Even within a deeply caring relationship the sex act can be blighted by past experience or an abusive childhood. We are complex creatures sexually, martyrs to our hormonal cycles, worn with juggling dozens of different plates, heavily dependent on mood, atmosphere and harmony. We barely get round to acknowledging the first rumblings of desire before we're engulfed by such a torrent of testosterone from the other side of the bed that we're left feeling winded.

Unfortunately, to the bewilderment of most men, the male physique does little for us, which is why, in reality, the current obsession with looks leaves most of us a little cold. The first time I saw the film of D. H. Lawrence's *Women in Love* there were a couple of elderly ladies in the row behind me. At the moment when the two leading men wrestle stark naked in front of the fire, their rippling biceps glowing seductively in the firelight, one whispers loudly to the other, 'Lovely carpet.' Personally, my mood is heavily dependent on seeing a tidy bedroom, but that's probably very Jewish. And what does a Jewish woman say when she's making love? 'Sam, the ceiling needs painting.'

I don't understand why God made such discrepancies between men and women, but that's how it is and that's what Peter and I have tried to explain to couples we're preparing for marriage. In very simplified terms, for women, intimacy is the way to sex, and for men sex is the way to intimacy, and outside a deeply committed, loving relationship, that's a potentially lethal cocktail.

The dictionary defines intimacy as 'close or warm friendship', but the word has become synonymous with sexual relations. Without the former, however, the latter are not intimate at all. As we saw in the creation story, the male failure is in relationship and he may have struggles in this area. Some men find it difficult to express their feelings. Many find it impossible to admit weakness. But for real sexual intimacy, vulnerability – a rediscovery of the original Adam-like nakedness – is essential, otherwise, even within marriage, the sex act is simply satisfying the appetite, as any other member of the animal kingdom does. There is no such thing as 'making love' to anyone as closed down and shut off as a snail.

Yet no human being, sexually active or not, can survive without intimacy. Sexuality expresses itself in all our relationships. Single and celibate, Jesus nonetheless had a number of 'intimates' – John, who lay at the last supper with his head on Jesus' chest; Peter and the other disciples with whom he could be transparently honest and completely himself; Mary and Martha, whose company he sought when he wanted to unwind. If we cannot find intimacy as a single person, we will never find it in marriage, and certainly not in sex. One of my greatest hopes for my children has been that they would grow up knowing that it is possible to be hopelessly and completely in love with the same person throughout an entire lifetime, and that I am as filled with passion for their father now as I was on the day we married, and am enjoying more and more the great gift of our union.

I realised recently with a sense of shock how few more years I have left to enjoy it – aggravated by the fact that, having crossed the magical age of sixty, I can no longer buy thrush medication over the counter. According to the Medicines and Healthcare Products Regulatory Agency, a government department (well it would be, wouldn't it?), women tend not to get thrush in later life – a delicate way of saying they don't have sex. Someone needs to tell them they're living in the Dark Ages. After all, the 'experts' – probably bright young things yet to see forty – tell us that as we get older, coitus may become a little less frequent, a little more difficult – though by no means impossible. Peter's grandfather was seventy-two when Peter's father was born. Admittedly, his wife was thirty-two! Even so, in old age she spoke quite freely of his passion in that department, so I have high expectations of future bliss. I have always thought that when one partner has a terminal illness the saddest moment in the relationship must be the last farewell to lovemaking, that very tangible expression of all that we have been for each other, soul, mind and body, for so many years. Jesus makes it clear there is no sex in heaven. There are probably very good reasons – there must be something far better. All the same, I had better make the most of it now.

Chapter 8

The Mothering Woman

You can't frighten me. I have children.

Fridge magnet

Giving birth is a gift given uniquely to women. Nothing can generate quite such joy or pain. Childlessness can be a woman's greatest sorrow – a dull, nagging ache, so much a part of her that the hurt still catches her off guard in later life. Fertility problems can seem a treachery of the body, a mockery, a denial of all the woman's hopes and expectations by a capricious, ungenerous God. The decision not to have children can make a woman a pariah, especially in the Church, where, for centuries, the 'creation ordinance' to go forth and multiply has been promulgated as a woman's most sacred duty. A woman who cannot bond with her child may face endless self-recrimination and guilt. And for the woman who loses a child, no grief or bewilderment is so great.

Even those blessed with the ability to raise their children in a secure, loving environment find that being a mother is the most demanding role they will ever take on. In none of the many relationships entrusted to woman is it more essential to speak words of life, and in none can that be more difficult. Thus far, I have been spared heartbreak, yet, even so, I would have to say that giving birth and mothering is a great deal more, and nothing like it is so often made out to be – even on *Call the Midwife*!

Having a child changes most women overnight. Suddenly, from some untapped, hitherto undiscovered source deep within, there wells up an emotion more powerful than any other. It is a fierce, frightening, protective, all-consuming kind of devotion. Now you know you will kill or be killed in defence of your cub. But then, as the months go by, you discover this little tyrant also has the ability, in tandem and equal measure, to provoke bouts of temper, exasperation and impatience you always thought you were far too nice to have.

One thing is certain – mothering has very little to do with the bland, pious and idealised images of the glowing, phlegmatic Madonna that have pursued women from the Renaissance. There she sits in serene soft focus with a gurgling, contented cherub at her breast. She obviously doesn't suffer from a milk deficiency, or cracked nipples. 'Ah,' say the voracious bottle-feeding adverts, contrary to the midwife's advice, 'for the luminous tranquillity of the problem-free modern mother, abandon the boobs and bring in the bottle.' This leaves many new mums feeling confused and inadequate whichever they opt for.

As a child I swallowed the saccharine image whole and thought it an unkind freak of nature that I had been granted a mother with the gentle equanimity of King Kong. She was engaged at seventeen, married at nineteen and, once the babies came along, bitterly resented her missed youth, and later her missed opportunities. With little else to occupy her, other than to make her home more perfect than anyone else's, she submitted to the endless demands of obsessive compulsive disorder, and our childhood world was dominated by a set of rigid rituals that held us, as much as her, in an unforgiving vice. By night, she was the party girl, dancing her demons away at the Blue Parrot nightclub, but that meant that her teenage brood had to be bathed and in pyjamas by 6pm, the house and children tidied and ready for the babysitter.

I would be a very different mother, I told myself, as I grew into resentful adolescence. One day I would live the proper dream. I would have a gingerbread cottage with honeysuckle growing up the wall, and newly washed, sweet-smelling nappies wafting gently in the breeze as they hung out in the summer sun. In reality, stuck without a car in the middle of Greater Manchester, these were my wilderness years. If one person had told me I might make a better mother of teenagers than babies, it would have released me from the guilt induced by the stifling and restless boredom I felt. But blessed with the ministry of encouragement, friends simply said, 'Just wait, it gets worse.'

Like most women, I wanted to be a good mother, and had a clear ideal of what a good mother should be – endlessly patient, caring, selfless and giving. Yet once the children arrived I constantly failed to live up to my self-imposed standards, and was consumed with the fear of getting it wrong and damaging them for life. What if my two cherubs suddenly metamorphosed into drug-taking, glue-sniffing, promiscuous little pagans? It would all be my fault.

Children come without a manual or personalised growth plan. Our major role model is usually our own parents, and that, certainly for me, was the very one I wanted to avoid the most. Until the day I heard myself speaking in my mother's voice! I marvel that mine are as well adjusted as they seem to be. Fortunately for them, they had a firm, patient, loving father, who made up for my inadequacies in the play and discipline departments.

Yet as I look back now, I don't think the secrets of child-rearing are completely directionless and arbitrary. Certain basic, ageless principles appear in story form in a manual for living that, unlike many of the other textbooks on the subject that become dated and countermanded, has survived the test of time.

The Bible contains an encouraging mixture of mothers who get it right and mothers who get it wrong. One thing is sure – there is no area of our lives where women, and even men, are more vulnerable, or more susceptible to fatal fond indulgence like King David, or to desperate counter-productive scheming like Rebekah.

In Matthew's Gospel, Salome, mother of James and John, asks Jesus if her two sons can have a special place on either side of him in his father's kingdom (Matt. 20:20–1). There is no attempt to disguise the naked maternal ambition. She has invested all in her two fine boys, and isn't afraid to voice her aspirations. What else should a Jewish mother want for her boys than the best? Jesus doesn't criticise her maternal pride. It's the prize that pride needs for personal fulfilment that he tackles. Following him has nothing to do with the all too human notion that success equals status.

Extra-special mothers

I always smile when I come across Salome and her boys. It reminds me of a wonderful single mother in Normanton, where Peter served his curacy. Joan Harding's life had never been easy. She was an evacuee during the Second World War, but when it was over, her family in Liverpool didn't want her back, but never told her the truth. She was seventeen years old before anyone ever bought her a birthday present. But the woman who had known so little love felt she had been given more than enough when she met with Jesus Christ. It turned her life around.

She raised her twin boys alone with limited financial means in the little former mining town in West Yorkshire, determined they wouldn't end up in the pit like most of the local lads. And she called them James and John, 'her sons of thunder', the nickname Jesus had given to his two disciples. They were real tearaways, eventually towering over their tiny mother. But tight discipline and immense love were meted out in equal measure. 'I think my mum did an amazing job of teaching John and me always to put God first, trust him for miracles (especially healing) and to love the Bible,' James told me. 'After my road accident, when I came out of the coma, she was the one holding my hand as I recovered from brain damage, and her greatest gift to me was to support me patiently as I had so much to learn again. She was so proud when I received my PhD in New Testament in 2006.' Joan was indeed very proud of her boys, but worldly status wasn't her objective. Her only ambition was that they would be followers of Christ, and that wish more than came true. After his ordination, James lectured at St Mellitus College in London in Missiology, and went on to become the Founder Principal of St Paul's Theological College, Kuala Lumpur, Malaysia, which is affiliated to St Mellitus. And John is Senior Pastor of Frontline Church, Wavertree in Liverpool.

When the Kings of Israel and Judah are named in the Old Testament, so are their mothers. Some stir their boys on to greatness; others are their downfall. Among the many positive models of mothering in the Bible are Hannah, the mother of Samuel, who released her son for a better cause than waiting on her in her old age; and

Eunice and Lois, mother and grandmother of Timothy, who trained him in the spiritual requirements of a mighty life calling.

But raising a child in the Christian faith can be as costly as it is rewarding. In the nineteenth and early twentieth century, a child with a calling to go to Africa, Asia or India as a missionary meant heartbreak for a parent. Once that child left for the other side of the world, a mother would probably never see them again. We can feel the immense pain behind such a sacrifice in the words of Amy Carmichael's widowed mother as her beloved daughter prepared to go to India.

> Yes, dearest Amy, He has leant you to me all these years. He only knows what a strength, comfort and joy you have been to me. In sorrow He made you my staff and solace, in loneliness my more than child companion, and in gladness my bright and merry-hearted sympathiser. So, darling, when He asks you now to go away from within my reach, can I say nay? No, no Amy, He is yours – you are His – to take you where He pleases and use you as He pleases. I can trust you to Him and I do . . . All day He has helped me, and my heart unfailingly says, 'Go ye . . .'[1]

When it comes to letting a child go to follow their destiny, we have a prime example in the most famous mother who ever lived, though women have been robbed of the chance of identifying with her by the pious, desexualised, inaccessible icon history has made of her. In his *Genesee Diary*, the spiritual sage Henri Nouwen says meditating on Mary's gentleness and softness enabled him to keep in touch with his feminine side, so that he wasn't deprived of it in an aggressive, competitive male world. But was Mary really soft and gentle, or is that wishful stereotyping? My feeling is that beyond the image, there is a flesh-and-blood Jewish Mama waiting to be rediscovered, a real woman with the joys and struggles of any mother, as tough as a Scouser bringing up her family in a deprived part of Liverpool.

Mary, an amazing mother

Mary's pregnancy is recorded by Luke in Luke 1. 'I have carefully investigated everything' (verse 3) he says, just like the doctor he is, with meticulous attention to medical details. He has obviously interviewed Mary at length about her obstetric history and established that this was a perfectly normal pregnancy and childbirth – it was only the conception that was extraordinary. Luke is so impressed with the woman and her account that he tells the tale through her eyes – one of the few scriptural narratives told from a woman's perspective.

The village of Nazareth was so small that even the Galileans would have only passed through it on their way somewhere else, yet this is the birthplace of one of the world's most exceptional women. Her name is actually Miriam, which means 'strong', for she is not unlike her namesake in the Old Testament – Moses' sister, who opted to accompany her brother through endless years of wilderness wanderings, and is a tough old boot. That's why God has singled Mary out. Her calling will require unusual reserves of inner strength and resilience.

Meanwhile, back at the heavenly ranch, the angel Gabriel receives the commission he has been awaiting for hundreds of years, since he appeared to Daniel to tell him it would take seventy times seven years for the Messiah 'to finish transgression, to put an end to sin, to atone for wickedness, [and] to bring in everlasting righteousness' (Dan. 9:24). The time has come to announce to the world that the prophecy is fulfilled. He is beside himself with excitement. God probably warns him, 'Don't get carried away, Gabriel. Remember, you're an angel and she's a mere girl. Don't frighten her.'

But Gabriel can't help himself, and announces himself loudly with a, 'Hello, Mary. Greetings, you special lady. The Lord is with you.'

And she is terrified out of her wits.

Take two. Gabriel remembers what he has been told and starts again. 'Don't be afraid, Mary, you're going to have a son – he will reign over the house of Jacob forever and his kingdom will never end.'

Typical of any woman faced with the impossible, Mary asks the practical, 'How, when I haven't slept with anyone?'

It is a question born of faith, not doubt. Since the day of her birth, the Scriptures have been the very foundation of her life. She knows with absolute certainty the Messiah will come – but what has it to do with her? It is the logistics that bother her.

The power of God will 'overshadow you', explains the angel Gabriel with great delicacy. And if that is still as clear as mud, she could always go and visit her elderly, infertile cousin Elizabeth, now six months pregnant – a visual sign, if ever there was one, that with God nothing is impossible.

Mary is satisfied – and that is amazing in itself. She has just been handed the humiliation of an illicit pregnancy, disgrace for her family and the possible loss of the man she hopes to marry. But there doesn't appear to be prolonged heart searching. It takes no more than a moment to yield her autonomy, her ambitions and her future to God. 'May it be to me as you have said.' This is surely the culmination of a short lifetime of surrender.

Every human being who has ever chosen to follow God comes inexorably to this moment of decision, like Mary, Ruth and Esther, when he asks us to choose between our dreams and his plans. Many of my career ambitions in the media had to be abandoned when I moved with Peter away from Coventry to the north-west coast. It felt, and often still feels, as if some part of me died, though I now see how it was all for the best. But that was nothing compared to the challenge Mary faced. Could she say no? I think she could, but God knows her well enough to know that she won't. After all, the most important cosmic event in history hinges on that yes. Her acquiescence is vital in terms of what she will be for the child she will carry, for she will raise a son who will take after her in his unflinching obedience to the Father.

'Blessed is she who has believed that the Lord would fulfil his promises to her!' says the elderly Elizabeth (Luke 1:45). I'm not sure I would have wanted Mary's blessings. God's plans do not carry an automatic exemption from suffering, illness or pain. At this stage Mary is aware of the enormity, but not the implications, of her calling. For Mary, the stigma is merely the start. She will face an uncomfortable birth in surroundings she would never have chosen, banishment from her village, the ignominy of being a refugee, the bewilderment of her son's ministry, the terror of watching him face trumped-up charges and the devastation of his terrible death. At

Jesus' *brith*, or circumcision, the prophet Simeon warns her that a sword will be plunged into her heart – hardly the most encouraging picture to give a mother at such a joyful celebration. But Mary knows now what to do with disturbing information. She simply tucks it away inside herself, like a handkerchief in a pocket, trusting that when the time comes she will be ready to get it out again. Moment by moment we are only given as much as we can cope with.

But like Esther and Ruth, Mary is no passive victim of circumstances. She grabs God's will by the throat, with joy, not self-pity, and in the great prophetic tradition of her antecedents and role models, Miriam and Hannah, proclaims the greatness of God and the coming of his kingdom. Her Magnificat is full of Old Testament echoes, the words and themes she has loved from childhood, but now they have personal significance, for a little nobody from nowhere has been given a place with her heroines in the history of her people, as they wait for God's promises to be fulfilled. God is the master of topsy-turvydom – for one day, when this extraordinary child of hers comes into his own, all the poor will be empowered, and all the powerful brought down to size.

For the first twelve years, Jesus' childhood is much like any other. After that 'silent night, holy night' of Bethlehem, where 'all is calm, all is bright', there must have been many other nights shattered by noise when Jesus screamed the house down, as babies do. Along came the other babies, Joseph's children, and packed into a basic, tiny home, didn't Mary sometimes lose her temper when Jesus got under her feet, or messed with the sawdust she had just swept up from under Joseph's workbench?

The turning point comes when Jesus is twelve, around the time of his bar mitzvah. His parents manage to lose him in a crowded Jerusalem during the Passover, one of the three pilgrim festivals they would attend annually as a family. In fact, Joseph and Mary are one third of the way home, a full day's journey on foot to the Galilee, before they notice Jesus isn't with them. Mary, who probably presumed he was with one or another of his favourite grown-ups in the Nazareth community, must have been, nonetheless, beside herself with guilt and distress, and her relief when she finds he hasn't been trampled to death or been kidnapped by white slavers is palpable. Instead, he is safely in the Temple discussing theology with the rabbis. Only when the initial relief wears off does the anomaly of it strike her. He's only twelve; a child, for goodness sake. Though he goes home willingly and never treats her with anything other than respect, from that moment, in some subtle way his priorities have changed. His first loyalty is no longer to her, and, given her strength of character, she isn't going to find that easy. She begins to see there is more to this child than she imagined. It is a salutary moment when the roles are reversed and we learn from our children.

Mary must have been especially close to her eldest boy after Joseph died. The firstborn son took on the family business and became the breadwinner. Then, while her other children married, as they usually did, Jesus stayed at home and presumably became her companion and confidante, as Amy Carmichael was for her widowed mother. Later, when he met the widow of Nain, he knew exactly how she felt.

Yet from the moment of his conception, she has always known that this special child cannot be hers to hold on to forever. She must have been living in dread of the inevitable separation. If letting go of our children is the greatest gift we can give them, it is also the most painful. On the day that Joel left home and our church, where he had been music director for nine months, to work in London, I went up to his empty room and found a single plectrum lying in the middle of the floor. I sat in a heap, feeling desolate, and grieved for the church's loss as well as my own.

When Jesus' ministry finally begins, it is not at all what Mary expects. Her quiet, respectful son mixes with the rabble, makes the worst sort of friends and has a fascination for the wrong sort of women. 'Isn't this Mary's son?' the local people sneer. Her reputation is ruined all over again – because of him.

On one occasion, she is so worried about him that she sets off with his brothers to find him – presumably to give him a piece of her mind – but can't get near enough because of the crowds. Worse still, a message is relayed back to her: 'Whoever does the will of my Father in heaven is my brother and sister and mother' (Matt. 12:50).

Is she stung by this apparent snub? She might well be, but she probably recognises it is necessary. Jesus is not disrespectful. He has to resist the attempt to keep him tied to her apron strings. He does not belong to her alone; he has the work of the kingdom to do. The umbilical cord is finally cut.

She eventually becomes one of a group of women from Galilee who leave Nazareth and follow the other disciples, providing for their needs, on a path that ultimately leads to betrayal and death. She can no longer intervene and make things right for him, pick him up and put him on her knee as she did when he was her little boy, save him from all hurt and harm, as we all instinctively want to do for our children. A sword is indeed plunged into her heart and the pain is almost unbearable.

As he hangs on the cross, Jesus sees it, and his last human act is to entrust her to John. 'Take care of her for me, John. Be to her what I would have been if I could. But I can't.'

She doesn't need to stay in that terrible place and watch his last agony, but she does, and presumably brings him some minimal comfort simply by being there. Finally, once it is all over, he is taken down from the cross and laid in her arms, where she cradles him one last time before laying him gently in the grave. This is not only the death of her child. It feels like the death of all the promises of God.

But disappointment and disillusionment do not cripple someone who has learned to wait and trust as she has. She too has her moment of resurrection. In the book of Acts she is with the other disciples, waiting for Pentecost, and she is as empowered by the Holy Spirit as they are (Acts 2). She becomes a mother to the infant church, a force to be reckoned with. Legend has it that when the persecution of Christians in Jerusalem broke out she went with John to Ephesus, to help lead a difficult, touchy congregation. For the greater part of her life she is single and alone, a widow whose child was cruelly and publicly put to death, but she doesn't resign herself to her misfortune, or opt for an early, easy retirement, sitting with her feet up in front of the fire.

No wonder God loves her. But when a member of the crowd shouts to Jesus, 'Blessed is the mother who grave you birth and nursed you', he responds, 'Blessed rather are those who hear the word of God and obey it' (Luke 11:27–8), firmly resisting any notion that Mary is greater than any other mother. Much as he loves her, he has lived with her and knows like any other child that she is not the perfect woman. At times she is difficult, at times demanding. Occasionally, she gets it completely wrong. But when it comes to faith and obedience there have been few to equal her.

Mary is no bland or faded Madonna. Like many women in difficult circumstances, she is strong and determined, practical and resourceful – a survivor. She is every woman who has ever given up or lost a child, every woman whose 'yes' to God has cost them their all, every woman who has walked alone in later years, yet remained faithful to the very end.

Pregnancy and babyhood – the desert years

Life's tough enough without having someone kick you from the inside.

Rita Rudner[2]

I had a Jewish delivery: they knock you out with the first pain; they wake you up when the hairdresser shows.

Joan Rivers[3]

Pregnancy was not what I expected and I felt dreadfully let down. For nine months I waited in vain for a serene, contented glow to suffuse my entire being, evident to all who came into contact with me. I think the very idea must have been created by men, who, feeling they ought still find a pregnant woman attractive, confuse the inability to move with contentment.

The first time I experienced morning sickness – now there's a euphemism if ever there was one for that dreadful, all-day nausea – I was gutting chickens and thought that was why I felt so squeamish. It was three in the afternoon, not the morning, and I was barely six weeks pregnant. Before we married I told Peter I had an iron stomach and was never sick. But for a full eight months, I never stopped. I was sick behind every tree, wall and lamppost in our street, while tutting passers-by muttered that the only thing worse than a drunken man was a drunken woman. Having conceived a much-wanted baby, how was it possible to long so much for the sea to stop heaving, and to be on dry land again? I felt I was going to die of it, and was greatly reassured when I read that Charlotte Brontë had.

But once a little seed has miraculously overcome all the obstacles and successfully tunnelled its way through the female underground system, there is no turning back. As the pig said to the hen over a cooked breakfast, 'You may be involved, but I'm committed.' And only God knows what that commitment will involve.

Nausea was just the first in a series of never-ending joys. Gradually, as the flesh expands, the skin creaks, groans and stretches like hardened leather, then cracks into fissures from naval to buttocks. Folds and pouches appear in the most extraordinary places. Purple veins make their way to the surface, then fork, split and thread into dozens of spaghetti junctions. The teeth disintegrate, fillings fall out, gums ulcerate, abscesses form in every area of decay – but at least the dentistry is free.

I told myself that Joel would be an only child. But it is one of life's mysteries how quickly the memory of pregnancy and childbirth passes into oblivion. Bruised and battered, stitched up like the Christmas turkey as you are, nonetheless any recollection of nausea, indigestion, stretch marks, swollen ankles, high blood pressure, discomfort, embarrassment, and pain as you have never known it, melts at the first sight of the bundle of hospital linen on your lap.

On top of all the discomforts associated with my first pregnancy, Abby sat on top of the cord and the placenta in the uterus, which may well have been a comfortable cushion for her, but meant I had a skull pushing my intestines into my diaphragm. I lived on antacids. The only comfort was that since Joel had hurtled down the birth canal from amniotic gloom into daylight, like a deep-sea diver coming up for air, having a second baby would be easier still. How could I be so wrong? But in those mediaeval days there were no scans to warn me or the midwives of the dangers ahead.

Abby's near non-existence has always left me with the feeling that she was a special gift. In the summer before she left home for university, in Peter's parents' lovely Balearic home, grieving for her going, I wrote down all I wanted to tell her about what she meant to me, in the form of a letter.

Dear Abby

In some ways I wonder whether it wasn't a mistake to come to Ibiza this summer of all summers – the last before you leave for university and the nest finally empties – for this house has been our only constant home down through the years and it holds so many memories. If your childhood is anywhere, it's here, and that's why I seem a little overwrought!

I keep getting glimpses of you as you were, with a little melon-shaped belly, elastic band wrists, wispy tendrils escaping from an excuse for a pony tail, and smooth olive skin, so beautiful I could hardly believe you were mine. I wanted to stop the clock and keep you just like that. But then, each stage was wonderful and had its compensations.

And here you are preparing for university, excited about the future, and here am I living in the past. Yes, I imagine it can be exasperating. I don't want to regret what has gone or use it to hold you back, but these memories belong to you. They tell the story of who you are today and that's why I want you to have them, for the more you understand your past, the more you can embrace your future. And there is nothing more I want than for you to see your dreams come true. I also want you to know how greatly loved you have always been, but I'll write it down, rather than go all mushy on you.

You were a surprise from the very beginning. We never expected to have a daughter. All our friends seemed to have two, or even three, of the same – all boys or all girls. Mixtures weren't in fashion. We automatically assumed therefore that we would have another boy. So when the consultant came out of the operating theatre, and presented Dad with a baby girl, he was speechless.

The indomitable Miss Baker, who was ready to sacrifice a night at the theatre for the sake of your safe arrival, thought it was due to the trauma of your dramatic delivery, and reassured him you were alive and well. But actually, I think we had both been very much at peace throughout the entire ordeal, very sure that you were safe in your heavenly Father's hands. But your earthly father could hardly say, 'Actually, it's her gender that has reduced me to this state.'

And there you were, in his arms, long before I was able to touch or see you, staring up at him from a bundle of blankets, as if you knew already who he was. And if he held you then as I saw him hold you later, it will have been with immense pride and tenderness.

I know he gave you back to God, just as we did together with Joel, seconds after his birth. We always thought of both our children as a gift, not a right, a temporary bequest entrusted to us for those all-important years. I never realised how temporary that was, how fragile my hold, how much it would hurt to let you go, until now, watching you stand on the threshold of independent womanhood. What happened to the precious moments and days which slipped through my fingers before I could catch or keep them?

I had badly wanted to give you a tranquil, gentle introduction to the world. Joel's birth had been disappointing. Wired up like a battery hen, a state-of-the-art techno-patient, I was a victim of medical science. Two midwives moaned about their nightlife and their men over the top of my bump, pausing just long enough to deliver the baby, cut the cord and dump him in my arms.

But in the end your birth was wrenched from my hands with a violence that left us all a little breathless. Dad said that the young nurse who took you up to the ward was shaking so much that she could hardly manage to press the lift button.

'Twelve minutes before brain damage. But we did it. Emergency procedures worked. Seven minutes. Isn't she lovely?'

They wheeled you to my bedside.

'We have a daughter. Look at her.'

I was aware of Dad's voice somewhere in the distance. I desperately tried to make some kind of enthusiastic sound, but all that emerged was a groan. I felt as if I had been run over by a steamroller.

'Make her look at the baby,' I heard a strange voice say. 'Otherwise she'll worry. She may think the baby hasn't lived.'

I remember thinking, 'Go away, you silly old bag. Of course I know she's alive. Just get me the morphine.'

Throughout the entire traumatic series of events, from the moment I felt the cord come slithering down like a giant snake, as they rushed me on the trolley to the theatre through endless hospital corridors, on my knees, head down, so that the cord would continue to function and not starve you of vital oxygen, I knew with a certainty beyond reason, with a calm that defied circumstances, that you were meant to be.

Later it worried me that I hadn't held you soon enough. I was terrified you might grow up with some deep-seated sense of rejection, because you were alone that first night, not touched, cradled or fed. We were studying Clinical Theology at St John's and a few of the students thought they had been damaged by their pre-birth or birth experiences. I had visions of you in years to come, confiding in a counsellor, 'I think my problems all stem back to the dreadful night of my birth when my mother didn't want to see me.' Yet I could not believe that a loving God would penalise you for what was neither my fault nor my choosing. Neither the pregnancy nor the birth followed the textbook, nor any plans I might have made.

I awoke at about four in the morning longing to see you, but of course you weren't there. They had taken you to the nursery so that I could sleep, and being a perfect patient I didn't want to be difficult by asking them to bring you to me. So I waited in the darkness, counting the minutes until day, praying that none of the trauma of the past nine months would do any lasting damage.

I needn't have worried. You are naturally the most joyous, free spirit I have ever met. I love that unladylike laugh that echoes across the hillside here and alerts every crowded room to your presence. Never lose it. I fought so hard to preserve it. I love the way you have always danced, instinctively like an African child, in the dullest churches to the direst hymns. There were times when I was tempted to stop you, to say 'shush', sit down, keep quiet, but that would have reflected my hang-ups, made you self-conscious, not God-conscious.

When they eventually brought you to me the nurse asked if I wanted to feed you, bearing in mind it wasn't always easy after a Caesarian. Joel had screamed every time I had held him anywhere near my breast and opted instead for fast food from a bottle. It had left me feeling a bit of a failure and a freak. The staff nurse placed a pillow over my stomach to cushion the wound, and laid you on it. You opened those heavily lashed, dark, almond-shaped eyes of yours and looked me full in the face, and I felt as if I had been hit, full on, by a tidal wave. I was shocked by the fierceness of the protectiveness I felt. It sounds silly but it mattered that you were a girl, one like me, a potential woman. I decided there and then to make the world a better place for women, the world you would inherit. I wanted you to have access to the moon, and the sun and the stars too, not to be earth-bound by artificial human ties. I could no longer under-stand how any man or woman could look at their baby daughter and tell her that in God's scheme of things she was an after-thought, second best, that it was a pity she wasn't a boy, for her horizons must now be limited.

Amazingly you fed and went on feeding, hungrily and happily. No screams, no rejection, just pure, untroubled tranquillity. The only person with the power to disturb your calm and sour your spirit was me. As I held you for the first time in my arms, that suddenly seemed an awesome responsibility. There were plenty of times when, like any baby, you screamed for no reason I could fathom, and after several hours I wasn't as patient as I might have been. It was later, as you let me know that you understood every-thing I said, that I realised that every cynical, harsh and unloving word would drive out spontaneity and joy, diminish confidence and tarnish the world that would claim you soon enough.

Your great-great Aunt Lucy Guinness, a pioneer missionary and writer, who had her children in her late thirties and died when they were very young, wrote, 'What in me impels my child to rise or fall?' I have always found that worrying, but have tried to live up to its challenge, even if I haven't always succeeded.

Today you lie stretched out on the terrace in a patch of sunlight, flexing one smooth and graceful limb after another, like a cat. The future looms unspoken between us. You are poised on the threshold of a new adventure that may eventually take you far away from me. I am so glad that because of your faith you go with an openness and freshness, not with the jaded, haunted look of thousands of young women who throng the paseo every night in search of some new, temporary pleasure.

I am so proud of the lovely young woman you have become. Brains are a help in this world, but Dad and I always believed character came before academic achievement. We place you firmly in the hands of one who loves you even more than we do, as we always have ever since that day when you so nearly didn't make it at all. You go with all our love, prayers and blessings, as well as the crockery, furniture, bedding . . .

Mum

Babies and I never really went well together. As my friend Serena puts it so appositely, 'Some are born mothers, some become mothers and some have motherhood thrust upon them.' When the press announced a new phenomenon known as 'the mum-at-home breakdown syndrome', I could quite understand it. I didn't have much patience with another individual crowding my space, interfering with my routine and disturbing my nights. It all stems from my big Myers Briggs 'J', the personality check that tells me I value order and planning. Having the carpet, walls and every other available surface smeared with jam, chocolate and banana was enough to drive any woman, let alone a 'J', to depression. I was cut off, de-professionalised, deskilled, de-personalised by life alone with a mini-tyrant inside four brick walls. And when I did go out, I seemed to become invisible, the lot of any woman with a hyperactive toddler imprisoned in a buggy.

I am the sort of person who prefers socialising with independent beings capable of serious, mature conversation, who entertain themselves then put their own toys away. That came, faster than I could have imagined. But meanwhile, I had never been so tired in my whole life. The comedian Milton Berle said, 'If evolution really works, how come mothers have only two hands?' There is no such thing as a non-working mother. And I'm not an expert. I only managed two.

The growing years

It is easier to become a parent than to be one. It's also easier to divest oneself of a husband than a child. A child is forever, not just for childhood, so the first principle of having one is to nurture one you like. But how? What blueprint is there?

> Like an eagle that stirs up its nest
> and hovers over its young,
> that spreads its wings to catch them
> and carries them on its pinions.
> The Lord alone led him.

(Deut. 32:11)

On holiday in France one year I watched, not an eagle, but a beautiful snowy white barn owl teaching her babies to fly. She lined her two up on a high window ledge, carefully explained to them what they had to do, then gave an impromptu demonstration – in other words, 'Do as I do, not just as I say.' Mesmerised, they watched her sweeping and diving, but when she flew back onto the ledge, they were reluctant to follow. They put out one claw, then the other, weighing up the risks, manifestly terrified of dropping fifty feet to the ground below. Patiently, she coaxed and cajoled them. She probably explained what wings were for. Eventually, hesitantly, they dared to venture out for a few yards, before diving back to the ledge for safety. The whole process was repeated several times under Mother Owl's unwavering scrutiny, each sally forth taking her babes a little further, until, by the end of the evening, they had developed a taste for freedom and there was no holding them back. Enchanted, we watched the three swooping and swirling joyously together in the night sky.

During those early years of high dependency, children observe their parents and model their behaviour and language, uncannily, on what they see. And all the time the crack between them and us is steadily turning into a crevice. They were nurtured inside us, but must learn to be who they are without us. It is vital to relate to and respect that otherness. The first time Joel was cheeky to us, when we had barely taught him to speak, I was completely taken aback. 'Hang on a minute, boy, we decided to have you. Who do you think you are? You wouldn't be here if it wasn't for us.' Actually, I didn't will Joel into existence. 'And if we are made in God's image,' a friend said to me, 'then so are they. We need to know that with our hearts, and not just our reason.'

Every mother's instinct is to keep her child at her side. I knew my children would have to learn to fly, so endeavoured to let them try out their wings rather sooner than perhaps I should. Since Abby was only five when I went out to work full-time, there was little choice. I warned her that if she wanted sandwiches rather than school dinner, she could make them herself. I can still see her, barely able to wield a knife, sitting at the kitchen table, honey from ear to ear, in her hair, up her nose, down her uniform, anywhere but on the bread. 'It's not that I like being sticky,' she announced one day, 'it's just that I've got used to it.' What a heel I felt, until she said with smug satisfaction, 'The other children complain about what their mums put in their sandwiches. They should make them themselves.' So early independence wasn't such a bad idea after all.

When Joel was born I set off on a one-woman mission to raise the first real new man. If anyone could do it, I could. Imagine my shock when the Sunday crèche organiser informed me that my three-year-old, when asked to tidy the toys away, announced, 'Let the girls do it.' Where had he seen that? How did I fail so soon? I had to admit to myself reluctantly that this was a person, not a clone. Nonetheless, if I had anything to do with it, this male person was going to be thoroughly house trained.

When he was a little older he was happy enough to conjure up the evening meal if I gave him a pound of mince, but heaven help me if I suggested what he might do with it. On the basis that creativity is an integral part of true freedom and independence, we put up with polka dot casserole – black specks floating in an unidentifiable milky substance. Today, unlike his dad, he's an imaginative cook – when a demanding job and fathering, clergy-spousing and DIY permit.

Just as he took control of his birth, Joel continued to do everything with gusto and determination. A person's character is there from the start. All it takes to fulfil its potential is a conducive environment – protection, information, discipline, the stability of their parents' relationship if that's possible and, most important, unconditional love. Above all else, deep within, a really secure child will need to know that love does not have to be deserved or earned. It is never temporarily withheld, never knowingly unkind. It covers a multitude of parental sins and failings. I think we have apologised to our children as often as they have had to apologise to us.

Affection and touch are the building blocks to meaningful relationships and real intimacy in later life – for boys as well as girls. When I am abroad I love to watch Italian men with babies and children. They adore them. It doesn't matter whose children they are, they cannot resist picking them up, throwing them in the air, kissing and cuddling them, while making the goo-goo, gaa-gaa and chutchy noises that would make a more reserved or macho man cringe.

For many centuries people have been hidebound by supposed male and female roles in child-rearing. But who defines what they should be and who should do what? The Bible gives no guidelines or advice in this particular matter. Ideally, making children and rearing them needs to be the parents' mutual activity and interest – which is why it can be fraught if they are apart. Peter and I discovered that when it came to comprehending our children and their very different needs, our complementary styles were very helpful.

When she was around nine or ten, Abby would have the most magnificent tantrums. Peter tended to confront them and demand she 'stop that behaviour immediately', which only made matters ten times worse. In the end he left her to me. For a while I was mystified by such an overblown response, then realised that she just couldn't bear to be seen to be in the wrong, whether she was or not. If I took her on my knee and explained the nature of the problem with a cuddle, good behaviour was usually restored. This is such a tender, wonderful picture of the motherhood of a God whose unconditional love restores calm to a wayward child. 'As a mother comforts her child, so will I comfort you' (Isa. 66:13).

Adolescence

Lullaby

Go to sleep, Mum,
I won't stop breathing
suddenly, in the night.

Go to sleep, I won't
climb out of my cot and
tumble downstairs.

Mum, I won't swallow
the pills the doctor gave you or
put hairpins in electric
sockets, just go to sleep.

I won't cry

when you take me to school and leave me:
I'll be happy with other children
my own age.

Sleep, Mum, sleep.
I won't
fall in the pond, play with matches,
run under a lorry, or even consider
sweets from strangers.

No, I won't
give you a lot of lip,
not like some.

I won't sniff glue
fail all my exams
get myself
my girlfriend pregnant.
I'll work hard and get a steady/
really worthwhile job.
I promise, go to sleep.

I'll never forget
to drop in/phone/write
and if
I need any milk, I'll yell.
Rosemary Norman[4]

At sixteen, Abby was half child, half woman. She still laughed uproariously at loud body noises, English tourists with no dress sense, spoonerisms and parental faux pas. She blew enormous gum bubbles which exploded in her face and sent us running for the white spirit, flew kites, lay on the floor without shoes, oblivious to the scent in the room, and told me off if I teased her father – though she did it to her heart's content. All the most important things in life were piled up somewhere in her bedroom, if she could but find them among the mounds of files and papers, empty glass bottles and other clutter gathering dust on her shelves, under her bed or tucked in corners. She was warm, curious, open, fun-loving, irresponsible, wide-eyed and full of wonder, headstrong yet totally dependent at the same time.

The secret of relating to teenagers seems to be to like them. They get heartily sick of being criticised, yet they meet it everywhere, usually from unpleasant elderly people, jealous of their youth and exuberance, whose rudeness sets them the worst possible example. Age is no excuse for bad manners.

I was spared the sullen sulking adolescent I was warned to expect. The early years of companionship paid off, but it still took time to persuade Abby that mutual trust and respect involved keeping her word about what time she promised to come in at night, and asking before she borrowed clothes, make-up, tights and underwear. My sister-in-law made my niece cringe with embarrassment by calling her mobile in the middle of a crowded students' union to find out where all her knickers had gone.

Abby's chubbiness took a long time to melt – but it did, almost overnight, in one great hormonal explosion. No wonder teenagers can be difficult. They have such a lot to contend with. My friend Rosemary thinks men's heads are dislocated from the cervical spine at birth. She takes as evidence for her argument her lovely, pubescent son, Mark – sensitive, thoughtful, raised and predisposed to be an entirely new man – yet whose emotions, she claims, still wander around like dismembered ghosts trying to find a body to inhabit.

I know exactly what she means. Every now and then, Joel and I had to have a lengthy discussion about what it meant to be part of a family. He was forever pursuing projects with such single-mindedness that nothing and no one else mattered. It's the steamroller mentality that earned his Guinness ancestors their millions and is shared by his father, uncle and grandfather, and many of the male of the species. Men need the modification that only the efficient, consistent workings of their emotional parts can ensure, and that's a hard call on their mothers.

My mother used to say, 'When your children are little, your fears are little. As they get bigger, so do the fears.' I didn't believe her. I was too busy juggling the childminding, worrying about feeding, teething, and other minor developmental and behavioural difficulties. How could child rearing get worse? But it did change. When they were little and tucked up in bed at night, at least I knew where they were. But once they're behind the wheel of a car, if they are out a moment past midnight, a thousand terrifying imaginings assault the imagination and keep a mother from her sleep. Every new adventure of theirs spells danger and terror. Yet I cannot let my irrational fears curtail their lives or hold them back.

It is so perverse. When they are at home there is no access to the TV or shower. They invariably beat you to the toilet, are in front of you at the mirror, in your favourite armchair, and even between you in your bed. You wish they were out so that you could settle down, just the two of you, to those newly rediscovered, more mature pleasures in life. Yet you know that will come soon enough. For now you must hold on to every wonderful moment, before the day dawns when you long for them to disrupt your routine and rob you of your privacy.

> Oh, time! be slow!
> it was a dawn ago
> I was a child

> dreaming of being grown;
> a noon ago
> I was
> with children of my own;
> and now
> it's afternoon
> – and late,
> and they are grown
> and gone.
> Time, wait!
>
> *Ruth Bell Graham*[5]

The nest empties

'Empty Nest Syndrome? Not me. I'm a professional woman. I have my career.' Or that was what I thought. I always laughed at the women devastated by their children's departure. 'I can't wait,' I used to say jovially. 'Life is far too full.'

Then suddenly it seemed the years had melted away, and with Abby's departure, they were gone. It had never occurred to me that I would lose a friend. Perhaps if she had been more difficult, argued more, been rude more often. There were moments – but that's all they were – moments. I found myself wondering where I would turn for advice on my spur-of-the-moment purchases, or who would tell me what to wear. When I had a house full of guests, who would say, 'Stop worrying, Mum, it'll be alright', or set the table with fancy serviette arrangements, or throw together a perfect pavlova?

I stand in the room that used to be full of knick-knacks, bric-a-brac, piles of papers, clothes and lists, and simply look. It is so painfully bare it echoes. Oh, bring back the mess. I'll never complain again. Her scent still lingers – a touch of the Calvin Klein,' mixed with a hint of foot odour. I don't like to think of her now, enclosed in such a small space. Her en-suite room at college is so small, she says that if she were a boy she wouldn't have to bother getting out of bed to go to the loo.

I passed her empty bedroom door three times last night when I couldn't sleep, and each time the sight of it left me with an empty sensation in the pit of my stomach. I stood still in the early morning chill, remembering the comforting sight of the sliver of light beneath the door whenever I came home late. I would knock gently, and wait for the soft, 'Yes?', then perch on the edge of the bed. She'd be reading, would pause to look at me, waiting for an explanation, as if I'm the errant child about to justify my lateness. Then she would relent, moving over and making room for me to get in next to her. We would chat about the evening's events and giggle at the foibles of friends. Eventually I would prize myself away. It's hard to say goodnight.

I blink – no stream of light under the door. Will I ever get used to the feeling of dismemberment? The books say you must bond with your baby – but no one helps you un-bond when the time comes. And this is for ever – the beginning of a new life for her. Dear God, please let it be the beginning of a new life for me, before I drown in self-pity. The past may have slipped through my fingers like water – yet the future waits. My most productive years are yet to come – aren't they?

A wish for my children

On this doorstep I stand
year after year
to watch you going

and think: May you not
skin your knees. May you
not catch your fingers
in car doors. May
your hearts not break.

May tide and weather
wait for your coming

and may you grow strong
to break
all webs of my weaving.
Evangeline Paterson[6]

I am so glad that as Peter and I looked at each other across the meal table, and came to terms with the vacant spaces on either side, that I didn't invest my all in my children. They always understood there was a pecking order, and that our first commitment was to one another. We always knew that, one day there would be just the two of us, just as we also know that, one day, one of us will be alone. It does fine-tune one's determination to live in the now.

But however much I enjoyed her company, Abby was not then primarily 'a friend', for my responsibility, like the mother barn owl, was to make her walk with her head held high into womanhood. I was fascinated to see this process from her perspective. Not easy for her either, it seems.

I'm sure that the body has a subconscious preparation routine for leaving home. I have a great relationship with my family. I wasn't unhappy at home, but at eighteen, my body was itching for a new adventure. I was desperate to get out. My mind had prepared itself to dispatch and the escape route was university, a whole world of independence, an abundance of opportunity and a plethora of mistakes to be made and faced.

I was struck by sadness in the weeks before I made the momentous leap to freedom. Although I would be back for each student vacation, I would never truly live and belong at home again. An inbuilt grieving system was at work, thinking of my parents alone at home. I'm so glad I've left. I realise I haven't stopped knowing them. I've begun to know them in a new way, and it's better for both of us.

My parents have been faced with living alone together again after twenty-one years and they seem to have taken to it rather well. I feel I ought to apologise for coming home and interrupting their shorthand conversation to ask what the heck they're talking about. Aside from that, we relate to each other now as adults.

They ask me for advice and tell me things they used to talk about only in code. I ask them for advice and still talk in code – there are some things parents shouldn't know.

There are things I have realised through leaving home. The way things are done in my house isn't the way they are done everywhere else. What has always been normal suddenly doesn't seem so logical, like why keep the wet and dry rubbish separate when the stuff to be recycled has its own box anyway? Little things they do, like never answering the question they have been asked, have become infuriating. My parents have foibles. They are faulted, heaven forbid. What's worse, they're aging. How dare they? They're not old, but they are definitely aging, and it seems inappropriate and thoughtless of them to do so while I am not around to supervise.

Even today, when they are grown with spouses and children of their own, I feel their every hurt, sorrow, pain, disappointment and rejection much more vividly than my own. They are my daily breath, hope and prayer, an integral part of me, yet completely separate and living their own lives. I can't imagine the pain of losing one of them, or of their rejection. It was hard enough letting them walk out of the door into their own lives – I knew then that I had raised them only to give them up. But now there are six grandchildren. And the whole process, without the same responsibilities, of course, repeats itself. My mother never warned me about that.

The woman is greater than the wife or mother

The woman is greater than the wife or mother and in consenting to take upon herself these relations she should never subscribe one iota of her individuality to any senseless conventionalisms or false codes.

Elizabeth Cady Stanton[7]

Mothering may well be one of the most important jobs in life a woman can do, but raising children takes up a very short part of it. It must always take its place in the context of the rest of our lives, and never become all-consuming; otherwise, what is left when the children are grown up and gone? It's fatal to try to find fulfilment through our children. They are, said 'The Prophet', Kahlil Gibran, like arrows from our bow. We have no control over their destiny. If they do provide us with fulfilment, it is a bonus, not an entitlement.

God forbid I should end up with that typical Lancashire epitaph, 'She was a wonderful wife and mother.' I have told Peter he can put anything he likes on my gravestone, that I was a source of endless fascination and frustration, an imaginative and interesting cook, an engaging and funny friend – but please, no reference to wonderful wife and mother! We women are so much more than the roles and stereotypes imposed upon us.

The Bible does not define men or women by whether they have children or not. Mothering is not for everyone, and the best mothers are not always the biological variety. My favourite aunt was unable to have children. It was a source of immense pain to her, but she was as much a mother to me as my own – more so at times. The unconditional love she lavished on me built my confidence and made an enormous difference to my life. I felt angry on her behalf when complete strangers would ask her why she never had children, as if every woman has the choice, as if it were any of their business anyway. I wanted to shout at them, 'She has. She has me.'

My second surrogate mother, after my beloved aunt died, was a short-lived but very special gift. I was speaking at a conference in London and had described how my mother had told me never to come home again once I became a Christian. Afterwards, I noticed a tiny black woman with penetrating dark eyes in a wonderful, well-worn face, holding back while I was bombarded by a queue of questions. Something about her patient dignity and determination captured my attention, and I finally managed to manoeuvre my way to her. She simply looked straight into my eyes, took hold of my hand, and said, 'Sound like you need a new Mama, girl. Can I be your Mama?' Then she reached out, and as I felt the warmth of her arms around me, I whispered, 'That's the best offer I've had in ages.'

We corresponded by card for some years, and every time I spoke anywhere within range of London, Irene was there, sitting quietly in the audience, making no demand, a gentle, praying, nodding presence, and afterwards, with a tight hug, a cup of tea and always profound wisdom and encouragement. My only regret was that we lived too far apart to see more of each other. One day the cards stopped coming. I looked for her, but never saw her again and reckoned, sadly, she must have passed on to higher things. And I guessed her family didn't let me know because they had no idea of the part she played in my life. But I have never forgotten the difference her loving support made.

Jewish mothers can be masters at pulling the emotional strings. How many of them does it take to change a lightbulb? None. 'Don't worry about me. I'll just sit here in the dark.' When I was baptised at the age of twenty-one, one of the world's most reluctant rather than joyous disciples, I thought I might never see my mother again. It was certainly the end of all her dreams of seeing her daughter marry a nice Jewish boy under the traditional canopy in the synagogue. But what I thought was the end of our relationship turned out, years later, to be its making. In time, she accepted my decision. Now we were two individuals with our own minds and no illusions about each other.

The writer Susan Hill wrote, 'The moment you have children yourself you forgive your own parents everything.' I see now that life wasn't easy for my mother. She never had the opportunities she so freely gave to me. Her world was constrained by the numerous expectations imposed on the women of her background. None of her intelligence, shrewdness and character was ever really put to its best use.

Whoever we are, whatever our roles, women as much as men are all called to take up our cross and follow our master. Yet many a woman over the years has used, 'But I'm only a wife and mother,' as their get-out clause. And somehow the children dominate the rest of their lives, and they miss their chance of speaking life to the wider world. And the world misses their contribution.

Yet who am I to speak about self-sacrificial motherhood? Nothing is sadder or harder than losing a child. I can't imagine what it must be like for my sisters in some developing countries whose children are taken into slavery, or die of disease and starvation. Mine haven't even emigrated to the other side of the globe. Nor have I sent a son to war. On holiday on the Greek island of Leros one year, I went into the tiny British cemetery to visit the graves of the seventy-nine British soldiers who heroically defended the tiny island in World War II. I laid a stone (the traditional Jewish way of remembrance) on the grave of the youngest – he had been a mere seventeen years old. Each of these boys was some mother's son, and had they been mine, I would have wanted a British visitor to give up a few minutes of their holiday to go there and say, 'Thank you for your sacrifice. You are not forgotten.'

In the days of the great Roman persecution of the early church, many Christian mothers were told to renounce their faith or watch the massacre of their children. Their courage in such extremes is beyond my comprehension. I cannot say what I would have done in their shoes. We can only know there must be a special grace given in such dire circumstances and, like Mary, who responded to God's perplexing calling with a trusting 'yes', believe that one day we will understand the why, and see it had some unfathomable purpose.

The influence of an inspirational mother

As I look back at my own life, a number of women – some married, but many single – have had a profound influence on the woman I became – more influence, in fact, than my own mother. It doesn't take a biological mother to give all, or the best mothering, and I am so grateful for the significant older women I owned as 'mother' in my heart. I don't know that they always knew what they meant to me and I regret now that I didn't tell them, but mothering doesn't always bring spoken gratitude. Yet every woman who is ever comforter, encourager, truth-teller, nourisher, example and inspiration is 'mother', as Mother Julian of Norwich was in the fifteenth century to the many who came to her tiny cell looking for wisdom, advice and love.

But all the same, I am just a little envious of those who had the privilege of being blessed with an inspirational woman as a birth mother. When my children were small we used to watch *Play School* on a tiny, second-hand, clapped out black and white telly. All we could see of the presenter, Floella Benjamin, were dangling, beaded plaits and a pair of sparkling eyes, but her warmth was infectious and the children adored her. How could we ever have guessed at the struggles that confident, beautiful woman had faced for acceptance in the UK?

She emigrated to Britain from Trinidad in 1960 at the age of ten, part of the Windrush generation, invited to be the workforce that would help get Britain back on our feet after the war. But there was scant welcome for the new arrivals. After the freedoms and space of living on such a warm and beautiful island, Floella found herself in one small room, shared with her parents and five siblings in a house full of other tenants, and a communal outside toilet. 'I expected everyone to treat me kindly and with respect,' she said later, 'but Britain was cold, unwelcoming, violent and bleak. I had to learn to live in two cultures fast if I was going to survive.'[8]

Her father was a professional jazz player who travelled the world. When there was eventually enough money to buy a property, Veronica, Floella's mother, known to her children as 'Marmie', decided to move the family upmarket where they would get the best schooling, health care and jumble sales! As they arrived to view a house in middle-class, white Beckenham, they were greeted by the police. Neighbours had called 999 saying black people were about to steal the fixtures and fittings from the empty house. Fortunately, one of the policemen was married to a black woman and called off his colleagues. But it was cold comfort. He warned Marmie that this kind of thing happened all the time.

'My wonderful, determined and charismatic mother defiantly folded her arms across her ample bosom, stared at the group of neighbours who stood watching and said loudly, "We are going to buy this house."' She did, and it was an object lesson for Floella – never to let opposition prevent you doing what you know is right.

The neighbours eventually moved out – after years of racial abuse and even dog mess through the letterbox – all except for the Polish family next door, who had been subjected to similar, hostile behaviour.

Marmie 'oozed wisdom and courage', and instilled a confident belief in her children that they could achieve anything. A good education was 'a passport to life'. But despite loving school, life for Floella was a constant struggle. If the gloomy weather, inedible school dinners and ongoing sense of not belonging weren't enough, she was constantly subjected to mean small-mindedness. 'Every day was a battle whenever I left the safety, comfort and security of my loving home, knowing I would have to face insults and abuse, from adults and children alike, as I walked the streets.' Going to the shops for Marmie could be traumatic for a child – she was ignored and repeatedly pushed to the back of the queue as though she were invisible. But there was no way she could go home without the shopping. Marmie would have sent her back to wait until she was served – an important lesson in perseverance, the smart way to confront bigoted behaviour.

Even churchgoing was an ordeal. Services were 'mild, controlled, unemotional', and nothing like as colourful as she was used to. So she tried singing loudly and joyfully, as she had in Trinidad, and overheard the white congregation muttering about her afterwards on the church steps. 'I see they're letting in that kind now. Is nowhere sacred?' Her family never returned and switched to one of the new West Indian churches, 'always full to the brim with people rejoicing out loud'. But the rejection she experienced at what should have been the safest place on earth hurt for a long time to come.[9]

Walking to the shops one day – she was around fourteen at the time – a boy of a similar age started shouting out the usual abuse. She was so incensed that she grabbed hold of the lollipop he was sucking and shoved it down his throat. As he started to choke, she had what she always felt was as a 'spiritual revelation'. A gentle voice in her head whispered, 'Floella, stop it . . . stop it now. You know who you are, you know your Marmie and Dardie love you, start respecting yourself too. You can't change the colour of your skin and if this boy has a problem with the colour of your skin, it's his problem, not yours. Start loving yourself Floella.' She pulled the lolly out of his throat and made up her mind from that moment on to use her brain, not brawn. Adversity would be an impetus for good, not tit for tat.

At sixteen, Floella was forced to leave school because her parents couldn't afford it. But she still did her A levels at night school, while working for three years in the accounts office of Barclays Bank. For a short while she had aspirations to become Britain's first black woman bank manager, but was disabused of that idea by her boss, who treated her as a servant. No black woman was ever going to rise through the ranks. Instead, encouraged by her father, she went for an audition for a West End musical, and got the part that would open the door to a successful career in acting – and a great deal more.

Presenting children's TV initiated her into her life's passion – to create a more open, joyful, meaningful world for children. Deploring the standard of children's TV in the eighties she created Floella Benjamin Productions, making programmes intended to inspire children with self-confidence and open their eyes to the cultural riches of diversity. So she accompanied them with children's books, and even lobbied three prime ministers for a children's minister, until her request was eventually granted in 2003.

From then on, her list of achievements must impress even the most tireless of campaigners. In 2001 she received an OBE for her contribution to television and became Governor of Dulwich College, an irony not lost on her, as this was where, forty years earlier, Marmie had supervised the boarders' laundry. In 2004, for innovation and excellence in making children's programmes, BAFTA honoured her with a Special Lifetime Achievement Award. In 2005, she received an honorary doctorate from the University of Exeter. In 2006 she was appointed Chancellor of the University of Exeter, and in 2008 a Deputy Lieutenant of Greater London. She is Chair of the Windrush Commemoration Committee, and Vice President of Barnardo's. In 2010 she became Baroness Benjamin of Beckenham, and finally in 2020, Dame Commander of the British Empire for services to charity.

The peerage is her favourite accolade. The 'Beckenham' in her title was a tribute to her Mum, who lived in the same house there until her death of bowel cancer in 2008. It was because of her, Floella claimed, that her traumatic childhood experiences in a cruel, hostile environment were used to build character and fortitude, and make her the woman she is today. 'As we rush blindly towards an uncertain future I hope and pray there are visionaries like Marmie among us. Inspirators who with sheer determination and force of character, will guide us along the path of common sense, togetherness and reason, and save this environmentally wounded, materialistic and socially unbalanced world from destruction, for the sake of our children.'[10]

Chapter 9
The Working Woman

It doesn't quite fit with an image of professional competency to break down and have a good cry in a meeting, not in front of a dozen or so hard-boiled managers, so I swallowed the golf ball in my gullet before the telltale signs of distress welled up and out, drenching the brilliant draft communications strategy of mine that my female colleagues were shredding with such relish. After all, why let frustration, disappointment, humiliation, or whatever emotion was driving me to display such weakness, spoil their fun?

I had wrestled with the document for days. I'm a journalist, not a strategist. I love stories not theories, creative thinking not abstract planning, meaningful words not management-speak. But there is one thing I have had to learn about the world of work – no one these days ever says, 'I can't,' or even, 'I won't.' Expediency requires digesting a 'how to succeed' web-blog and becoming an expert in five minutes – with the jargon to prove it. On a positive note, this means that some of us are being stretched in ways we never imagined possible. On the other hand, the fear of losing face can make a lot of normally pleasant people pretentious and defensive. As I discovered that afternoon.

I am no expert in the theory of communications, and opt for instinct and experience rather than dreary manuals, but I still thought my strategy was quite good. On reflection, I suspect the people around that table thought so too, hence the barrage of criticism. Naively, I'd always believed in a quasi-sisterhood – a world where women have an unspoken commitment to support each other in the workplace because we are not as combative or competitive as the men. We are, I thought, relational, caring, collaborative, sensitive, supportive team builders. Beware stereotypical suppositions!

Four resolute senior managers with flexed claws inflicted more than superficial wounds to my pride. I managed to stay calm, and, at the end of the meeting, made myself smile and thank them all for their time and contribution. More determined Christian duty than team leadership principles, but it left me as shredded as my strategy.

Female posturing had wreaked havoc on my unwitting, but nonetheless misguided, sense of female superiority, and left me determined to gain an understanding of the underground currents that make women unkind to one another. All of those present had worked hard and faced a great deal of male competition to achieve the senior management positions they were in. Why had we so little respect for one another? If we now take our achievement for granted, are we not in danger of throwing away women's unique contribution to the workplace?

Women of my mother's generation never had such opportunities. In the little West Yorkshire mining town where Peter served his curacy I was shocked to discover that the women had always worked – as farm workers, domestics and factory hands – the menial jobs that were beneath a man or, basically, the jobs men didn't want to do. During the Second World War, within weeks of having a baby there would be a knock on the door and a 'Come on, love, you're needed at the munitions factory. Never mind breast-feeding. Put the babe on a bottle and leave her with your mum.'

My own mum had never worked. As late as the 1950s a woman who was a teacher or an office or health worker would be expected to resign her post when she married. Some kept their status a secret for many years. Then came the 1960s and the pill and, whether it was true or not, women appeared less of an employment risk.

In the ancient Hebraic tradition, a man's highest calling was to study the Torah and fulfil religious duties. What he needed was a woman with the strategic ability to run the home and fund it with a family business. It is still the case today for some of the ultra-orthodox. The landlady of my first student flat was a rabbi's wife. In the book of Proverbs, the husband of such a paragon sits with the elders at the city gate (see Prov. 31:23). In other words, he debates and interprets the law, and when necessary, hands out wise advice and judgement to all who come for help – a sort of early Citizens' Advice

Bureau with legal clout while their women were not only the home makers, but the breadwinners too.

A vigorous woman is hard to find

A good woman is hard to find,
and worth far more than diamonds . . .
She shops around for the best yarns and cottons,
and enjoys knitting and sewing.
She, is like a trading ship that sails to faraway places
and brings back exotic surprises.
She's up before dawn, preparing breakfast
for her family and organizing her day.
She looks over a field and buys it,
then, with money she's put aside, plants a garden.
First thing in the morning, she dresses for work,
rolls up her sleeves, eager to get started.
She senses the worth of her work,
is in no hurry to call it quits for the day.
She's skilled in the crafts of home and hearth,
diligent in homemaking.
She's quick to assist anyone in need,
and reaches out to the poor.
She doesn't worry about her family when it snows;
their winter clothes are all mended and ready to wear . . .
She designs gowns and sells them,
brings the sweaters she knits to the dress shops.

(Prov. 31:10–24, *The Message*)[1]

If ever woman was capable of multitasking, this woman is. Among her lines of business are real estate, farming, market gardening, fabric design and fashion retail, to name but a few. Her prowess in sales and marketing, her charity work, her cuisine and house management are second to none. Far from criticising her neglect of her family, the writer praises her ability to work from dawn to dusk, and holds her up as an example to follow.

The Hebrew adjective *chayil*, traditionally translated 'virtuous' or 'of noble character' (or rather weakly as 'good' in *The Message*), actually means 'forceful' or 'vigorous' – like a merchant ship in full sail – big, bold and brash. It ploughs its way through the ocean with such grace and power that smaller ships move out of the way. I am not sure that this particular image of woman is a favourite in most churches. It hardly fits the old, hard-to-shake-off stereotype of gentle, acquiescent domesticity. In fact, it's more New York Jewish, upfront and direct, than mild and deferential.

The Proverbial woman is no meek little creature dependent upon the protection and provision of her man. She has her own land and bank account. 'Her arms are strong' says the NIV translation (verse 17). She's a tough cookie, both physically and mentally, a shrewd negotiator and businesswoman, so woe betide anyone who mistakes her for a soft touch. Yet the hard-nosed career and highly pressured life don't make her a harridan in the home. Her husband and children adore her. They rely on her because she is organised, dependable, even-tempered and wise. She doesn't make them pay for the stresses she encounters in the workplace. Their lives run like clockwork; there is always food in the fridge and clean underwear in the drawer. But this paragon does not owe her organisational ability, integrity and strength of character to management or lifestyle textbooks, but to her godly principles. Work, home and faith are fully integrated.

Manifestly this is not a universal prototype. Not all women have such financial resources or stamina, but I wonder why this model of godly womanhood has been so stalwartly ignored for so long. Admittedly, it is a hard act to follow, but the whole point of a role model is to expand our horizons. In his commentary on Proverbs, Derek Kidner describes her achievement as 'the full flowering of domesticity', which today seems a bit of a put-down, but he was writing in 1964 before it was really acceptable for a woman to be the breadwinner. Even so, he is forced to admit that this woman's world is 'no petty and restricted sphere', but rather that, 'Here is scope for formidable powers and great achievement'[2] and, I would add, both in and out of the home.

Doomed to be domesticated

Throughout most of the post-war years the Church supported the secular, middle-class notion that a woman's place was limited to the home, whether she loved or loathed it, was contented or frustrated. And in some homes today, particularly in the USA, reactionary theology still rides roughshod over women's feelings and calling, limiting them to the 'restricted sphere' of playing second fiddle.

My husband Peter says that his realisation of the innate equality of women in the workplace came in the early 1980s, almost as a revelation, shortly after he had left teaching to go to St John's, Nottingham, to train for ministry. Until then, he was 'the victim of a deeply ingrained chauvinism of which I was simply unaware, and wasn't highlighted for me until I attended a sociology lecture at Nottingham University. I suddenly realised that despite a good working relationship with senior female colleagues I still thought of them as earning pin money. Even then, a man can be very egalitarian in his working relationships with his colleagues, yet still expect a woman in the home to back and support him, subsuming her wishes to his. It is a shock when she develops her own career and the whole structure of the relationship has to be reordered.'

It was as well he had that revelation when he did. Within a year of moving to Nottingham I had started writing, mainly as a way of getting my head and hands out of the nappy bucket. Whenever the children were at playschool or asleep, at lunchtime, in the evening, in the early hours of the morning, I worked over a hot word processor. And gradually, unsought opportunities began to open the door to the working world. I had never really thought about the financial benefits that lifted us out of the need for Family Income Support. Mainly, I revelled in the chance to find out who I was, other than wife and mother.

Abby had been at school a month when the phone rang, and Central TV's Head of Education and Religion offered me a full-time post as a researcher. I was both excited and terrified.

'What will we do with the children after school? How will we manage?' I asked Peter, almost willing him to restrict me to my safe little domestic nest.

'We will,' he reassured me. 'I can be at home doing administration, and if I can't, someone will help out.'

The job involved much travelling and occasional overnight stays. Peter and I had to learn to juggle our respective roles, and discover that neither of our jobs was more important than the other – even if his was the Christian variety (and what a bizarre division of the sacred and secular that idea is). Each, in turn, took precedence.

On reflection, I think there were times when the children would have loved to be greeted from school by the smell of fresh baking, and a stereotypical mother, round and rosy-cheeked, in cosy sweater and pom-pom slippers, with a dusting of flour down her pinny and in her hair.

'Why aren't you there when we get in from school like other mums?' Abby asked one day.

'Because Dad is. How many other children have Dad waiting for them?'

She thought about it for a while and ran off, satisfied. When it came to playing Dad, was always more fun anyway.

Peter felt he ought to try his hand at cooking, since following a recipe was manifestly a doddle for a trained engineer. For his first little trick he thought he might try croissants. I described in detail the difficulties he might encounter when working with a yeast and puff pastry mix, and he and a fellow clergyman decided to plug the gap in their education with a cookery course. They spent many a happy Friday morning fending off questions from curious old ladies about what employment might give two young men a day off in the middle of the week. After twelve weeks he graduated successfully with a great deal of theory, but little practice. The truth is he simply doesn't enjoy cooking enough to resist disappearing into his study to do just a little bit of sermon preparation or to make a few vital phone calls, while the casserole is burning to a cinder on the ring. His lasagne was excellent, but it took all day to make and involved around a week's worth of pans, to the disgust of our two reluctant dishwashers. In the end, I excused him from duty and took over kitchen duties again, except in times of dire emergency and desperation. At least he tried. And he still comes and chops onions for me. And runs the family finances, which would bore me silly. Though he taught his methodology to Abby, and she enjoys it more than her man.

As in so many other partnerships, we discovered, ultimately, that there can only be one chief executive in the home – whichever one ensures the children have clean school uniform on a Monday morning. Since that privilege usually falls to women, it is small wonder that 80 per cent would work only part-time given the chance. A successful career costs women more than we ever imagined. A survey in *Good Houskeeping* in 2002 revealed that 90 per cent of women believed that better opportunities had made life more pressurised, less manageable and less enjoyable.

'Women don't want to go back to the bad old days,' said journalist Polly Toynbee, 'but we're living through a tough transition period, a half-made female revolution where old and new cultural expectations clash to create unbearable pressures.'[3] A woman's stressed brain, she said, was like a washing machine, churning with thoughts of the shopping, dinner money, birthday cards, cleaning, ironing, and a thousand other worries as they strive to prove they're as good at their job as any man. A friend of mine whose husband's pay was such that she had no choice but to work from the moment her baby was born, said to me wistfully, 'Most women's lives are a compromise, juggling to do the best they can with what they've got.' Though the introduction of family-friendly, flexible working policies in some organisations has made life easier, it isn't always possible.

In the West, despite the new world of opportunity, women are still finding it difficult to get to the top, and to earn equal pay when they do.[4] The government target for women in leadership of the top FTSE 350 companies was 33 per cent by 2020. In 2019 the Hampton-Alexander Review, an organisation committed to achieving that target, showed that there had been few signs of any change in the under-representation of women at the very top of Britain's biggest businesses. Although there were now more than 900 women on the boards of the best-performing companies, wrote the Chief Executive, Denise Wilson OBE, only twenty-five women were chairs, and even fewer were CEOs. Little had changed in the past few years, and to achieve the government's target would mean that one in every two FTSE 100 executive appointments in 2020–21 would have to be a woman.

But Hampton-Alexander has one other key objective – to up the number of women at boardroom level. Since October 2019, 32.4 per cent of those positions have been filled by women across the top FTSE 100 companies, up from 12.5 per cent since 2011, when 152 companies still had all-male boards. Only two companies now have no women on their board. An achievement in equality? Or are many companies simply fulfilling their government obligations with tokenism? After all, the non-executive role, usually part-time, is so much less demanding, or influential.

This can be disheartening for the capable women who would like to think that competence and expertise are, at last, the only criteria for heads of business organisations. Chris Cummings, chief executive of the Investment Association, said that promoting women into executive posts wasn't simply a nice idea. 'The research is clear: firms with diverse boards and management teams make better decisions, drive innovation and outperform their less diverse peers.'[5] So perhaps the late Paul Tournier wasn't altogether wrong, after all. Though, like Hampton-Alexander, he might have still been waiting to see the realisation dawn on the business world.

John Drane of Aberdeen University suggests, however, that women are less likely than men to reach the top, not so much because they are passed over, but because they haven't the same drive to reach it. 'Whereas men have generally inclined to put career consolidation ahead of idealism and intimacy, women more usually consider the effects that their lifestyle choices will have on others, especially those with whom they are in close relationships.'[6] For some women, such as former Prime Minister Theresa May, and Professor Anne Garden, former Dean of Medicine at Lancaster University, 'the top' may demand the sacrifice of never having children, although surveys have discovered that children do not necessarily resent their parents for not giving them enough time. What they want is quality time – parents who are not stressed out of their minds, irritable and distracted when they get home.

The controversial clinical psychologist, Dr Jordan Peterson, Professor of Psychology at the University of Toronto, supports the notion that women might prefer a post on a company board because it leaves them time for what they see as more important – namely, relationships. Dr Peterson began recording his lectures and uploading them onto his YouTube channel in 2013. His videos have had more than 65 million views, making him something of an internet celebrity, but they also created a furore among many younger women. He claims that because men and women are different culturally and biologically, equality of opportunity will never mean equality of outcome. Men are more interested in things, women in people, so despite current, limitless choices for women, more women will go into nursing, while more men are engineers. He believes therefore that it is a waste of time to weight senior job opportunities in favour of women. No legislation to minimise our cultural differences can alter biological differences, so it is pointless for the left-wing ideologues to try to enforce them with political correctness.

But this goes no way to explaining recent research from 500 scientific institutions worldwide that shows that while half of science students are female, only four are professors.[7] Tensions with work–life balance are a problem, but the report primarily blames a historic, unconscious bias, poor pay, harassment and a lack of networking opportunities. That makes it hard to retain, let alone promote, gifted women in a world where, given half a chance, they excel. Since Marie Curie, only fifteen women have won the Nobel Prize for science. Not nearly as many as there might have been if women had not had such a fight to be heard and valued.

If society is predisposed to a culture of male dominance in the workplace, it surely ought to be challenged in the name of a fairer, more balanced society. It is true that women will take a break from their career to have babies, or become carers of frail parents and other family members, or suffer distressing symptoms with the menopause. If they do, surely that's worth greater recognition, accommodation and respect. And extra support rather than exclusion – in the name of the ultimate benefits even those experiences bring to the workplace and society in general.

Why can't a man be more like a woman? Or vice versa

We were on holiday in rural France, on a makeshift 'beach' in a bend of a river, cordoned off for swimming. On a platform ten yards out, with no verbal communication other than whoops and shrieks, a dozen twelve- to fourteen-year-old boys endlessly wrestled and manhandled each other overboard in the effort to be the only one left standing. Despite the occasional half-hearted warning whistle from a lifeguard, they went on throwing each other in, dragging themselves back onto the platform and getting themselves thrown in again for several exhausting hours, oblivious of any risk to life or limb.

As I watched this masculine, adolescent rough and tumble, I wondered whether boys ever grow out of it, and whether, in fact, most of the manufacturing industries and management structures throughout the world are simply a more refined version of this particular game. Each boy was determined to be the only one on the platform, master of his universe, and when he achieved it, albeit for a moment, he jumped and cheered and thumped himself on the chest like King Kong.

It took a long while before they realised that superiority could be accomplished by cunning as well as brute force – that creeping up from behind could be more effective than confrontation in launching another boy into the water. Whoever was pushed overboard was far less likely to pull their attacker down with them.

We went through a phase in the 1980s of believing that men and women were basically the same, that 'anything he could do, she could do – and probably better'. It was, of course, a nonsense. His physical strength meant he was always going to win a race or a game of squash. By the 1990s, we were beginning to accept the idea of gender differences, and writers like Deborah Tannen, Professor of Linguistics at Georgetown University, were confirming that men and women behave very differently, and that it is reflected primarily in our conversational styles. In fact, she says, women are often prevented from rising to key positions by the way in which we communicate. It is a very strange irony that one of our unique and essential design features, our ability to 'speak life', should become the means to deny us the opportunity to do so.

Some of the differences between the genders are indeed biological and innate, as Jordan Peterson suggests. Research based on observing children at play shows that boys tend to be more 'project' oriented, girls more 'people' oriented. After an hour, two boys will have concentrated so hard on the task, they will know little more about each other than at the start. Two girls, however, will have discovered each other's age, family status, likes and dislikes. The task will have been secondary to the relationship.

But those differences are then modified and developed by cultural and social expectations as children grow up, which is why we have to be very careful about making sweeping generalisations about men and women. Boys in a group tend to play at one-upmanship. When they are out at night in a gang, they walk in a pyramid formation. They boast, brag, swagger, banter, hand out their orders and hold forth with confidence, deploy any number of little strategies to ensure, whatever they feel like inside, that they are the leader and not the runt at the bottom of the pile. But many men, like my introverted, gentle husband, feel very uneasy in that kind of company and prefer social groups where admitting fear and self-doubt is not seen as weakness.

According to Tannen, groups of girls, on the other hand, are more likely to link arms and walk side by side. They make suggestions to each other; they don't give instructions. They don't like to sound too confident or certain, lest they draw attention to themselves. If one of them does try to stride out ahead, the others will rein her in. Being superior, bossy or a boaster isn't nice. So girls, when they grow up, however bold or retiring their personality, will have learned to adapt their conversational style to an acceptable feminine way of speaking.

That day at the river beach, when Abby and her friend Helena swam out to the platform to join the boys, they played a very different game. They sat quietly on one corner, enjoying the sun and chatting, ostensibly ignoring the performance around them, but watching, always watching. And as soon as the boys were out of the way, they stood up together and dived gracefully into the water. Tannen describes the way in which these dynamics affect our different styles of communication in later life:

Conversational rituals common among men often involve using opposition such as banter, joking, teasing and playful put-downs, and expending effort to avoid the one-down position in the interaction. Conversational rituals common among women are often ways of maintaining an appearance of equality, taking into account the effect of the exchange on the other person, and expending effort to downplay the speaker's authority so they can get the job done without flexing their muscles in an obvious way.[8]

The differing styles have had a major impact on the workplace. Men tend not to ask questions as it may reveal their ignorance and put them in a 'one-down' position. Like the doctor who couldn't bring himself to ask, 'Nurse, which kidney are we removing today?' and took the wrong one out – a mammoth disaster that could so easily have been avoided. Women do ask questions, but have to run the risk that they may be considered incompetent for it.

Because they are more used to vying for centre stage, men tend to appear more confident, though, if they are like my husband, there's a strong chance that the more certain they sound, the less sure of themselves they actually are. They ensure the boss is kept informed of their achievements, prepare the pathway to promotion and then negotiate bigger pay packets than their female colleagues.

Women, on the other hand, tend to temper what they say, lest they be accused of self-aggrandisement or of sounding aggressive. We are more tentative, more aware of the impact of our words on the recipient, and the feelings they might provoke. In the context of the NHS, a female doctor or nurse will usually be far less direct and forthright in breaking bad news. Women downplay their certainties, while men downplay their doubts. Since women prefer consensus, a female manager or head teacher may seek out the opinions of others, but that can be counter-productive, for it may suggest she doesn't know her own mind. Not only that, unless she explains quite clearly that she reserves the right to make the final decision, those whose views do not appear to be represented in the outcome of a consultation may feel annoyed at her apparent high-handedness.

Because men are more used to aiming for the superior position in a hierarchical world, they will feel more comfortable about handing out their orders. Few women can deliver a list of instructions, no matter how reasonable they might be, without someone referring to them as 'Mummy' or 'schoolmarmy'. The press said Margaret Thatcher was bossy. Actually, she was the boss. Though many of the policies of the male prime ministers who followed her were equally prescriptive, none of the press accused them of being 'Nanny'.

When we lived in Coventry I was part of an ever-expanding group of women who commuted into Birmingham. The differences between men and women in the workplace were evident even on the journey in. We women had an enormous amount of fun, sharing our holiday snaps, family anecdotes, TV programmes, favourite shopping haunts and restaurants. As the group grew, so did the noise. No subject was taboo and giggles soon began to turn into raucous laughter. Every day the same men got on the train, but they never acknowledged or addressed each other or formed themselves into a group. They stayed in their own individual little worlds, hidden behind their newspapers, and, as the weeks went by, their hostility became palpable. They moved further and further down the train away from 'those women', occasionally raising their eyes above their paper and half-moon spectacles to stare at us with disapproval.

Those were the 1990s, when women were positively encouraged back into the workplace – for our people and management skills, our preference for teamwork and collaboration. This was our chance to excel, but few of us ever made it to the top because men, like those on the train, dismissed our chatter as 'small talk'. It may well have oiled the wheels of the average office, but few men set any store by the relationships it created. To our male commuting colleagues we were a group of silly, senseless females, not serious workers, though we all went to responsible jobs.

A new kind of role model

In the 1990s a new kind of woman appeared on our TV screens and captured the heart of men and women alike. *Prime Suspect*'s Detective Inspector Jane Tennison was a woman in a man's world – tough, rough, clever, witty, and still very sexy. Now in her late seventies, actress Helen Mirren has never escaped the image she created. But I had my own DI Tennison – a woman I admired more than any other I have ever met.

Raised in a strict Brethren home where women's submission to men was part of the natural order, Ruth Winterbottom left school at sixteen to work as a machine operator in the treasury department of the Ormskirk Urban District Council. However, after exchanging it for a career in the police, she finally became the first female Divisional Commander of Police in the country. She was as tough as Jane Tennison, but with a graciousness, compassion and dignity that Tennison never quite managed.

In the last half of the twentieth century the police force really was the great bastion of macho superiority, as portrayed in *Prime Suspect*. As a student I went to the local police station in Manchester to report a stolen cassette player. The catcalls as I walked along the corridors and thinly veiled sexual innuendos from the constable on duty were threatening and offensive, and left me feeling I never wanted to go near the police again. So Ruth, and her alter ego, Jane Tennison, filled me with profound satisfaction. I loved to see the male bobbies nod their heads and utter a deferential 'Ma'am' as she went by.

As Ruth rose through the ranks, managing the men was not easy. Lynda La Plante, writer of *Prime Suspect*, got it right, she once told me. Being a lone woman in a boys' club had its moments, but most of the time it required foresight and shrewdness. The senior officers were chummy and clubby. When they went out together for a drink or to play golf, they left her behind. The lower-ranking men constantly tried to catch her out. She had to be one step ahead of them all the time, proving she had the stamina, the courage and the unshockability, rather than the intelligence, for the job.

One night, when she went back to her office, she found the door closed and the lights off, which was unusual. Still in the dark, as she made her way to the switch she became aware of two large mounds moving on her desk. Fortunately she loved animals and went and picked up one of the two Peruvian guinea pigs that had been placed in her in-tray. That was when she heard the sound of male laughter behind her. She had passed the test, but, she told me, 'It made me realise that it would take more than government legislation to eradicate sexual discrimination.'

Meanwhile, she became a trailblazer, paving the way for Pauline Clare, the first female Chief Constable in the country – in Lancashire, Ruth's own force. Many of her achievements were because of, not in spite of, being a woman. It became apparent to her that in a male-dominated police force and judicial system, crimes against women were not handled sensitively. In 1986, when the Home Office issued a new set of directives on the treatment of victims of rape and domestic violence, Ruth was responsible for setting up the Rape Crisis Centre in Lancaster, one of the first in the country. 'We provided bright, sympathetic surroundings, a bath where women could sit for a long, warm soak, a comfortable change of clothing. It was all so obvious you wonder how it was missed for so many years. We also created a play area for children with a two-way mirror so that they could be interviewed in a more sympathetic environment. The first little girl asked where the doll's house was. It was an oversight, but fortunately, a local garage generously came to our rescue.'

But Ruth believed the most significant change she saw over the years was in the traditional police attitude to crimes against women. 'There had always been the suspicion, in the days before the morning-after pill, that a woman was claiming rape to cover herself in case she was pregnant. What was she doing walking home alone at one in the morning? What did she expect if she wore her skirt that short? If a wife didn't like domestic violence why did she put up with it? There was an underwritten assumption that a woman must deserve what she got. Despite the fact that it was abundantly obvious, for example, that a woman with four children and no money could hardly walk away from tyranny.'

She was desperately disappointed that despite such a radical shift, convictions in rape cases were still so hard to get. 'But injustice will always be the greatest frustration for anyone in the police. I lost count of the times I watched someone I knew was guilty walk from the court scot-free. Those are the times I thanked God I believed in an ultimate judgement and an afterlife.'

The major challenge, with her final promotion, was how to make the most of the opportunity without sacrificing any of the femininity and courtesy she had fought so hard to maintain. 'I remember being told that if I wanted to get to the top in the police I would have to learn to drink, curse and swear like a man. They were so wrong. My femaleness was meant to soften and mellow a male-dominated world, to make it an easier place for the men.'

Her first call-out as a very young policewoman had been to a house where a fifteen-year-old girl lay dead in the bath, having tried to abort a shameful and unwanted pregnancy. It fell to Ruth to inform the parents. The trauma was immense, but back at the station there was no one to help her come to terms with her shock. This was routine policing. She was made to understand very quickly that to reveal emotion of any kind was unacceptable. Any copper who couldn't cope shouldn't be in the Force. But she never forgot how she felt that night.

As a superintendent she found she could do what no man in the force could do, simply by dint of being a woman. 'I gave the men permission to cry. They would never have cried in front of another man. It would have been station news. It would have affected their promotion prospects. And oh how policemen need to cry. They develop mechanisms for self-preservation, but you can only harden yourself to a certain degree. I've seen very powerful men break down. And I've cried with them over their domestic problems, or over a job that was just too hard to bear. I didn't want any young policeman or woman in my care to feel the lack of support I felt for all those years. It may not seem a great deal, but I hope that as a woman I've been able to give the men permission to be real about how they feel.'

It was evidently more than enough for the men and women she led. At her funeral, bishops, judges, local dignitaries and hundreds of policemen and women of every rank filled Lancaster Priory to show their love, respect and admiration for a woman who had shown them such understanding and support.[9] Few women I had met had touched so many lives with her ability to use what was best in being a woman and a Christian for the enhancement of everyone with whom she came into contact. She once said to me, 'A friend asked me one day how I reconciled having such power at work, when it was denied me in church. She wanted to know whether it was my humility. I told her I didn't think of what I had at work as power, more as responsibility. A superintendent should look after the staff; listen to their problems and their pain.' This was a woman who didn't fight what she couldn't achieve, but saw what she could, and lived it to her last breath.

Women and their media stereotypes

The media and film world, that arch creator of caricature, has not been kind to the working woman. After the end of World War II, women who didn't crawl back into the home, particularly single women, were seen as formidable and unfeminine. In the fifties and sixties, big, busty, battle-axes like the *Carry On* matron, or the Peggy Mount harridan, or Alistair Sim in drag as the headmistress of St Trinian's were the butt of a great deal of fun. They emasculated weedy, wimpy little men.

In the seventies the idea of female independence was still incredibly threatening. Women only went to work out of necessity, and when they did they worked in shops, like Mrs Slocombe in *Are You Being Served*. They were divorced, sad, and couldn't get or keep a man. No career woman had any chance of a happy, fulfilled domestic or emotional life.

In the eighties, enter the vamp. The powerful *Dynasty* woman with false eyelashes and shoulder pads to mask her insecurities clawed her way to centre stage. In the Thatcher era, powerful women knew how to squeeze a man where it hurt. They were desirable, but disastrous in the long term. The film *Fatal Attraction* personalised and polarised the struggle between the evil career woman and the good little housewife and mother.

By the nineties the roles had been reversed. Detective Inspector Jane Tennison drove her way to the top by being as tough as a man. The long-suffering men in her life had to compete for her attention, and her relationship with them was often subsumed by her passion for her job. Career success and domestic happiness were still not compatible.

The dawn of the new century heralded a new type of working woman, who supposedly gave voice to anxieties and neuroses of countless of her kind. Like Bridget Jones, Ally McBeal was the single girl with a big man-shaped hole in her life. 'Society is made up of more women than men and if women really wanted to change it they could,' she claimed. 'I plan to change it. I just want to get married first.' On the outside McBeal was a legal big shot; on the inside she was an insecure, vulnerable, hurting little girl with no self-esteem because she had no man. Life on the other side of the glass ceiling turned out to be one huge disappointment. Domestication is what a woman really wants, but the show ended and McBeal never got it. That old *teshuqah,* the yearning for male affirmation and approval, still pursued women and prevented us having the impact we could and should have. It took the media more than half a century only to come full circle from Bette Davis' words in *All About Eve*:

> Funny business, a woman's career – the things you drop on your way up the ladder so you can move faster. You forget you'll need them again when you get back to being a woman. One career all females have in common is being a woman. Sooner or later we've got to work at it – no matter how many other careers we've had or wanted. In the last analysis nothing's any good unless you can look up just before dinner or turn around in bed and there he is. Without that you're not a woman, you're something with a French provincial office or a book full of clippings, but you're not a woman.[10]

In 2012 Birgitte Nyborg, a minor centrist politician who, against all the odds, became the first female Prime Minister of Denmark, appeared on our screens in a series called *Borgen,* or *Government.* Here at last, I thought, was a realistic appraisal of the effects of a powerful woman on society and power's effect on her. Until, inevitably, she too had to choose between the man she'd been happily married to for many years and the career that demanded her all. Would the stereotyping never end?

In 2019 a new phenomenon emerged. In the award-winning BBC drama series *Killing Eve,* lead writer Phoebe Waller-Bridge recreated Villanelle, the murdering female psychopath from Luke Jennings's books. She told Andrew Marr that it was 'refreshing and oddly empowering' to create violent female characters after decades of

television in which women are the victims. 'In some ways it's important,' she admitted, 'because it shows the brutality against women.' On
the other hand, she thought women were tired of seeing themselves
'on slabs the whole time and being beaten up'.[11] But perhaps something is lost when we're forced to descend to the behaviour we abhor.
It certainly brings little equanimity to her heroines.

So how do women win in the workplace?

If research told us that the new, housetrained man was a figment of
our imagination, could the media also be right, that few female
workers defeat the stereotypes and successfully bring a wholesome
femininity into the workplace? To return to that awful day at my
workplace when my brilliant communications strategy was shredded
by my female colleagues and I was left a crumpled heap, it certainly
would appear that it wasn't happening in mine. Much of Deborah
Tannen's theory appears to disintegrate in the face of female posturing. In many ways it seems worse when it comes from a woman than
from a man. It feels like a betrayal, for if our calling is to speak life to
the world, we turn it on its head and speak death when we resort to
put-down. Someone's self-esteem, enthusiasm or confidence invariably takes a knocking.

A few days after that apocalyptic meeting, I asked a colleague how
she felt it had gone, fully expecting her to commiserate with me. She
didn't. She told me how pleasantly surprised the female managers
from her hospital had been. Fortunately, I was using the phone, so
she couldn't see how far my jaw had dropped. What I had overlooked was that the communications strategy had grown out of the
joining of two NHS trusts, each deeply hostile to the other. Her
managers had come, fearing that because I had written the strategy
rather than someone from their own trust it would put my organisation in a superior position. In other words, I had set myself up to be
knocked down. Female egalitarianism demanded I be put in my
place for pushing myself forward. The men, quite happy with my
apparent one-up position, simply read what I had written and took
it at face value with an occasional, 'Mmmm, very good,' or, 'Yes, that

seems fine,' while the women resorted to comments like, 'We don't use language like that in a public strategy,' or, 'Our managers won't accept that.'

In the end, my refusal to challenge their rudeness, my aim to be collaborative and all-encompassing, my silent prayers that I would not rise to their barbs or spill my insecurities all over the table won the day. I had been suitably chastised. They were pleased with their achievement. The strategy was still intact – almost – and adopted, but in jargon. On that occasion I saw quite clearly that a woman's communicational style is not always superior to a man's – not if she dare not challenge the status quo. It may even be counter-productive. Jargon is simply a curtain to hide our insecurities.

In 1998, Professor of Social Sciences Judy Wajcman believed women had no choice but to become more like men if they wanted to be successful. Her comparative study of senior men and women managers showed that though female executives were being encouraged in business school to forego the more aggressive style, they managed in much the same way as senior men. 'Like their male counterparts, women find it hard to be soft.' She manifestly didn't meet Ruth Winterbottom. All the managers she interviewed believed there were differences of style – the male being more into command and control, the female preferring cooperation and consultation. A staggering 80 per cent of the men claimed they wanted to manage in a more collaborative manner; in other words, more like a woman. The problem they identified was that the culture of British business, driven by downsizing, left them with no choice. A tough market economy had produced a more hierarchical structure, more control from head office or government. One male manager gave a frightening description of what the workplace had become, but it explained a great deal. 'We have returned to the sixties military style of management by brutality, shout louder, hit them harder and threaten them to death until they are frightened and they do what they are told.' Wajcman concluded that in this kind of hostile environment, women had no option but to manipulate the macho ethos. 'My research shows that to be successful, women have to learn to tailor and adapt how they manage to the dominant masculine culture.'[12]

But are we now still stuck in Wajcman mode, or was Tannen right, that once men and women learnt to understand their conversational differences they would become more accepting of each other's behaviour? Possibly the latter, because we are certainly more confident. Without resorting to the power suits, we dress and speak in a way that says we want to be taken seriously, and have rejected the cultural conditioning that made us apologise for our very existence. It means we have stopped believing or pretending that we are not the capable, gifted beings we actually are. It means we're discovering at last that we really are the Proverbial Woman, vigorous, dignified and strong, and have started to sound like it.

There is never any excuse for not being gracious, courteous and affirming of others. But there are times when, like Jesus himself, women may find themselves having to be a little more confrontational than we might like, particularly if we have to deal with an 'alpha' male or King Chimp – and they are still very much around. In his need to prove his supremacy to other men, a macho alpha male needs women who fawn on him, and finds dealing with women who confront him unbearably threatening.

My friend Chris, once a respected senior manager in Marks and Spencer, maintains there are two ways of dealing with men who find it hard to cope with intelligent, confident, capable women. We can be manipulative, flutter our eyelashes, collude and pretend to swoon in their shadow to get what we want. Or, when the lion roars or stamps his feet, we can remain unfazed and seek to bring him from a childish into a reasonable or adult state, hoping that, in the end, we earn their grudging respect. The latter approach, though harder, seems to me to be more in keeping with the *kenegdo*, or 'eyeball to eyeball' treatment described in Genesis.

'Women, if they but realised it, have such wisdom and negotiating skills at their fingertips,' says Chris. 'No man at the top will ever have to make the decisions the average woman will make in a lifetime. We don't need to become tough or manly, but simply put the best part of us – our adult relational skills – to good use. It's in some men's nature to want to dominate, but women have always had the power to help them develop a gentler, more egalitarian approach. The trouble is we allow emotion to govern our reason. We think our power lies in their wanting us. But we deceive ourselves. These men want anybody who says, "I'm here for you, I'll be your mother." If we want to change things we need to understand that.'

Chris makes no pretence of any religious interest, but this secular explanation of how men and women should relate is the closest equivalent of the creation story I have ever heard. Woman resists *teshuqah*, her need for male approval, uses her communication skills instead to help man yield his need for domination, and bingo, equality and complementariness. Thank you, Marks and Spencer.

Of course, the problem with making sweeping generalisations is that there are always exceptions to the rule. The alpha male is only one small category of men – even if they often end up as top dog. There are all the other layers of men in the pyramid – the 'mothering' or 'nurturing' man, who often ends up in human resources (or 'human remains' as one of my colleagues called it), the enthusiast, the introvert, the intellectual, the team player, the gentle and sensitive, and so many more. Ultimately, we wouldn't want men to be anything other than male – certainly not an extension of us. Where would the fun be in that? But for a man, if he is honest, the higher he rises, the lonelier work becomes. He doesn't make friends as women do. He watches his back, his side and his front, and there is nothing more welcome than a straightforward, supportive female colleague he can trust.

Chris believes that because they are more hardened to competition and posturing, men are more mentally equipped to cope with the cut and thrust of the Western business world. If she is right, then maintaining our uniquely feminine style, asking questions, consulting the team, treating our colleagues as equals is more, not less vital in the workplace. The secret is becoming more direct, more honest, more challenging, without losing our sensitivity to the way others around us are feeling.

The rights and wrongs of the workplace

After several years as a researcher at Central Television I was wooed by a brand new BBC local radio station in Coventry to present a three-hour daily lunchtime programme. A year later the station manager who hired me was promoted and replaced by a new man from the West Midlands, with a brief to replace the current team with presenters from a defunct radio team who were still on long-term contracts. I was out of a job overnight. It was a blow – both to my pride and to our finances.

As my initial anger at the injustice began to subside, I realised I had a choice – to give control of my life to the new station manager and rail publicly against his behaviour, or to place myself firmly in the hands of the Almighty, a boss who is never unjust and never deflected from whatever good plans he has in mind for us. The latter seemed by far the wisest plan, and instantly I felt less resentful, calmer and at peace. I walked into the new station manager's office with all the dignity I could muster and firmly and gently told him he had no right to break my contract. I would stand down in favour of the presenter he had in mind, but would work out my last months in some other capacity. I also decided not to join in the general backstabbing.

'You're better out of it,' said my ex PA on the phone one night, shortly after I had finally left. 'The atmosphere is awful – weeping, wailing and screaming in the corridors. I noticed you didn't do that. I guess that was because of your faith?'

As it happened, she was right. A new parish for Peter had become available up north, and we were free to go. Not only that but, for me, it opened up a new career in NHS communications, which I loved so much more than media work, while the new station manager in Coventry, barely more than forty, dropped dead in the car park – probably stressed out of his mind by all the hiring and firing he was forced to do. No human institution has the right to bully or bulldoze its employees. Too many women unwittingly play the pushover, but speaking life may mean standing up to the system and speaking up for justice and for the values that really matter.

Biblical wisdom insists a worker must be paid a fair wage and on time – and that seems to suggest equal pay for an equal job. Even babysitters, usually young women, are entitled to a gift and proper care. And every worker should – in theory – only work the hours for which they are paid. My previous boss in the NHS was a man who knew how to thank and apologise – rare but important courtesies in the workplace. If he saw a light in my office when he left the building at night, he would knock, put his head round the door and say, 'Go home. Whatever it is you feel you have to do, it will wait.' And he was right. It amazed me how often subsequent bosses, often female, put me under pressure to work late, or an extra day, because 'it's absolutely vital'. In a real crisis, that was fine. But more often it was the result of disorganisation and mismanagement, and I became less tolerant of picking up other people's omissions.

Apparently, women's tendency to overwork is the basis of our over-rated reputation for multitasking. The jury on this particular cookie has been out for some time, but one Australian study[13] seemed to show it was a myth. Women, apparently, find it just as hard as men to switch attention from one task to another, because two similar tasks compete to use the same part of the brain. Dealing with several issues at once can make us feel we're multitasking, but the brain can only focus on one project at a time. It's more likely that in order to succeed, women simply work harder and do more, adding domestic chores and emotional responsibilities to the demands of work. Or perhaps, contrary to the findings of the study, we have actually trained our brains to deal with more than one issue at a time out of necessity?

Whatever, multitasking may be what we have to do, or it may be about driving ourselves — out of fear, guilt, perfectionism or a desire to please. It is hard to be assertive enough to say no, to be the first to say goodnight and leave the building, to admit to ourselves we cannot do it all. But leisure is not an optional extra. If God set us an example, who are we to argue? Observing a Sabbath is one of the most ignored commandments in our shop-till-you-drop society — at our peril! It wasn't simply one of God's better suggestions. It wasn't even a chance to recover from clapped-out exhaustion. Or because it's essential for a balanced, healthy lifestyle. It was meant to be a taster of the joys of the life to come, when all work will cease to be necessary, and humans will know the wholeness of mind, body and spirit they were always meant to enjoy. Since the days of the Roman Empire, the Jewish Sabbath, with its compulsory observance of a full twenty-four-hour rest, from sundown to sundown, has always been a useful tool against workaholism. 'I have to go home now — it's my religion!' may well be worth a try.

When she was Chairman of a Health Trust, whether she was in the middle of a board meeting or not, at lunchtime on Fridays, Rabbi Julia Neuberger would say, 'I'm off now. It's time for the family.' It was her way of challenging a work-obsessed culture, of saying that home was a place of equal importance, of giving permission to her colleagues, especially the men, to leave. And they found her leadership life-enhancing.

Bullying in the workplace is an all-too-common way of exploiting women's desire to please, by making them anxious, willing to work longer hours than they should. And women can be just as guilty of it as men. Take, for example, the allegations of bullying made against Home Secretary Priti Patel in 2020. In this, as in most issues, there is no room for women to take the moral high ground. Diminishing others by demeaning, harassing and excluding them is usually a way of dealing with some sense of inadequacy in ourselves.

It is hard to find the best way to deal with this unacceptable exercise of power and dominance, but Jesus provides an interesting model. He was shamelessly bullied, threatened, mocked, scorned and belittled by the authorities, but was never anyone's doormat. He was made a public spectacle, yet bore it with a dignity and courage that left his integrity intact and ultimately earned him the grudging respect of most of his persecutors.

His secret is revealed in the Sermon on the Mount. 'Turn the other cheek' (Matt. 5:38–41) does not mean 'let yourself be a pushover'. A backhanded slap on the cheek is regarded in the Middle East as a statement of contempt. But Jesus insists we should refuse to be insulted, by offering our assailant the other cheek to slap as well. In other words, it was a form of passive resistance, a way of standing your ground with self-respect and dignity.

Another secret is to remain completely unfazed, or if that isn't possible, to appear unconcerned. It is imperative, in the face of bullying, to breathe deeply, hold your head up high, look the abuser straight in the eye and never, never let them know how intimidated you feel. 'It is fairly exhilarating,' one woman manager said to Deborah Tannen, 'to be able to stare hostility straight in the face and manage to remain unmoved.' It took her thirty-five years to learn this particular trick.[14]

Another, depending on how clever and manipulative the abuser, is assertive confrontation – gently and firmly pointing out the bullying tactics, holding our ground and repeating our decision that it must stop. It might risk losing a job, a tough decision if no other income is coming into the home, but ultimately that needs to be weighed against the cost to our mental health and wellbeing.

Bullying should always be reported. New working directives on whistle-blowing make it a little easier, but institutions exist to protect themselves, not the employee, and it is a courageous step to take – especially if colleagues defend their position rather than what they know to be the truth. 'Shopping' anyone can feel like an admission of defeat. This is especially true of sexual harassment. Unfortunately, every institution, including the Church, has its share of sexual predators who feed their need for power by playing cat and mouse with every woman in their sphere, cleverly covering their tracks by pretending to be a domesticated pussy rather than the rapacious tom. It may even be the boss or the minister who has got away with appalling behaviour for years, simply because no one has dared to challenge or report it.

When I first began working in the religious department of Central TV, I was a naive newcomer to the office world, and was shocked when one particular director, who made a public show of his Christian piety, called me into his office for some very unwanted prayer and attention. 'Don't worry about it,' one of my colleagues confided in me, when I sheepishly shared my concerns with her. 'He does it to us all. At least you won't feel left out! We think it's probably his diabetes getting out of control. Just make sure you're never alone with him.'

That was easier said than done when we ended up on a film shoot together at the Swanwick Conference Centre in Derbyshire and I had a bedroom with no lock on the door. I heaved a huge chest of drawers across it before I went to bed, but spent a sleepless night, full of terrors, convinced I heard him outside. One Friday evening some months later, after we had all left for home, he tried his technique on a woman in another department. By Monday morning he had been suspended amid a blaze of publicity in the tabloid newspapers.

For me, the incident raised many questions about why we in the religious department had had such a misguided sense of loyalty and sympathy that we colluded in his behaviour. Of course his diabetes had nothing to do with it. Common sense should have told us that. Some were genuinely fond of him and didn't want him to lose his job. Others knew his wife and didn't want to upset her. Our producer, who saw what was going on, had offered his team no protection or support.

Thankfully, times have changed. But unless women know the limits of a little harmless flirting and are prepared to say when they find touch and innuendo embarrassing and uncomfortable, it will continue unchecked, and even escalate. If management is not prepared to listen or offer their support, it may be essential to find work elsewhere. When integrity, self-confidence and mental health are threatened, there is no shame in walking away – especially if the complaint is left on record. Many a woman has found herself vindicated at last – even if it is years later.

I once had to leave a job I loved when my close friendship with a very senior colleague became a weapon levelled at her integrity. It was yet another case of female jealousy and resentment, and it caused me much heart-searching, but in the end there was nothing else I could do to preserve the reputation of someone I loved and valued, and who had a far more important role to play than I did.

Give work your best shot

I would earnestly ask my sisters to keep clear of both jargons now currently everywhere (for they *are* equally jargons); of the jargon, namely, of the 'rights' of women, which urges women to do all that men do, including the medical and other professions, merely because men do it and without regard to whether this is the best women can do; and of the jargon that urges women to do nothing that men do, merely because they are women, and 'should be recalled to their sense of duty as a woman' and because 'this is woman's work' and 'this is men's' and 'these are things women should not do' which is an assertion and nothing more. Surely

woman should bring the best she has *whatever* it is to the work of
God's world without attending to either of these cries.

Florence Nightingale[15]

Florence Nightingale made nursing a respected career for women.
But her standards were high. She called on her girls to eschew
marriage in order to do what they were called to do. Why would any
woman want a man more than the chance to make her world a
better place? Today, thankfully, we can have both. But there is an
onus on us to make work as pleasant, challenging and creative as it
can be.[16] A first-rate teacher inspires their pupils, a good manager
instils self-confidence and self-worth, a caring health professional
speeds up the recovery of their patient, a professional housewife or
househusband makes their home a place of rest and recreation.

Years ago, when she was Chief Executive of the Bro Taf Health
Authority in Cardiff, I met Dr Gill Todd when I spoke at a meeting
for female heads of NHS Trusts. A committed Christian, she applied
her faith to the task in hand, and had brought another young woman
with her, whom she was mentoring and preparing for a future senior
management role. The young woman explained that Gill would give
her up-and-coming young managers a small geographical area of
their own, so that they could get to know the local population and
commission the healthcare they needed. It was a visionary, creative
approach to training, and they respected the trust she placed in them.
But not all young women have such fine role models.

Too many women who have had to fight their way to the top
'pull the ladder up' on younger female colleagues instead of offering
them opportunity and encouragement, because they don't see why
the next generation should have it any easier than they did. Flexible
working hours and allowances for childcare appear unnecessary
luxuries that mock the dedication and sacrifice they were forced to
make. Or perhaps they simply feel threatened by younger talent. But
this is not giving our best. It is women behaving badly, jealously
guarding our territory without consideration or compassion. It is
having a very strange, protective idea of our own achievements.

Some early women missionaries thought their pioneering work
so difficult that when they went home on furlough they recruited

only men. Some years ago I remember being shocked to hear that a well-known female church planter had deliberately handed her 'baby' to a group of uniquely male leaders before she moved elsewhere. Despite all her work in setting up a new church, only men, she told me, would be up to the task of leading it. This isn't merely 'pulling up the ladder', but slamming the hatch door in your sisters' and daughters' faces. And there has to be another way for women of faith.

Work cannot be our entire world – even if it feels like that by the end of the week. Yet, for all its frustrations and foibles, it is a gift and can be a privilege, so much more than just earning our daily bread. And even if Tournier's assessment in the 1950s of women's contribution to civilisation when every industry was thrown open to her influence was somewhat overblown, we do have the potential of standing with the men to make our workplace a happier, better place.

Chapter 10

A Woman of Experience and Maturity

A few years ago I found myself on the speaking circuit of a group of women's literary lunches where the average age of the membership was around seventy-five. Those who managed to stay awake for my post-luncheon address were exposed to a rendering of Jenny Joseph's wonderful poem, *Warning*, with it's first line: 'When I Am an Old Woman I Shall Wear Purple'[1] – long before it became an almost cult phenomenon. There were loud, affirming cackles throughout – whether because they thought they were purple-wearers or still planned to become purple-wearers I couldn't quite work out. Because the truth was that a group of less likely geriatric delinquents would be hard to find. Their perms, frocks and glittering paste brooches were utterly conventional. They referred to me as 'Mrs Guinness' throughout, however many times I told them my first name, and spoke to each other in the same formal, deferential language. But if you can't blow a raspberry at the establishment at seventy-five, when can you?

As this world's pleasures slowly loosen their grip and eternal joys become more real and imminent, we should, in theory, be released from the earth-bound necessity to conform, satisfy and please. We could start to say what we really think and feel and get away with it, forgiven because we might just have a touch of dementia. But I meet few truly liberated eighty-year-olds, largely, I think, because they still fear the consequences of speaking their mind.

A friend of mine described how, during a stay in hospital, the elderly woman in the bed opposite was denied the use of a commode because the staff were 'busy'.

'She's an angel,' whispered the patient, pointing to the departing nurse's back. My friend could hardly believe what she was hearing.

The denial of the commode was only the culmination of repeated unpleasantness and rudeness.

'No, she isn't,' my friend retorted, 'she's anything but.'

But the older woman had no intention of letting the truth penetrate her reason and either destroy her illusions or galvanise her into assertive action. It was manifestly safer to live with great physical discomfort and keep the peace, than rob an angel of her halo by reporting her to her manager, as she should have done.

Nothing disabused the nurse about her views – that old ladies are weak and ineffectual, a willing butt for her frustrations and passive victims of her anger. The largest employer in the UK, the NHS is frequented by women more often than men, is staffed by many more women than men, yet can be the most hierarchical and oppressive of regimes. It is staggering that there need to be government directives to explain to NHS staff how to show elderly people courtesy and dignity. Even the best of nurses tend to shout at them as if they're automatically deaf, or worse, speak to them as if they are children. 'Come along now, Gladys, let's just pop you into bed, shall we?' And they take an arm that quivers to order, and 'just pop' Gladys with barely disguised intolerance into whatever out-of-the-way piece of space is ascribed to her.

If I were Gladys, I'd tell the nurse where to pop herself in the most robust English available to a Christian, or swing a fast right hook. But Gladys wouldn't dare do either. A lifetime of ladylike subservience, of never acknowledging or expressing her own needs, of putting everyone else first, has rendered her passive. She submits to the indignity of being called by her first name, which she hates, and plays the nurse's game by pretending to be the frail, hard-of-hearing, helpless old biddy with the cracked, worried little voice everyone associates with old age.

Woe betide anyone who treats my 92-year-old Jewish Mama as a pathetic old dear, despite her shock of silver-white hair. Her voice has never lost its inimitable ability to shatter glass at a hundred yards. And she can still reduce the most hardened workman to pulp with her Thatcher-esque gift for wielding words like a machete.

'I'm sorry,' grovelled the male manager of her local Tesco when she once complained loudly and in full about the quality of the service. 'The problem is the girl on the till.'

Now if there is one thing my mother cannot abide, it is a

pompous male manager who blames his defenceless, unsuspecting junior workers – especially if they are female. So she drew herself up to her full five feet, looked him straight in the eye and remonstrated, 'On the contrary, a store is only as good as its manager.'

At eighty-four, my mother-in-law, a strong-willed, determined woman, used to snap, 'I'm not an old lady yet,' when we tried to take her arm to help her across the road. When her body finally began to give up, a junior doctor arrived at her hospital bed and said, 'We're going to operate, Mrs Guinness.'

'Oh, are you?' she replied. 'Well, it's my body and I think I'll be the judge of that.'

'Of course,' he demurred, a grudging new respect in his eyes.

There was an eighty-four-year-old woman in the New Testament who was equally outspoken, a wonderful role model for any woman who fears that the aging process may creep up on her unawares and divest her of her usefulness before her time.

Anna, defier of convention

There was also a prophet, Anna, the daughter of Peanuel, of the tribe of Asher. She was very old; she had lived with her husband seven years after her marriage, and then was a widow until she was eighty-four. She never left the temple but worshipped night and day, fasting and praying. Coming up to them [Mary, Joseph and the infant Jesus] at that very moment, she gave thanks to God and spoke about the child to all who were looking forward to the redemption of Jerusalem.

(Luke 2:36–8)

The spirit of prophecy had been silent in Israel for more than 300 years. The traditional view was that God would only speak directly to his people again in the dawning of the new Messianic age. According to the Pharisees, one thing was sure – no prophet would ever come from Galilee.

On every account Anna defied convention. She was a woman, a prophet and descended from Asher, the tribe that had settled in

Galilee. She even preceded the fulfilment of the prophecy in the book of Joel that 'Your sons and daughters will prophesy, your old men will dream dreams, your young men will see visions' (Joel 2:28). Even then, she was too old to be a daughter any more, and she was certainly not an old man.

But this widow was not a frail little woman, dependent on her family and society. She had only had seven years of marriage when her husband died – much like my husband's grandmother, Grace. Grace was only twenty-seven when she married the aging but well-known preacher and writer Henry Grattan Guinness in 1903. He was forty years her senior and their relationship caused a great stir and not a little criticism in evangelical circles. But they were blissfully happy and had two sons, born when Grattan Guinness was seventy and seventy-two. In old age, she would speak, with wistful girlish pleasure, of the seven years they had had together and say that they had provided her with more than enough passion to last a lifetime. She never married again but, despite an ultra-conservative Brethren upbringing, challenged the conventions of Edwardian society by going out to work so that she could bring up her two boys alone. Not to mention campaigning for women's suffrage and birth control.[2]

I imagine that Anna, like Grace, was a feisty individual. They must have both been fairly tough to survive alone as women in their respective societies. Who knows why Anna chose never to marry again at a time when it would certainly have been the norm. Perhaps she too had been married to an irreplaceable man, and felt there could never be another human substitute. Since children were no longer a priority, perhaps there was another way of using the unexpected freedom she had been given. So she joined a group in Jerusalem known as 'The Quiet of the Land'. It was an Order of contemplatives who withdrew from society and devoted themselves to praying for the coming of the Messiah, never knowing if they would live to see the fulfilment of their hopes and dreams.

After all those years in the Temple precincts, one day must have dawned much like another. Until, out of the corner of her eye, she catches sight of a young couple slowly climbing the steps with their precious bundle in their arms. She smiles to herself as she observes the special radiance of so many new parents – despite the exhaustion and broken nights. She turns away, but something different about this particular family makes her look again. Now her throat tightens and her breathing quickens. She cannot take her eyes off the couple and their baby, as they continue their hesitant approach towards the high altar, bringing a poor little offering of thanksgiving.

Suddenly, they're intercepted by that cantankerous old natterer, Simeon, who, despite the continual teasing and mocking laughter of the other sages, has always insisted he will see the Messiah before he dies. Well, if Simeon seems to think that this is it, and he can now die in peace, there can be no mistake. Her stomach turns cartwheels of joy.

Gently, she takes the precious baby into her arms, then hurtles around the Temple like a virago, shouting to all the scholars, teachers and holy men and women, gathered in the silence to wait and pray for the Messiah, that he is here. Mary and Joseph must have wondered what kind of an eccentric has grabbed hold of their baby, but he doesn't make a murmur. As for Anna, what does she care how others will see her? This is her moment. As every cool and shady corner of the Temple now begins to yield its human shadows, curious to see what the fuss is all about, she holds the baby high above her head and publicly proclaims him the Messiah of Israel.

I imagine Mary and Joseph were glad to have the baby safely back in their arms. Were they aware of the significance of the restoration of the prophetic voice, heralding a new messianic age? It's in maturity that Anna becomes the first woman to proclaim to the world the good news of the incarnation.

Mature achievers and Peter Rabbit

Once a woman passes the fifty-year landmark, like a good cheese or wine, she may be at her best – if 'the best' involves wisdom, experience, discernment, a demand for authenticity, the power to let bygones be bygones, the ability to encourage potential in others and the grace to laugh at her own foibles. Her children, if she is fortunate to have any, are grown up, while her energy, if not at its height, shows no sign of abating. The sky is the limit, suggest magazines like

Good Housekeeping. We can, apparently, start a company, write a book, tour the world with a backpack, find love for the umpteenth time or cycle across China! Some female television presenters these days are even over fifty, we are reminded, month after month, when the same women appear on the front cover. Sometimes, we're told, the very mature are not without sex appeal, women like Dame Judi Dench or Dame Helen Mirren, or that paragon of survival, Mary Berry – who probably owes more to reaching men's bellies than raising their testosterone levels. And though it may over-egg the pudding in the name of anti-agism, *Good Housekeeping* does buck the trend of most fashion magazines, occasionally resorting to models over the age of seventy. And it does leave some of us with a warm glow. Meanwhile, to function at all, the churches now depend on the ministration of mature women – often running the show, while the men make the coffee and tea, and sometimes a meal for the entire community.

So age, apparently, need be no obstacle for an energetic, determined woman, motivated by faith and vision. It may even be an advantage. Some of the most heroic women have been well past their prime when their life's calling came, and perhaps the timing was not altogether arbitrary.

At forty-seven, Corrie Ten Boom was a sedate, middle-aged, unremarkable single lady who had lived a very sheltered life in her small but much-loved native town of Haarlem. That changed in 1939 when war broke out and Holland was occupied by the Nazis. 'Lord Jesus,' she prayed, 'I offer myself for your people. In any way. Any place. Any time.'[3] She began hiding Jews in a secret room above the home she shared with her widowed father and older sister, Betsie, over Casper Ten Boom's watch repair shop. She and Betsie were eventually betrayed to the Gestapo and found themselves in Ravensbruck Concentration Camp. The physical indignity suffered by these two sheltered, no-longer-young women was immense, but their inner, spiritual life remained intact as they prayed for those who subjected them to such sustained humiliation.

In 1944, shortly before Corrie was released, Betsie died, but Corrie fulfilled her last wishes by travelling the world to preach the power of forgiveness. Her ministry only ended when she was in her eighties and a stroke left her without speech and paralysed. Even then, those who met her were bowled over by the radiance of this incapacitated old lady.

Mother Teresa, perhaps the most famous Christian woman of all time, was born in Albania to a peasant family in 1910. She was forty when she set up a new order, known as 'The Missionaries of Charity', to work among the poor in Calcutta. She was in her sixties before her work gained any international recognition, and in her eighties when her public witness had its greatest impact. She urged every human being to smile five times a day at someone they didn't like, and attributed her life's achievement, like Corrie Ten Boom, to placing herself entirely at God's disposal. 'Put yourself completely under the influence of Jesus, so that he may think his thoughts in your mind and do his work through your hands, for you will be all-powerful with him who strengthens you.'[4]

The wonderful, late Helen Taylor-Thompson OBE, who turned the Mildmay Hospital into the foremost European centre for the care of people with HIV, was a human dynamo well into her nineties. She was in her late sixties when her most important life's work began.

Helen, at nineteen, was recruited into the SOE (Special Operations Executive), Churchill's secret army of spies and saboteurs. A back injury, sustained in fighting off a senior officer who tried to rape her, prevented her being parachuted into France and killed, as most of her female colleagues were. She smiled when she described to me her decision not to report the man for the sake of his family – aware of the terrible irony that he may well have saved her life.

But it wasn't until the 1980s, after years of running a family business, that she took on the Department of Health to save a dilapidated Christian charity hospital from the bulldozer, with no idea what she was supposed to do with it. Someone said to her, 'Helen, Mildmay was opened to combat cholera, a nineteenth-century epidemic. What if Mildmay has been rescued to fight a twentieth-century epidemic? Haven't you heard of HIV?' She hadn't, but by the time she was in her seventies she was chair of the first dedicated hospital in Europe for the palliative care of people with AIDS, raising millions of pounds, recruiting an outstanding staff, establishing its pioneering work in Africa, fighting stigma and playing host to Princess Diana.

In 1995, along with others, Helen organised the 'Great Banquet', when 33,000 people in London, of every background, race and colour, rich and poor, politicians, police and vagrants, sat down and ate together. Out of it sprang CAN, the Community Action Network, a conglomeration of largely young entrepreneurs who shared a commitment to using their business expertise to tackle social injustice. In 2019, the network was renamed 'The Helen Taylor-Thompson Foundation' in her honour.

Meanwhile, in 2000, Helen founded Thare Machi Education (TME), and chaired it from a wheelchair until her death in September 2000 at the age of ninety-six. In Uganda, Kenya, South Africa, Malawi, India, Cambodia, Congo, Zambia and China, TME education uses interactive DVDs in local languages to educate young women in disease prevention, to enable them to transform the poor communities in which they live.

There have been many older women who have decided to forego comfortable retirement for the betterment of others. One of my favourites made no statement about personal faith, but her achievement was so special, and her personal bequest so great, that I think her story deserves to be told. In 1923, when she was fifty-eight, writer and illustrator Beatrix Potter embarked upon a new career that would bring pleasures more lasting than any of her books. She had no idea when she bought Troutbeck Farm in the Lake District that upon her death, eighteen years later, she would eventually bequeath the entire Monk Coniston estate – 4,000 acres of land, fifteen farmhouses and dozens of cottages – to the charity she helped to found: The National Trust.

Throughout the 1920s, while agriculture was in the doldrums, the well-to-do came to the Lake District in droves, looking for holiday homes or building plots along the most picturesque vantage points of the lake shores. Capitalists bought up land and forests for businesses and hotels. None was aware of how corporately destructive on the landscape their individual pursuits would turn out to be. But Beatrix Potter could see it only too well, and feared that some of the most pleasurable pursuits would be lost to the public forever. Despite substantial earnings from bestselling children's books like

The Tale of Peter Rabbit, The Tale of Squirrel Nutkin and *The Tailor of Gloucester*, she did not have enough money to buy the Monk Coniston estate outright, but knew, if she was to save for others this part of the Lake District she loved the most, then she had to find it.

Born in London in 1866, Beatrix Potter had fallen in love with the Lake District from her very first family holiday there, when they had rented Wray Castle for three months in the summer of 1882. Only in the countryside, where she could give free rein to her profound affinity with nature, did she feel truly, completely alive. She drew and painted everything she saw, with reverent attention to the tiniest detail. Even the common toadstool became an object of fascination and beauty, thanks to her pen.

The Potters were strict, strait-laced, rather unloving parents, who believed that once their only daughter reached her late thirties and was still single, she would devote the rest of her life to caring for them. Her success as a writer and illustrator had been a shock to them. So was the announcement of her engagement to her publisher, Norman Warne. They were bitterly opposed to her marriage, and not a little relieved when her intended died suddenly of pernicious anaemia. But instead of playing the dutiful daughter, Beatrix decided to establish her independence anyway. In 1905, seven weeks after Norman's death, she bought Hill Top Farm in the village of Near Sawrey, with its breathtaking views over Esthwaite Water to the hills of Coniston beyond. 'My purchase seems to be regarded as a huge joke,' she wrote to Norman's brother, Frederick. 'I have been going over my hill with a tape measure.'[5]

She continued to live in London, but spent as much time in Near Sawrey as she could, renovating the house and helping her tenant farmer get the farm in good working order. It was the best possible therapy for grief, and the next few years were Beatrix Potter's most fruitful, as her 'friends' at Hill Top provided the inspiration for Jemima Puddleduck, Jeremy Fisher, Tom Kitten and Samuel Whiskers.

In 1909 she bought a second farm in Near Sawrey – Castle Farm – with professional advice and support from a local firm of solicitors, W. H. Heelis and Son of Ambleside and Hawkshead. William Heelis, the bachelor son who specialised in land contracts, was very taken with the determined woman writer from London and soon proposed to her. Beatrix's parents were furious. She was forty-six and they were getting frail, but in 1913 they begrudgingly gave their blessing to the marriage, and she and Willie began their new life together in Castle Cottage in Sawrey. From then on, farming, not writing and drawing, took first place in her life.

Ten years later she acquired Troutbeck Farm and, when its tenants died in 1926, decided to run it herself with the help of local shepherd Tom Storey, who encouraged her to build up her celebrated flock of Herdwick sheep. But it was at the age of sixty-four in 1929 that she faced her greatest challenge. The Monk Coniston Estate, comprising 2,500 acres of land around Coniston Water, including seven farms, and some of the area's most magical vistas and glorious beauty spots like Tarn Hows, came on the market. It was more than she could ever afford. But in 1930, she clinched a cliff-hanging deal with the newly formed National Trust, persuading them to share the £15,000 cost of the Monk Coniston Estate, which would become theirs on her death. She wrote:

> Those of us who have felt the spirit of the fells reckon little of passing praise; but I do value the esteem of others who have understanding. It seems that we have done a big thing; without premeditation; suddenly; inevitably – what else can one do? It will be a happy consummation if the Trust is able to turn this quixotic adventure into a splendid reality.[6]

Managing the entire estate well into her seventies, she was a familiar figure in her tweed skirts, gaberdine, green wellingtons and battered hats, choosing tenants, collecting rents, repairing hundreds of dilapidated buildings, putting up fences, mending walls and supervising the felling and planting of trees. Willie kept the accounts, and her lavish spending on ramshackle buildings was a source of constant marital disharmony. But she was determined to do everything she could to hand over her estate in pristine order.

This was a woman who managed to gain acceptance and respect in an exclusively male world. Children found her rather formidable and unapproachable, but the children's story writer was shy and had no idea how to relate to them. The locals had no idea of her fame. She was just Mrs Heelis, farmer, Herdwick sheep breeder and supporter of hill farming. 'I am in the chair at the Herdwick Breeders Association meetings,' she wrote to a friend in the 1930s, when she was its president. 'You would laugh to see me amongst the other old farmers – usually in a tavern! after a sheep fair.'[7]

Every summer for many years, Peter and I spent a reading and walking week with friends in a house built in the 1920s with lovely views over Esthwaite Water and within walking distance of Tarn Hows. 'Fellfield' belongs to the Anglican Diocese of Liverpool, thanks to the generosity of a previous bishop, who left his lovely home for other clergy to enjoy. There is a restfulness and peace about the place that seems to sink deep into the soul. From the moment I crossed the threshold, it always felt like home, and I often referred to it affectionately as my spiritual timeshare. It was a wonderful privilege to be able to stay there, and I'm also glad, perhaps selfishly, that one woman managed to limit the number of properties built in its vicinity and to give me and thousands of others unlimited access to Coniston Water. When Beatrix Potter died in 1943, her bequest was the largest ever made to the National Trust. She had effectively saved the Coniston area from the few with means who would have exploited it, for the many without means who dearly love it. And the National Trust was now a viable force to be reckoned with.

Beatrix Potter simply did what she had to do, and was fortunate enough to have the vision and resources to do it. Helen Taylor-Thompson, Mother Teresa and Corrie Ten Boom had no financial resources when they committed themselves to their life's grand projects, yet succeeded all the same. When asked by Kenneth Clarke, Secretary of State for Health, how she intended to raise the money to run the Mildmay Hospital, Helen Taylor-Thompson once said to me, quite simply, 'I get down on my knees and I pray, then I get up and I work.' None of these remarkable social entrepreneurs thought of herself as 'just a woman'. Gender had no place in their heads. There was too much to do. Each of them seems to have worked harder past retirement age than before it. So it's probably a good idea, as one gets older, to cut oneself free from ties and be ready for the truly great adventure.

Losses and compensations

Get even. Live long enough to be a source of aggravation and anxiety to your children.

Bumper sticker

There is so much more I would like to achieve and so little time left in which to do it. When I was younger I thought that the mind would adjust automatically to the changes in the body. But it doesn't, and we are left in an almost permanent state of shock – especially when I catch sight of myself in a shop window and wonder who the old bag with the saggy skin can be.

One of the nice things about growing older is that the old *teshuqah* begins to lose its power. Any respect we gain is for character alone, and there is no need to worry about being attractive to men any more – except one, if we're fortunate to have one – and such odd things are happening to his body that he doesn't seem too concerned about what's happening to yours. Men swell and droop, moult and sprout every bit as much as, if not more than, women, and find it just as hard to admit they're not quite the fine specimen they thought they were at thirty-five. My mother-in-law once said to me, you know he's getting old when you say, 'Darling, let's go upstairs and make love,' and he says, 'Sorry, my love, which do you want, because I can't manage both any more.'

Apart from taking short breaks in Sidmouth or Eastbourne, where the average age of the population seems to be about eighty, I don't know many easy ways of feeling young – especially when young women stand up in the Tube and offer you their seat. I still love to whizz down the water flume at the local swimming pool, ignoring the bemused giggles of teenagers in the queue and the disapproving expressions of their parents looking on, but usually end up with back-ache. I still wear a bikini, but reckon I look like an elderly woman who wishes she hadn't lost the battle with gravity. I spend hours gardening in France, but can barely move when I stop for the day. How galling that I should just have acquired the bug for it, when I no longer have the physique! These pleasures will no doubt soon be added to the list of bereavements I can't escape. So I will simply find some that I can.

There are small bereavements almost from the moment we are born. I remember being surprised when Abby, at eight, told me she missed many childhood freedoms that being grown up no longer allowed. 'You can't suck your thumb in public, or take your comfort rag to school, and you certainly can't be sick on the floor, because everyone thinks you should be old enough to be sick in the toilet.'

I shall simply have to accommodate the losses, as we do, often unwittingly, throughout life, kiss them sadly goodbye – and dwell on the compensations instead. I enjoy swimming more than ever – though I can't swim thirty lengths before breakfast as my eighty-eight-year-old friend, Rachel, could. I can be as eccentric as I choose to be. And though I know I won't live long enough to see the fruition of my meagre efforts in the garden, someone will enjoy the legacy I've left them. And besides, I still have my moments. Abby and I were shopping in the more sophisticated atmosphere of Ibiza town one day, where gorgeous grey-haired continental men with lean and weather-beaten good looks know how to value experience and maturity. So when I heard from behind us, 'Guapa, guapa,' 'Pretty, pretty,' whispered unmistakably in my ear, I turned with anticipation, fully expecting to see a sophisticated, muscular Spaniard with wonderful eyes and a fine jawline. Instead, there stood two bald-headed, heavily jowled, leering old boys with paunches, who looked as if they had about one hundred and seventy years between them. Abby had hysterics and they fled.

French men still think Brigitte Bardot is gorgeous – at eighty-six. Every now and then, from a great distance, I manage to achieve a wolf whistle. So why, in our UK culture, do women of a certain age become invisible? What is attractiveness? Surely more than superficialities?

Some years ago, John Cleese made a fascinating TV documentary on the human face. He interviewed an American plastic surgeon who had been so distressed that his attempts to repair congenitally malformed faces seemed to make matters worse, not better, that he set off on a quest to discover what constituted our concepts of beauty. He gathered thousands of photographs of so-called beautiful people of every race and nationality, and came up with a prototype of the perfect face. With their large eyes, full mouths, dainty chins and well-proportioned features, many celebrity faces fitted his model. But as John Cleese pointed out, and I couldn't have put it more succinctly if I had tried, today's celebrity status symbols are rarely worthy of the unearned fame they acquire. Their contribution to beauty is small since it won't survive much past their thirtieth birthday.

He then went on to examine photographs of Nelson Mandela, Mother Teresa, Gandhi and other genuine superstars, people whose faces radiated the strength and beauty of their characters. They were compelling, profound and wonderful faces, proving that attraction is so much more than society's limited, superficial, skin-deep assumptions. They had put a great deal of unwitting effort into creating the crevices, cracks and laughter lines that constituted the faces of their later years. By the time we are seventy, every wrinkle reflects the prevailing emotions in our lives – strength, bitterness, joy, anger, malice, love, purity, achievement and failure. The face is a visible diary or record of all we have felt and done throughout our lives. Ugliness and attractiveness go on growing. Neither dies before its owner. At seventeen, said Mother Teresa, we have the face we are born with. At seventy, we have the face we deserve.

I think I'd like a tee shirt that has 'No, it is NOT my age' stretched across its front. Thence I shall graduate into a delinquent, eccentric geriatric with long hair, big dangly earrings, ruffled gipsy skirts and outrageous boots, exploring and enjoying all the freedoms denied me by my various roles as respectable worker, mother and minister's wife. I want to be more liberated, not more tied or restricted, as my life progresses, but I suspect that depends on the stamina of the body, although I have met many women for whom a zimmer frame has been no limitation.

One of aging's greatest compensations has been becoming a granny. Being a grandparent seems to turn the least sentimental woman into a doting softy, showing off her latest photos, videos and WhatsApps to anyone polite enough to give her the time of day. I always vowed I wouldn't be that kind of grandmother. But in ignorance, I lied. What is this emotional tidal wave that drives away all reason the moment we hold that new life in our arms? A grandmother has, of course, carried her daughter's children in her own uterus in the form of the eggs that would one day become her grandchildren. But that doesn't explain the identical response to a son's children. An article in the *New York Times* in 2016 suggested there must be 'grandmother hormones'.[8]

According to the psychologist Gerard Kennedy, grandchildren find strength to cope with problems, security and stability from grandmothers who provide emotional warmth, a sense of protection and care, and a role model, rather than a set of imposed values. As a child, I missed out. My father's mother was the stereotypical frail, faded, elderly Granny Rose who paid me little attention, even when I paraded around in her felt hat with the long ostrich feathers. My mother's mother, only forty-two when I was born, was a chain-smoking, whisky-swilling fashion icon, too vain and self-centred to show me much in the way of affection, but I coveted her interesting wardrobe, especially the hooped petticoats, and asked if she would leave them to me in her will. Now it's my turn to work out who gets what in my will, though I doubt my granddaughter will want my wardrobe. She's twice my size for a start.

It was very different for Abby. This is how, in adolescence, she described the importance of her grannies in her life:

Grannies are great inventions. Both my grandfathers died when I was young, so my grannies became my main education and entertainment.

My paternal grandmother was a wise and witty woman. I wasn't sad when she died as she was old, ill and ready, confident of her destination. It was about a week later when I cried, remembering how we had made earrings out of string and gems from her button box, how I would eat salad only for her because she would make it into a clock-face and test me on my telling the time.

Her recipes for cheese dreams, curried eggs and 'boiled Granny dressing' are part of our family tradition. I always felt a little timid in her five-foot-seven presence, but could never hear enough about her Canadian childhood and wartime motherhood. I used to gaze in wonder at her papery skin, infinitely soft and traced with thousands of sunshine lines. Everyone always said she was a real lady. Her memory makes me hope I will be remembered in that way when I am gone. How wonderful for people to discuss your life with admiration and slight envy.

It was she who impressed on me the importance of etiquette. The word 'ladylike' began to haunt me when I sat, ate, talked or walked. I have to admit I'm grateful for it now, just as I'm grateful for being beaten hands down at Scrabble by one granny and at Kaluki by the other.

The 'other', my mother's mother, is very different and she is still very much alive, which is useful. One evening, when I was very small, I stood in my favourite Andy Pandy pyjamas and watched eagerly as she prepared for bed. When she finally turned and asked what I wanted, I said, 'I'm waiting for you to take your teeth out.' She thought it was very funny, but then, all my friends' grannies had false teeth and it was a great disappointment to find that I was unlucky enough to have a granny whose teeth were all her own. However, she too is armed with recipes that no one else can imitate: we live for her chopped herring and chopped liver, not to mention the gefüllte fish and chicken soup. The routine evening cuddle is completely reliable, but quickly forgotten when the cards come out with the coppers for betting. There were private celebrations when I grew taller than her; there will be public ones when I finally win a round of Kaluki.

A grandmother can be a real gift to her children. She is the only woman in the world who will never tire of hearing them brag about the exploits of her grandchildren. She can be an occasional child-minder, a listening ear when parents are distracted. But she can be a source of irritation too – spoiling them with gifts, allowing little chocolate treats just before lunch or letting them stay up past bedtime, undoing all the good behaviour and habits the parents try to instil. But if the relationship between the parents and their parents becomes fragile, if it's terminated through misunderstandings or divorce, or if it is neglected, as it is in so many families where children make no effort to visit aging parents, the loss to all can be incalculable. Like most relationships, it needs a large dollop of time, effort, honesty, appreciation and forgiveness – on both sides.

Grandchildren, in their turn, are God's way of keeping us young and active – especially if they are so terrified of going down the local slide that you have to let them sit on your knee. My grandchildren have all had a battery-operated toy musical box, and they know that one particular tune on it will always make Granny dance like a virago. Strange how often they choose to play it. They make us laugh, they make us play, they draw out reserves of tenderness we weren't sure we still had.

We all need children and young people in our lives – if for no other reason than to prevent us from becoming completely out of touch with the world. So if we're not blessed with grandchildren, borrow some. There are so many single-parent families around us, so many families with no grandparents nearby, all needing surrogate grannies.

It's never too late for long-term goals

During one of the many NHS rejigs, one or two of my younger female colleagues began jostling for the new jobs. They rushed round in ever more demented circles, giving every hour to their work, determined to become senior executives. All power to their elbows, I said to myself. I was just glad it wasn't me. Those of us who were a little older sat and watched them, feeling bemused and just a little superior. We felt there were more important things in life than hoisting ourselves up the career ladder.

Then suddenly, without so much as a tiny push, the door swung open in front of me, and like Alice in Wonderland I fell through it, and landed with a bump and a shock in a fairly senior management job. I felt vaguely schizoid – lamenting the freedoms of part-time paid work, yet excited at the challenges and privilege of having such a responsible job at my stage of life.

A mere four years later, when yet another NHS reshuffle would have incurred a four-hour daily commute, it was hard to let go. But by then, Peter and I were wondering about spending more time in France, before we were too old to plunge into a new adventure. That had always been the dream – since we married. It just took longer to come true than we ever anticipated.

Women will say to someone who is underpaid, never promoted and given a tiny pension, 'Never mind, as long as you're happy, that's all that counts.' It may be true, if there is enough to live on, but a man would rarely say the same. Most men plan, remain focussed, and quite often succeed in their aims, even though their drivenness may drive the women in their orbit to despair along the way. 'You can't stop Niagara,' my mother-in-law used to lament, when my father-in-law had launched himself into yet another project. He was still in full flow, handing out his orders, on his deathbed.

But if a person has no goals, nor will they achieve them. Women are not always good at having identifiable objectives. We say things like, 'Well, I might try to become the managing director, but on the other hand, I might have another baby.' We don't always allow for a strong sense of calling, and, if we're not careful, one day can follow another without foresight or focus. I have met very few women who had a clear idea of what they wanted to achieve in retirement, other than, 'Well, I'll have a holiday, then I'll paint the house, and then I'll just see.' I can fairly well guarantee, if there is a man in their lives, 'just seeing' will be an endless round of chores, while he pursues his latest project or indulges in his favourite sport. We need our own interests and passions.

Mother Teresa and Corrie Ten Boom, like Anna, were single. Helen Taylor-Thompson had a very accommodating husband. But what they all shared was a vision for building the kingdom of God that extended far beyond the temporary goals of career success and watching the children grow up.

The new army of retirees has a great deal more energy than their parents, but are also confronted with more expectations – to become tireless voluntary workers, to care for grandchildren so that their children can pay the mortgage, to be responsible for elderly parents because social care is so badly funded. We are rarely able to fulfil every expectation that confronts us. There is a life to be lived, before we are in a position when we can no longer cope with the aches and pains of our wearing bodies. Voluntary work can make a huge difference to the wellbeing of society; grandparents can leave a legacy of unconditional love; exercise is necessary and good for us; and culture and reading stimulate the brain cells and stave off dementia, and ensure we are neither bored nor boring. It is important to hang on to our vision, and remain stalwartly true to the person it has taken so long for us to find. There are responsibilities we may have to take on, but we can say no to the things we don't have the resources or will to do.

One annoying thing about age is the worry that every 'minor health problem' could potentially be our last. Time races away with us, so it's vital to capture the moment and enjoy it, if, and as much as, we can. The Jews are not very clear about life after death. All we leave behind, they say, is our good name and reputation. How do we want to be remembered? How many lives do we fill with joy and purpose? It's a very good guide to how we live.

A model woman

> Teach the older women to be reverent in the way they live, not to be slanderers or addicted to much wine, but to teach what is good. Then they can urge the younger women to love their husbands and children, to be self-controlled and pure, to be busy at home, to be kind, and to be subject to their husbands, so that no one will malign the word of God.
>
> (Tit. 2:3–5)

Malice and booze, according to Paul, can sometimes be the weaknesses of women's later years. Or at least, that's what Titus is up against in the church he leads. Instead, they are to be role models for younger women in love and kindness and purity. The Greek word used here for 'to urge or to train' is *sophronizosin,* an unusual word that means 'to bring to their senses'. According to theologian Gordon Fee, Paul is still concerned about more of those misinformed young women, like the ones in Ephesus, who are using their sexual attractions to lead young men astray. What better way to disabuse them than for older women to get alongside and encourage them to abandon pagan ways and wise up to their responsibilities.[9]

My generation of women used a great deal of energy fighting for the right to preach and lead. Some, like me, remained laywomen, while others were certainly trailblazers in church ministry. But I have heard many younger women in church leadership today complain that they have had to forge their own way with few role models, relying on men to open the door for them. When Ruth Hassall, our church youth and children's worker in Lancaster, helped to lead a training day for future leaders, several participators expressed surprise afterwards that Peter had given her such a key speaking role. Ruth was taken aback by their reaction. 'I think in their hearts they were still expecting the inevitable moment when he or another male leader would say, "Ruth, go and put the kettle on,"' she said. But Peter recognised that Ruth was an important role model for the women who were there, and that giving her the floor would say more about equality in leadership than any words that would pass his lips. And it was Ruth who organised a mentoring scheme for the young women in the church, linking them up with older women who would listen, reflect on their issues with them, pray for them and be there for them in a crisis.[10]

As I look back now, I have to admit that, apart from my husband, few church leaders gave me any real encouragement, advice or guidance in my own speaking ministry. In fact, I received a great deal more support in my secular, professional life. How we need women in their sixties, seventies and eighties who will mentor younger women, not condemning their choices with a 'we know what is best', or projecting their own disappointments with a 'take my advice and go out to work as soon as you can, otherwise you'll just be a drudge like I was'.

Life is a gift without a handbook. In poverty, persecution and suffering, Jewish women throughout the ages learned that, 'You can't stop the birds of tragedy from flying over your head and dropping their business on you, but you can refuse to let them nest in your hair,' and passed on their secret of their tenacity from one generation to the next. From girlhood, women need more encouragement to be adventurous. Apparently, when a job is advertised, men will see the 75 per cent they can do and go for it; women will see the 25 per cent they can't, and not bother applying. What an opportunity for older women to put their wealth of experience as worker, minister, wife, mother and godmother to positive use, inspiring the next generations to bigger and better dreams.

I'm not a natural mentor – in the formalised sense. I'm too much of a grasshopper. And I wouldn't encourage any young woman to do as I have done in France and attend a church that doesn't allow for women in leadership – unless there is a geographical or cultural necessity. I have no choice – this is the only informal church for fifty square miles. But for fourteen years I have scratched away at their pre-suppositions and culture, taught in alternative groups, done online seminars. And occasionally, Peter 'shares' his sermons with me to make a point. And I now get a loud cheer from all the women when I do. How long can the church council hold out?

We may not be able to change the entire world, but we can encourage the women in our small corner to feel more confident, more equipped to live in it. Empowering women to influence every level of society – economic, political, social and spiritual – will have an impact on all kinds of major policy choices. 'The function of freedom,' said the writer Toni Morrison, 'is to free someone else.'[11]

Called to change the world

To return to the start of this journey through the world of woman, I have been privileged in my lifetime to live through one of the most remarkable revolutions of all time – the dawning of a new era for the female of the species. In 1973, as I was just setting out from university – a bright-eyed and bushy-tailed hopeful – a well-known Bible scholar had just published a commentary on the book of Exodus. In chapter 38 there is an interesting, throwaway verse (verse 8) that most of us miss. It describes how the 'women who served at the entrance to the tent of meeting' gave away their mirrors to be melted down to create a metal sink where the priests could wash their hands. Who were these women and what did they do? In his commentary of 1973, theologian Alan Cole suggests, 'The verb translated minister is rare and interesting . . . and probably stands for some form of organized sanctuary service, whether cleaning or sweeping (in which case many a Women's Guild has its prototype here).'[12] Women's Guilds, the Women's Institute – dedicated to cleaning and sweeping? I doubt that description would have pleased them, even then. A greater put-down would be hard to find.

Cole admits, with an element of condescension, that they may be women who sang and danced at the festivals, like Miriam. However, contemporary theologians now agree that these were more likely to be women of influence, of devout and pious character, who spent a great deal of time in prayer and worship, the forerunners of Anna, the prophetess. The gift of their mirrors was probably their way of renouncing the world for a season. They must have been holy, as my magnifying mirror is one of my most prized possessions and to part with it would be a sacrifice too far.

Nothing demonstrates so powerfully how interpretations of the Bible depend on the lenses of cultural conditioning and preferred theology. But it also shows just how far the Church has travelled in less than fifty years. In 1973 I don't know that I would have questioned Alan Cole's assumption that 'ministering women' meant teams of cleaners. By the time Abby was born, eight years later, I knew I wanted to create a better world for women than that. But is it?

The dawn heralds a new day, and is but a beginning. Women can now be pastors of churches in countries such as China, South Korea, Japan, Singapore, Turkey, Latin America, and in many parts of Africa – though the last data, published by the World Bank in 2014, showed that men filled 80 per cent of these leadership roles.

There is still much to be achieved, in the West and elsewhere. As long as the oppression of women continues across the globe – exclusion, domestic violence, child marriage, female genital mutilation, legalised rape, honour killings, the denial of education, and poverty of every kind – there can be no resting on our laurels.

The more I research and write and speak about what women have to offer, the more convinced I become that equality is not just an optional extra for the Church – a matter of cultural and personal preference. The equality of men and women, established in the book of Genesis at creation, affirmed by the ministry of Jesus and the gift of the Holy Spirit at Pentecost, is one of the distinctive features of Christianity, marking it out from most other faiths. It is a persuasive argument for the relevance of what we believe, and a powerful tool in our hands for changing the world. Such is the influence of women that their liberation and education is one of the prime targets of the World Health Organization in bringing physical health and mental wellbeing to the nations.

The emancipated American black slave, Sojourner Truth, who set out in 1843 with twenty-five cents in her pocket to travel the coast campaigning for women's rights, said:

If the first woman God ever made was strong enough to turn the world upside down all alone, together women ought to be able to turn it right-side up again.[13]

Together we have the power to change hearts, lives and whole cultures. The founders of the National Childbirth Trust, who campaigned for childbirth to be treated as a perfectly normal though uniquely special event, rather than an illness, were initially regarded by a superior, hostile medical profession as a few wacky women. In the end their tenacity was rewarded – even if it was too late for them. Ingrained cultural attitudes were overturned. Mothers were given more control. Labour was no longer such a brutalising experience.

It would have taken much longer for women to achieve their political rights without the determined effort of the suffragettes. In many African countries and some European countries, such as Switzerland, women still didn't have the vote as late as the 1960s.

Sometimes our own personal achievements seem so very, very small, but I wonder whether we ever really know how much of a difference we make. I lost a lovely friend in France who was shocked to find she had terminal cancer in her late sixties, because her mother had lived well into her nineties, and there was so much else she had planned to do before her boat was called in. But as I have reflected on her life in the short time we knew her, I was struck by the legacy of love she left behind. She was a gifted, caring doctor and had made her mark in France in so many ways – in her professional capacity as a female role model for staff and students at the university medical practice in Poitiers, in her friendships with a raft of elderly British ex-pats who barely knew the language and were totally bewildered by visits to the GP and hospital. In her spare time, she never refused a medical diagnosis, a prescription for emergency medication or minor ailments, advice and reassurance, or a lift to a hospital consultation, with an accompanying translation service. On a daily basis she calmed dozens of anxieties and restored peace to countless families. I miss her hugely when I find a new mole, or have a bout of cystitis. But she also furnished my garden with dozens of cuttings that have brought me such pleasure. Everywhere I look I see something of her in the flowers and plants I love. That was a life well lived. She was perhaps the epitome of what Paul was advocating in his letter to Titus. So can we really have it all? Yes, we can. But it may not always look like 'all'. It may not even be what we expect, and it may not be all at once.

We don't always recognise the opportunities and power we have. And perhaps, like Queen Esther, an ordinary woman in so many ways yet called to use the little she had for the good of many, we women in the West, whose freedom has been won at such a price, have been called 'for such a time as this' to take up our creation calling and speak life and liberty into this beautiful, yet wounded world. Without two working wings, a bird is grounded, ineffectual. If industry, institutions and governments, not to mention the Church, want to rise up and fly, they desperately need the voices of women. Otherwise they will only have half the expertise, half the capability, half the potential and half the achievement.

— The End —

Acknowledgements

Writing an autobiography and making a spiritual will are practically the same.

Shalom Aleichem

Writing is such a terribly presumptuous occupation. Who am I to add my few drops to the ocean of words already in existence? How can I justify sharing my paltry experience with the world? My only defence is that, now in later life, I have a passion to see younger women with the confidence to benefit from the gains my generation fought so hard for and won, that they might live out their calling with boldness and faith. Our world still needs an army of campaigners, reformers and missionaries, like Catherine Booth, Mary Slessor, Florence Nightingale and Josephine Butler, who risked their reputations, their peace and sometimes their very lives, to change the face of their nineteenth-century world.

So thank you to all who have made a contribution, however unwitting – to those who initially goaded me into speaking on the subject publicly at a time when it didn't earn any woman brownie points, but it did make me do the homework; to the brave individuals who heard me and challenged me afterwards on my woolly thinking and made me go back and study again; to the churches and organisations like New Wine and Spring Harvest, who took the risk of allowing me to lead seminars on women and authority when it was still regarded as a controversial and radical topic; to Andy Lyon at Hodder for his infectious excitement over the book, and constant encouragement, and to the great team who work with him; to psychiatrist Angus Bell, former Head of Mental Health for the

North of England, who at times shared the platform with me and showed that a man could share the same views. His humour and insights on the subject of gender have always made me laugh – and made me think hard, and that is so necessary.

I don't know that I would have ever dared stray into this subject without the support of my children. When Joel came home from university many years ago, in immense frustration at the attitude of his fellow students, he said, 'I know you believe it's right for women to play a leading role in society and the Church, but how do you argue it? You'd better write it'. And now he is a clergy spouse himself. For his wife, Sarah, the decision to be ordained was not a career choice. No one in their right mind would give up being a senior occupational therapist manager for the cut in pay and cost in stress. But the commitment, passion and energy with which they embrace the calling never ceases to challenge me. I have learned so much from them, and it is thanks to their encouragement and insights that I have updated and rewritten most of the book.

I didn't know when I suggested to Abby, so long ago, that she write up her experiences of adolescence that they would be such a revelation – ouch! But I appreciated the ruthless honesty of her contributions – on good days. And I was thrilled that she was happy for her adolescent thoughts to be shared after so long. Now a senior manager herself, juggling motherhood with the demands of the job, I marvel at her skills and value her insights, so many shared here. And her friendship, perception and support always.

Thank you to Julian and Suzanna Farnham, for painstaking proof reading, and to those who read chapters and scribbled helpful comments on them, or inadvertently released tiny treasures I snatched from the ether. I apologise if I didn't warn you that I was going to regurgitate your words. I'm a journalist. Everything I see and hear is grist to the mill. Please don't stop speaking to me. Everything we say will be shouted from the rooftops one day anyway. As my original editor, Amy Boucher Pye did an extraordinary job of weaving mounds of jumbled, raw material into a coherent whole, and became a valued friend in the process. I always tell her how much I valued her 'literary liposuction', and now especially her gracious, generous preface to the book.

And a special thank you to my husband who has been a 'head' in the true sense of the word – a source of life, release, encouragement, confidence, theological insights, love and IT know-how, even to the point of spending two whole evenings sorting out the endnotes, which were jumbled by a technological glitch. He has been as much a partner in the production of books as he has of babies, and for whom I have never merely been a 'backup'. But then, show me the Jewish Mama who is!

Risk being unliked. Tell the truth as you understand it. If you're a writer you have a moral obligation to do this. And it is a revolutionary act – truth is always subversive.

Anne Lamott[1]

Endnotes

Preamble: Sometimes it's Hard to Be a Woman

1 *The Yorkshire Ripper Files: A Very British Crime Story*, BBC 4 (March 26–28 2019).

2 Professor Stephen Hawking, 'The Five Most Powerful People in Britain are Women', *The Daily Telegraph* (20th March, 2017).

3 Daisy Goodwin, 'Equality Lulls Viewers into a False Sense of Security', *Radio Times* (13–19 October, 2018).

4 Virginia Nicholson, *How Was it For You? Women, Sex, Love and Power* (Viking, 2019).

5 Dr Christina Scharff, 'Why so Many Young Women Don't Call Themselves Feminist', BBC News (6 Feb, 2019), https://www.bbc.co.uk/news/uk-politics-47006912 (accessed 18 December 2020).

6 Kath Sansom, 'Lives ruined as damage viewed as "women's problems"', BBC News (8 July 2020), https://www.bbc.co.uk/news/health-53307593 (accessed 18 December 2020).

7 Anke Samulowitz, Ida Gremyr, Erik Eriksson, and Gunnel Hensing, '"Brave Men" and "Emotional Women": A Theory-Guided Literature Review on Gender Bias in Health Care and Gendered Norms towards Patients with Chronic Pain' (25 February, 2018), https://www.ncbi.nlm.nih.gov/pmc/articles/PMC5845507/.

8 Gypsy Rose Lee, *Gypsy: A Memoir*, (Frog Book, 1999).

9 Rosa Silverman, 'Women Mean Business', *The Telegraph* (13 March 2018).

10 Maya Angelou, 'Phenomenal Woman' from *Pheonomenal Woman: Four Poems Celebrating Women* (Random House: 2011).

11 https://www.jkrowling.com/opinions/j-k-rowling-writes-about-her-reasons-for-speaking-out-on-sex-and-gender-issues/.

Chapter 1: The Life-Giving Woman

1 Augustine, *On The Trinity*, 7.7.10.

2 Origen, *Selecta in Exodus*, 17.7.

3 Quoted by Elaine Storkey, *Contributions to Christian Feminism* (Christian Impact, 1995) p. 48.

4 Moulana Majaz Azami, *Guidance for a Muslim Wife* (South Africa: Madrasah Arabia Islamia, 1990). There is a good deal of wise advice for women on relationships and raising children in this little booklet, but also the undoubted message that she serves God by serving her man.

5 Elaine Storkey, *Scars Across Humanity: Understanding and Overcoming Violence Against Women* (SPCK, 2015).

6 Christabel Pankhurst and Elizabeth Cady Stanton, who led the suffrage movement in the UK and USA respectively, were deeply committed to the Christian faith and renowned preachers.

7 At her keynote address in 1971, Aileen Hernandez, the African-American lawyer, civil rights activist and President of the National Organisation for Women in the USA, called the women's movement 'the last great hope of civilisation'. Writer and feminist Barbara Ehrenreich said that the assumption of female superiority, or at least 'a lesser inclination toward cruelty and violence', was more or less beyond debate.

8 Patricia Cornwell, *A Time for Remembering: The Ruth Bell Graham Story* (HarperCollins 1986), p. 202.

9 Quoted from an interview with Giles Brandreth, 'My Idea of Heaven', *The Sunday Telegraph* (5 April 2001).

10 Stan Goff, *Borderline: Reflections on War, Sex, and Church* (Cascade Books, 2015).

11 Helen Fielding, *Bridget Jones's Diary* (Picador, 1996). Film released 2001.

12 Matthew Henry, *Commentary on the Whole Bible, New, One Volume Edition*, ed. Rev. Leslie F. Church (Zondervan Publishing House, 1961), p. 7.

13 Paul Tournier, *Marriage Difficulties* (SCM Press, 1967).

14 Sirach 25:24 (Good News Translation ® Today's English Version, Second Edition. Copyright © 1992 American Bible Society. All rights reserved).

15 'Therefore, just as sin entered the world through one man, and death through sin, and in this way death came to all people, because all sinned' (Rom. 5:12).

16 Derek Kidner, *Genesis: An Introduction and Commentary* ed. D. J. Wiseman (IVP, 1967).

17 Carol Ann Duffy, 'Mrs Tiresias', *The World's Wife* (Picador, 1999). Reproduced with permission of the Licensor through PLSclear..

18 Gordon J. Wenham, *Word Biblical Commentary: Genesis 1–15* (Word Books, 1987), p. 81.

19 Miriam Grossman MD, 'A Psychiatrist's Letter to Young People about *Fifty Shades of Grey*', 11 February 2015, https://www.miriamgrossmanmd.com/an-open-letter-to-young-people-about-fifty-shades-of-grey/ (accessed 18 December 2020).

20 Susan Foh, 'What is the Woman's Desire?' *Westminster Theological Journal*, 37 (1975), pp. 376-83. Susan also suggests that submission is the cure.

21 Virginia Nicholson, 'Peace, Love and Predatory Men', *The Sunday Times Magazine* (24 March 2019).

22 Chimamanda Ngozi Adichie, 'We should all be feminists', TED talk, 14 April 2017, https://www.ted.com/talks/chimamanda_ngozi_adichie_we_should_all_be_feminists/up-next?language=en (accessed 18 December 2020).

23 Chimamanda Ngozi Adichie in conversation with Lisa Allardice, *The Guardian* (28 April 2018).

24 Jane Hansen with Marie Powers, *Fashioned for Intimacy* (Baker Pub Group, 1997).

25 Mary Stewart van Leeuwen, *Gender and Grace: Love, Work and Parenting in a Changing World* (IVP, 1990), p. 117.

26 Sarah Hopkins Bradford, *Harriet Tubman: The Moses of Her People* (New York: Citadel Press, 1974), p. 29.

27 Ibid, p. 30.

28 Ibid, p. 32.

Chapter 2: The Manipulative Woman

1 Eva Ibbotson was unique and I admired her enormously. Raised in Vienna, she wore flowing skirts and had a ponytail, and always seemed very exotic to me. She later became a very popular writer of children's fiction.

2 Anne Dickson, *A Woman in Your Own Right: Assertiveness and You* (London: Quartet Books, 1982).

3 Jackie Manson, *Look Who's Laughing* (London Palladium, 1999).

4 Laura Doyle, *The Surrendered Wife: A Practical Guide To Finding Intimacy, Passion And Peace With Your Man* (New York: Simon and Schuster, 2001).

5 Kathleen Bliss, *The Service and Status of Women in the Churches* (SCM, 1952). p. 183.

Chapter 3: The Assertive Woman

1 Tamara Cohn Eskenazi and Andrea L. Weiss (eds), *The Torah: A Women's Commentary* (URJ Press and Women of Reform Judaism, 2008).

2 Lynn McDonald (ed.), *Florence Nightingale on Society and Politics, Philosophy, Science, Education and Literature* (Wilfrid Laurier University Press, 2003), p. 395.

3 *The Salisbury Poisonings*, screened in three episodes on BBC One, 14–16 June 2020.

4 W. P. Livingstone, *The White Queen of Okoyong* (Hodder and Stoughton, 1950) p. 148.

5 Alan Burgess, *The Small Woman: Gladys Aylward* (The Reprint Society, 1959), pp. 254–5.

6 Burgess, *The Small Woman*, pp. 110–11.

7 Matthew 10:28, *New Light Bible* (Hodder and Stoughton, 1998).

8 Quoted in Jane Robinson, *Josephine Butler: A Very Brief History* (SPCK, 2020).

9 Joseph Williamson, *Josephine Butler: The Forgotten Saint* (The Faith Press, 1977), p. 97.

10 Josephine's letter to sister, Harriet, April 1883, quoted in *A singular* Glen Petrie, *A Singular Iniquity: The Campaigns of Josephine Butler* (Macmillan, 1971), p. 208.

11 Julie Bindel, 'A heroine for our age', *The Guardian* (21 September 2006).

Chapter 4: A Woman of Little Status?

1 Dr Leonard Swidler, *Women in Judaism: The Status of Women in Formative Judaism* (Scarecrow Press, 1976).

2 Hyam Maccoby, *Judaism in the First Century* (Sheldon Press, 1989).

3 Professor Shmuel Safrai, 'The Place of Women in First-century

Synagogues', *Jerusalem Perspective* (Sept/Oct 1993). Shmuel Safrai (1919–2003) was Professor Emeritus of the History of the Jewish People at the Hebrew University of Jerusalem.

4 Maccoby, *Judaism in the First Century*, p. 61.

5 For more information on the Jewish festivals, see *The Heavenly Party* by Michele Guinness (Lion, 2019).

6 Acts chapter 2 doesn't tell us how many were gathered there, simply that the disciples were 'all together'.

7 12 July 2013.

8 Daniel 12:2: 'Multitudes who sleep in the dust of the earth will awake: some to everlasting life, others to shame and everlasting contempt.'

9 Dorothy L. Sayers, *Unpopular Opinions* (Victor Gollancz, 1946), pp. 117-8.

10 Dorothy L. Sayers, *Are Women Human? Penetrating, Sensible and Witty Essays on the Role of Women in Society* (Eerdmans, 1971).

11 Lady Dorothy Hosie, 'Jesus and Women', in Lavinia (ed.), *The Hidden Journey: Missionary Heroines in Many Lands* (SPCK, 1993).

12 R. T. France, *A Slippery Slope? The Ordination of Women and Homosexual Practice – a Case Study in Biblical Interpretation* (Grove Books Ltd, 2000), p. 3.

13 Luke 8:1–3. Joanna and Junia have the same root in Hebrew and Latin.

14 On 6 July 2002, the religious correspondent of *The Times*, announced that a paper by Professor Richard Baukham, containing evidence that Junia, the Apostle, was a woman, was being studied by Church of England leaders debating whether women should be ordained bishops. 'The discovery suggests that society was far less patriarchal than previous research has shown . . . The assumption that the leading apostles were all men has been one of the most unassailable arguments against the ordination of women bishops. If the claim that Joanna and Junia were the same person and that Junia was a woman and an apostle is accepted, the argument for women bishops will have been all but won.'

15 Aristotle, *The Politics*.

16 Quoted in Elizabeth Ann Clark, *Women in the Early Church* (Liturgical Press, 1990), p. 37.

17 Byrne, *The Hidden Journey*.

18 Stephen Neill, *A History of Christian Missions* (Penguin, 1964). Neill retired early due to ill health, he claimed. But there were allegations about his sexuality and that he slapped his clergy.

19 Maccoby, *Judaism in the First Century*, p. 56.

Chapter 5: The Silent Woman?

1 Romans 16:1. Alvera and Berkeley Mickelsen, 'Does Male Dominance Tarnish Our Translations?' Obedience to Whose Word? *Christianity Today* (5 October 1979), pp. 23–7.

2 Antonia Fraser, *The Weaker Vessel* (Knopf, 1984), p. 122, quoted in Susan C. Hyatt, *In the Spirit We're Equal: The Spirit, the Bible, and Women, A Revival Perspective* (Nashville, TN: Hyatt Press, 1998), p. 77.

3 Hyatt, *In The Spirit We're Equal*, p. 77.

4 Deborah Tannen, *You Just Don't Understand: Women and Men in Conversation* (HarperCollin,s 2013). Deborah has written thirteen books, all still in print. She has inevitably been criticised in academia for making sweeping generalisations that can appear to stereotype women but, personally, I found her work very helpful in understanding the differences in the way women and men communicate with one another.

5 This view is also supported by James Moffatt *The First Epistle of Paul to the Corinthians,* (Hodder and Stoughton, 1943). Calvin took a very similar line, though he managed to argue that while it may be necessary for a woman to speak in public from time to time, it shouldn't be a regular feature of church services.

6 Gordon D. Fee, *The First Epistle to the Corinthians, The New International Commentary on the New Testament* (Eerdmans Publishing Co, 1987).

7 For example, Junia which appeared in the original Greek manuscripts being altered to Junias in mediaeval translations, to make the Apostle appear to be male.

8 William Barclay, *The Letters to the Corinthians: New Daily Study Bible* (Saint Andrew Press, 1956).

9 Richard Clark Kroeger and Catherine Clark Kroeger, *I Suffer Not a Woman: Rethinking 1 Timothy 2:11-15 in Light of Ancient Evidence* (Baker Publishing Group, 1992) is devoted entirely to 1 Tim. 2:11–15 and, because of the authors' in-depth knowledge of classical Greek language and culture, is an invaluable study of the text.

10 Richard and Catherine Clark Kroeger, *I Suffer Not a Woman.* Interestingly, in his *Analytical Concordance to the Bible* (Lutterworth, 1879), Robert Young defines *authentein* as 'to use one's own armour'.

11 Fee, *The First Epistle to the Corinthians.*

12 R. T. France, *A Slippery Slope?* p. 3.

13 France, *A Slippery Slope?*, p. 22.

14 Josephine Butler, 'Woman's Place in the Church', in *Review of the Churches*, *Vol 2* (Feb-April 1892), p. 343.

15 Hyatt, *In the Spirit We're Equal*, p. 220.

16 Quoted by Jill Evans, in *Beloved and Chosen: Women of Faith* (The Canterbury Press, 1993), from Sheila Fletcher, *Maude Royden: A Life* (Basil Blackwell, 1989), p. 162.

17 Tannen, *You Just Don't Understand*, p. 202.

Chapter 6: The Submissive Woman?

1 1 Peter 3:2, from A.M. Stibbs and A. F. Walls, *1 Peter, Tyndale New Testament Commentaries* (IVP, 1959), p. 125.

2 William Dalrymple, *From the Holy Mountain* (HarperCollins, 1998), p. 37.

3 Psalm 118:22, Katherine C. Bushnell, 'Lesson 37: Headship in the New Testament', *God's Word to Women* (Ray B. Munsen, 1923), paragraphs 282–91.

4 Hyatt, *In the Spirit We're Equal*, 1998), p. 247.

5 S. Bedale, 'The Meaning of Kephale in the Pauline Epistles', *Journal of Theological Studies*, 5 (1954), pp. 211–15.

6 S. T. Lowrie, '1 Corinthians XI and the Ordination of Women as Ruling Elders', *Princeton Theological Review*, 19 (1921), pp. 113–30.

7 F. F. Bruce, *I and II Corinthians* (NCB, 1971).

8 Gordon D. Fee, *The First Epistle to the Corinthians*, p. 502. Both the RSV and NIV say a woman should have a 'sign of authority' on her head, but the Greek simply says, 'authority'. The Living Bible translation, 'a woman should wear a covering on her head as a sign she is under a man's authority', is completely erroneous.

9 Matthew, *Commentary on the Whole Bible Vol. 1-1* (Hendrickson, 2008, first edition 1706). (See Genesis 2:21–5.)

10 The Greek word for 'angel' is the same as 'messenger', so it is just possible that Paul was referring to messengers from other churches, who might be so shocked to see a woman with her hair uncovered that they would be distracted from enjoying the benefits of her ministry during worship.

11 Demosthenes, *Apollodorus Against Neaera*, III, 122 (384–22 BC).

12 Plato, *Symposium*, 180, 192.

13 Lucian, *Erotes*, 51, cited by Hyatt, *In the Spirit We're Equal*, p. 250.

14 Laura Doyle, *The Surrendered Wife*.

15 Canon Lucy Peppiatt has written two books on the subject of Paul and women: *Unveiling Paul's Women: Making Sense of 1 Corinthians 11:2–16* (Wipf and Stock publishers, 2018); *Women and Worship at Corinth: Paul's Rhetorical Arguments in 1 Corinthians* (Wipf and Stock Publishers, 2015).

16 Colin Brown (ed.), *New International Dictionary of New Testament Theology Vol 3* (Exeter: Paternoster, 1978).

17 'Social Focus on Men' carried out by Office for National Statistics.

18 The results of the survey cited above, initiated by Joshua Generation and undertaken by Christian Research, were published in *Quadrant*, May 2001.

19 Libby Purves, *The Times* (12 June 2001).

20 The story is recorded by E. C. Dawson in *Missionary Heroines of the Cross* (Seeley, Service and Co, 1930), pp. 212–13, and repeated in Byrne, *The Hidden Journey*. French reprint: Mme C. Rey 1892 *Une Femme missionnaire, souvenirs de la vie et de la mort de Mme Coillard* (Hachette Livre et la Bnf. 2016).

Chapter 7: The Sexual Woman

1 Sayers, *Are Women Human?*, pp. 117–18.

2 Quoted in Rosie Nixson, *Liberating Women for the Gospel* (London: Hodder & Stoughton, 1997), pp. 27–28.

3 Marie Stopes and William Rogers, *Birth Control and Libel* (A. S. Barnes, 1968), p.76.

4 Nicholson, *How Was it For You?*

5 Evangeline Paterson, 'Advice to daughters'.

6 Sayers, *Are Women Human?* pp. 22-3.

7 Hugo Gryn with Naomi Gryn, *Chasing Shadows* (Penguin, 2000), p. xxix.

8 It is now medically clear that incidents of cervical cancer do not relate to the number of partners a woman might have had, and that even single women should have a regular smear test.

9 *The Guardian*, 16 July 2001. Chandra Levy's body was found about a year later.

10 Archibald D. Hart, *The Sexual Man* (Word, 1994).

Chapter 8: The Mothering Woman

1 16 January 1892, quoted in Elizabeth Elliott, *A Chance to Die: The Life and Legacy of Amy Carmichael* (Revell, 1987), p. 55.
2 Rita Rudner, *Naked Beneath My Clothes* (Viking, 1992).
3 Joan Rivers, 'Blonde with Dark Roots', Live at the London Palladium, 2006).
4 Rosemary Norman, 'Lullaby', Rosemary Palmeira (ed.), *In the Gold of the Flesh: Poems of Birth and Motherhood* (The Women's Press Ltd, 1990).
5 Ruth Bell Graham, *Sitting by my Laughing Fire* (Word Books, 1977). The late Ruth Bell Graham WAS the wife of evangelist, Billy Graham. © 1977 The Ruth Graham Literary Trust, used by permission. All rights reserved.
6 Evangeline Paterson, *Lucifer at the Fair* (Taxus, 1991).
7 Margaret Foster, *Significant sisters: The Grassroots of Active Feminism* (Vintage, 2004), p. 224.
8 Floella's story is taken from Floella Benjamin, *Coming To England* (Macmillan Children's Books, 2016, first published 1995); 'Floella Benjamin – a Windrush Story', https://www.blackhistorymonth.org.uk/article/section/the-windrush/baroness-floella-benjamin-a-windrush-story/; and Floella's website, www.floellabenjamin.com (websites accessed 18 December 2020).
9 Twitter, 11 February 2020, the day the Church of England apologised for its racism towards the Windrush arrivals. It cannot change what was, or the loss of all that cultural richness and relationship, but it can perhaps contribute to a new appreciation of the uninhibited joy in worship that was forfeited and create an openness to receive the gifts that different cultures bring.
10 Floella Benjamin, *Coming to England*, 1995.

Chapter 9: The Working Woman

1 Eugene Peterson, *The Message, The Old Testament Wisdom Books in Contemporary Language* (NAV Press, 1996).
2 Derek Kidner, *Proverbs: Tyndale Old Testament Commentaries* (Leicester: IVP, 1964), p. 184.
3 *Good Housekeeping* (June 2002).
4 'Hampton-Alexander FTSE 250 Executive Committee Report', 13 November 2019.

5 BBC News, 'Little sign of change for number of women in top roles', 13 November 2019.

6 John Drane, *The McDonaldization of the Church* (Darton, Longman and Todd, 2000), p. 175.

7 *Cell Stem Cell* (September 2019).

8 Deborah Tannen, *Talking from 9 to 5, Women and Men at work: Language, Sex and Power* (Virago, 1994), p. 23.

9 After retirement Ruth Winterbottom went on to become Chair of the Lancashire Ambulance Trust and, ultimately, High Sheriff of Lancaster. It was during her year in that role that she discovered she had only months to live, but she continued making public appearances up to her death of lung cancer from passive smoking at the age of sixty-one.

10 *All About Eve*, 1950, written and directed by Joseph L. Mankiewicz. Bette Davis played Margo Channing, a legendary actress about to be ousted by a new, brighter star in the firmament.

11 Phoebe Waller-Bridge on *The Andrew Marr Show*, BBC, 2019.

12 Professor Judy Wajcman, 'We Can't Take "Man" Out Of Management', *The Guardian*, 7 November, 1998. Professor Judy Wajcman is a member of the Research School of Social Sciences at the Australian National University. Her research, 'Managing Like a Man', was carried out while she was a research fellow at the Warwick Business School and published by Polity Press.

13 Leah Rupanner, 'The Conversation', *Science Alert* (15 August 2019).

14 Tannen, *Talking From 9 to 5*, p. 190.

15 Appendix to 'Notes on Nursing, What it is and What It is Not' (1860) quoted by Margaret Forster in *Significant Sisters*, p. 95.

16 Ephesians 6:9 'And, masters, do the same to them. Stop threatening them, (NRSVA).

Chapter 10: A Woman of Experience and Maturity

1 Jenny Joseph 'Warning' from *Selected Poems* (Bloodaxe, 1992) © Jenny Joseph, reproduced with permission of Johnson & Alcock Ltd.

2 Michele Guinness, *Grace: The Remarkable Life of Grace Grattan Guinness* (Hodder and Stoughton, 2016).

3 Corrie Ten Boom, *The Hiding Place* (Hodder and Stoughton, 2004).

4 Malcolm Muggeridge, *Something Beautiful For God* (HarperOne, 2013), p. 67.

5 Susan Denyer, *Beatrix Potter and Her Farms* (National Trust, 1992).

6 Denyer, *Beatrix Potter,* p. x.

7 Denyer, *Beatrix Potter,* p. x.

8 Dominique Browning 'The Bliss of Grandmother Hormones', *New York Times* (7 May 2016).

9 Gordon Fee, *New International Biblical Commentary, 1 and 2 Timothy, Titus,* (Hendrickson Publishers, 1988), pp. 186–7.

10 Ruth is currently Director of Discipleship for the Blackburn Diocese.

11 Toni Morrison, Barnard College commencement address, 1979.

12 Alan R. Cole, *Exodus: Tyndale Old Testament Commentaries Volume 2,* ed. Donald J. Wiseman (IVP, 1973).

13 Quoted in a speech made by Sojourner Truth at the Women's Rights Convention, Akron, Ohio, 1851.

Acknowledgements

1 Anne Lamott, *Bird by Bird: Instructions on Writing and Life* (Canongate, 2020).